Rahnieda Rose

D0312450

306642 JY 11.95
MHR

Madame
Benoit's
Microwave
Cook Book

Madame Benoit's Microwave Cook Book

Mme. Jehane Benoit

McGraw-Hill Ryerson Limited
Toronto   Montreal   New York   London

Madame Benoit's
Microwave
Cook Book
Copyright © Jehane Benoit, 1975.

All rights reserved. No part of this publication may be
reproduced, stored in a retrieval system, or transmitted in
any form or by any means, electronic, mechanical,
photocopying, recording, or otherwise, without the prior
written permission of McGraw-Hill Ryerson Limited.

ISBN 0-07-082291-3

5 6 7 8 9 10 BP 4 3 2 1 0 9 8 7 6
Printed and Bound in Canada

Design by Maher & Garbutt Ltd
Photography by René Delbuguet

To Wendy and Rob who brought the wonders of microwave cooking into my life.

Contents

Introduction

I have cooked with a microwave oven in my home for some years now and am convinced that before the end of the century all our housekeeping will be planned around the use of this exciting new appliance. One has only to think back over the past 50 years to see how many new pieces of equipment have come into our kitchens, and what a long way we are from the wood stove, to realize that changes that once were considered impossible are now with us and here to stay.

Changes are occurring, too, in our lifestyles and eating habits, and appliances such as the microwave oven are opening up a truly liberated future for the man or woman in the kitchen. The deep freeze and microwave can be complementary: we now have a whole range of convenience foods of all types, frozen and instant, so that it is possible to take precooked frozen foods from the freezer and instantly defrost and cook them with the microwave oven.

If you are the kind of person who values time, convenience, economy and saving labor, as well as delicious and nourishing food, you will love to cook with your microwave oven.

That is why I'm so excited to be able to pass on many of the recipes that I have tried and tested. In addition to recipes that I have worked out just for the microwave oven, I've also learned how to convert many of my old favorites to microwave cooking. Once you've learned the principles of microwave cooking and have tried some of the recipes in this book, you too will be able to do the same.

With a microwave oven, cooking takes approximately one-third the time it takes to cook conventionally, leaving you more time to do odd jobs around the house, to play with the kids or for leisure time. Not only will the time spent in your kitchen be lessened, but the elderly, the handicapped or the young around you can also prepare their own food without fear of burns, overcooked foods, hot dishes, etc.

My book will give you only a small idea of just how wide and exciting the world of microwave cooking is. I know that it will bring a new and adventurous flexibility into your life.

You will also find it is easy to switch from the gas or electric range to the microwave oven if you are willing to reorganize your food and thinking to this style of cooking. Initially you will find that cooking with microwaves is quite different in many respects to conventional cooking and for a while you may find that being unable to do things automatically as you did in the past may slow you down a little. However, this is only temporary and once you've become used to cooking with microwaves you'll wonder how you ever cooked the conventional way.

It is important to read these introductory chapters before beginning to cook with your microwave oven.

1. How Your Microwave Oven Works

Microwaves are electromagnetic energy waves with short wavelengths and high frequencies. You're familiar with wavelengths on your radio, and in relation to these the wavelength of microwaves is in the area of the shortest radio waves, just below those of infra-red waves and visible light. Microwaves are generated by electrons from electric current passing through a special vacuum tube called a magnetron. Like other electromagnetic waves such as TV, AM or FM radio, radar, ultra-violet, etc., microwaves can be transmitted, reflected or absorbed by various substances.

In the case of the microwave oven, the magnetron produces the energy for cooking. The moisture molecules in food absorb this energy and the very rapid rate of vibration of the molecules (friction) produces the heat within the food. This heat is produced to a depth of between 1 and 1¼ inches by the microwave energy and is conducted to the rest of the food the same way as conventional cooking. As you will see, the food is actually cooking itself. This makes cleaning up easier, because you don't get food baking on the dishes, and the oven cavity stays cool.

It is possible in some makes of ovens that the magnetron will be damaged if the oven is operated with no food in it to absorb the energy. The energy can be reflected back from the cavity to the magnetron under these conditions. The same effect is caused by a large quantity of metal in the oven which disturbs the wave pattern. To see if this is the case with your oven check the instructions provided by the manufacturer. Leaving a cup of water in the oven when not cooking will eliminate chances of accident, but is a little inconvenient.

The safety standards for microwave ovens are extremely rigorous and unless a door is tampered with, there is no risk whatsoever of any injury through radiation. Unlike X-rays, microwave energy has no cumulative effects nor does it ionize. You would immediately feel a burn if you were exposed to microwaves, just as you would if you sat out in the sun all day, for the sun is also a form of radiation.

It is impossible for your oven to emit radiation with its door open.

For full care and maintenance instructions, refer to your manufacturer's manual.

Basic Oven Construction

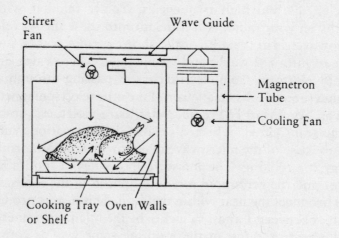

Stirrer Fan

Wave Guide

Magnetron Tube

Cooling Fan

Cooking Tray Oven Walls or Shelf

Power Source

The power source consists of a transformer and condenser. The transformer increases house current at 115 V. to the high voltages necessary to operate the magnetron.

Cooking Fan

The fan blows air over the magnetron to cool it. The air is then usually circulated through the oven cavity to carry steam and moisture away from the food.

Waveguide

Microwaves pass down the waveguide into the cavity where they spread out as shown, reflecting off the metal walls.

Cooking Tray

The cooking tray raises the food off the floor of the oven so that it can cook from below. Usually the tray is made of glass and is removable but some are sealed in.

Stirrer Fan

Because microwaves are a type of radio wave, they have peaks and troughs. This results in "hot spots" and "cool spots" in the oven which gives uneven cooking. One solution is to rotate the food constantly. Most ovens, however, have a stirrer fan which has metal blades at an angle to deflect microwaves from the waveguide into the cavity. As the stirrer turns, it rotates the wave pattern and evens out the cooking.

On the outside of the oven are the door and timer.

Door

Most microwave oven doors have a metal screen which keeps microwave energy in but allows you to see what is happening inside the oven. Some open to the side, some are hinged at the bottom and drop down.

Timer

The timer controls cooking times. Most allow precise control over short cooking times where it is crucial not to overcook, as in the case of cheese or eggs, as well as longer cooking times for large items. There are different types as follows:
1. two timers — one for short times, one for long times.
2. two-speed timers — really two timers in one. Two-speed timers are identified by short intervals (5-15 seconds) on first part of scale, longer times (usually minutes) on second part.
3. Digital timers — this type gives precise minute and second control.

Browning Systems

Large items will brown in the microwave oven, but assistance is required on smaller items such as chops or items which cook very quickly. There are several ways to do this:
1. Browning Utensils: These are often supplied with the oven by manufacturers. A utensil made by CORNING WARE is also generally available. They contain a material which absorbs mi-

crowaves. When placed in the oven the dish becomes hot. The longer it's heated, the hotter it gets. The method is to preheat the utensil in the oven, so that when the food is placed on it, searing occurs immediately. When the utensil is put back in the oven, the food will cook through the combination of heat from the utensil and the microwaves. The food has to be turned over halfway through cooking to sear the other side.

2. Element: This is similar to a broil element in a conventional range. Again foods must be turned as the element cooks only the side of the food facing it. This method of browning lengthens the cooking time because the element and magnetron cannot both be on at the same time. The oven would draw too much power for a 115 V. circuit. The heat from the element in the cavity does cause some extra work in cleaning the oven and also precludes the use of many regular microwave utensils such as paper, plastic, etc.

Defrost

This feature is described in Chapter 4—Defrosting Guide.

Variable Power Levels

Microwave ovens with variable power levels are becoming more common and range from those with two power levels to those with several or an infinite number of settings between very low and full power. This is similar to selecting different temperatures in a conventional range. One use for this feature is in defrosting, but it is also useful for certain foods which are better cooked at lower power levels, e.g.,

eggs and custards—because they can easily be overcooked at full power

stews—which are better simmered

economy cuts of meat—which require slow cooking for tenderizing

leftovers—are also better reheated at lower power level as slowing the heating allows the temperature to equalize throughout the food without starting to cook around the edges

In short, there is a real benefit to this feature and it is one worth having.

Turntables

Some ovens have this feature which rotates the glass tray with the food on it. This gives the same effect as that achieved by the stirrer fan, i.e., even cooking of the food.

Touch Control

Instead of mechanical timers or switches, some ovens feature an electronic solid-state control. This is a more elegant method of controlling the oven, but the mechanical timers do the same job. Solid state controls can be expected, however, to be more reliable and versatile. Cooking or defrosting times are entered by touch as with a calculator or push-button telephone. The clock is digital and usually serves as a time-of-day clock when not controlling the oven.

Types of Ovens Available

Countertop

This is the usual type of microwave oven, designed to sit on the kitchen counter and operate at 115 volts. There are two basic types:
1. Full sized 600-650 watts cooking power. *The times in this book are for an oven at this power level.*
2. Compacts. Smaller, lighter and, hence, more portable. Usually 450-500 watts and, therefore, slower than full-sized countertop ovens.

Over/under Range

A double oven range with the bottom oven being a conventional range (gas or electric) with surface burners. The top oven is basically a full-sized countertop microwave built into the range. *All the cooking times and recipes in this book should apply to this range.* The main advantage to this type is a saving of counter space.

Combination Oven

A full-sized range or wall oven with both microwave energy and conventional heat in the oven cavity. This can be used as a conventional range, solely as a microwave oven, or with both energy sources simultaneously.

The advantages are that it saves space and also has full cooking capability with none of the limitations of countertop ovens.

Since two energy sources are used at the same time, the recipes in this book are not suitable, although they could be adapted. Follow the manufacturer's instructions for cooking times.

The recipes in this book have been tested in an oven with a stated cooking power of 650 watts, which is the standard wattage for the majority of ovens. These ovens actually put out about 600 watts. To test the power of your own oven to see if it is within this range, place a cup filled with 6 ounces of cold water from the tap in the oven and see how long it takes to boil. It should be boiling in $2 - 2\frac{1}{4}$ minutes. If it is not quite boiling in this time, then you will probably have to add a minute or so to most of the recipes or subtract if it was boiling before the given time.

2. Getting Acquainted with Your Oven

The Many Functions of a Microwave Oven

Calling this appliance an *oven* is misleading for it has the capability to boil, fry, sear or steam and, in fact, do most of the regular top-of-the-stove jobs. In this respect, it is particularly good for making those sauces which often call for a double boiler, constant stirring and attention, and more often than not result in burnt saucepans when cooked on top of the stove. Vegetables, too, are really at their best cooked the microwave way, for very little water is required and they retain both color and flavor to the full.

Most people know what a boon a microwave oven is for serving convenience foods. You don't even have to warm the oven or defrost frozen convenience foods in advance. Pop them in the oven for a few minutes and they will be piping hot and tasting better than you ever thought they could. But this is not the whole story. With microwave cooking all foods are convenience foods.

If you are one of the many families now going back to using as many fresh foods as possible, the microwave oven is for you, because even if preparation takes a little longer than for convenience foods you will save tremendously in cooking time and produce better quality results. I've tried to give plenty of recipes for all types of cooking.

The microwave oven has yet another advantage over your conventional range in that it enables you to defrost foods rapidly, often as part of the cooking process. If you have unexpected guests or forget to take the meat out of the freezer, you can still have dinner on the table in a very short time.

One thing that your conventional oven can do better than the microwave oven is browning. But even here, there are ways to get

7

around this. For instance, most foods that are cooked in the microwave oven for longer than 10 minutes will brown automatically — roasts, poultry, etc. However since the air in the oven remains basically at room temperature, browning is not as complete as in a conventional range where the air is at 300-400°F. If you prefer a crisper surface, then you can place meat or poultry under your broiler for a final few minutes of cooking. Small items such as steaks, chops, hamburgers, will not brown and, in this case, there are a variety of alternatives. First, some ovens come with special browning utensils for this very purpose — see my chapter on Utensils. Secondly, you could use complementary cooking as I've suggested in some of the recipes. Complementary cooking is using your conventional range and microwave oven together. Or for hamburgers, meat loaf or similar items, I've used a coating of Kitchen Bouquet or soy sauce which gives a nice brown look when cooked. In the case of cakes the problem can be solved with icing or a topping.

One of the most practical features of the microwave oven in my mind is the fact that it is possible to reheat previously cooked foods in next to no time without drying out or loss of flavor. In fact, everything tastes freshly cooked, including steaks, pancakes and particularly vegetables, which are never successful when warmed up the conventional way. There are a thousand and one things that can be warmed in the microwave oven—rolls, breads, pies, cocktail tid-bits, and particularly baby foods and bottles. These latter are real time savers especially when baby's yelling for his bottle to warm.

Just think of all the added conveniences this will afford you. If you're part of a family that eats staggered meals, passing like ships in the night, so to speak, then it's possible to cook a full meal, serve individual portions onto dishes and refrigerate one for a latecomer when he or she arrives home. It's easy just to take the plate out of the refrigerator, put it straight into the oven and in seconds have a piping hot meal which tastes freshly cooked.

For those people who don't have a browning utensil or prefer items such as steaks, chops, pancakes, or waffles cooked the conventional way, it's simple to make an extra batch, freeze them and reheat in your microwave oven when required. They'll taste as fresh as the day they were cooked and think of all the time you can save.

Another advantage, and one that I find so useful when I have to leave home and travel for a few days or a week at a time, is that I can cook individual meals for my family, refrigerate or freeze them, remembering to indicate on them what they are and how long they will take in the microwave oven. They then take one out each evening or lunchtime, pop it in the oven for the given time and have a meal ready in minutes. They don't even do the washing up, just stack the dishes into the dishwasher! If that isn't convenience, then I don't know what is. And what's more, they say they've never been so well fed in my absence, thanks to the microwave oven.

It wouldn't be honest of me not to point out the limitations of microwave cooking here. They do exist, although the microwave oven itself is far more versatile than either the oven, broiler or surface elements of a regular range. The regular range can do all types of cooking only because these different means of getting heat into the food are all combined in the same appliance.

One limitation of the microwave oven is in the quantities of food you can cook. It is fine for a family or 4 or 5, but not for cooking Thanksgiving dinner for all the relatives. The cooking times become too long to make it worthwhile.

Another limitation shows up with some types of baking, although there are many things that can be baked in the microwave oven. Remember that the air in the oven is at room temperature. In a conventional oven the air is very hot. It is the drying action of this hot air that forms the crust on bread and browns pastry. Obviously this won't happen in a microwave oven. These things can be cooked in the microwave but will have a different texture and appearance than you are used to.

Finally, some of the less tender cuts of meat should be slow cooked in a conventional range so that tenderizing will occur in the meat. The use of marinades and liquids in cooking will give the tenderizing action. Whether it is enough depends on the particular cut of meat and your personal taste. I find most meats cook perfectly satisfactory in a microwave oven.

Before You Start to Cook

Time, not temperature, is the guiding factor in cooking with a microwave oven. Instead of setting time and temperature, you set only your minute timer.

The time needed to cook food in the microwave oven is based upon three things: the starting temperature of the food, the quantity, and the density.

Starting Temperature

If food is taken straight from freezer or refrigerator it will take longer to cook than if started at room temperature.

Quantity

The greater the quantity of food, the longer it takes to cook. Remember that the cooking power of your oven is approximately 600 watts. One potato will take 4 to 5 minutes to bake because all the energy goes into the single potato. Two potatoes will take 7 to 8 minutes because the energy is now divided between them.

Density

If a food is fairly dense, such as meat, it will take longer to cook or defrost than a food that is more porous. For example, a frozen chop will take longer than a slice of frozen bread.

This is another reason why foods are cooked one after the other in a microwave oven and not simultaneously as with cooking with a regular range. The foods would cook at different rates so that some would be done, others not. Also, as I've just pointed out, there is no saving in time by cooking foods all together. Foods cooked individually, one after the other, will take the same overall time and be done to perfection.

Another area where the different densities of foods make a difference is if you are reheating several items on a plate together, because naturally they too will absorb the microwave at different rates. I've found that the most satisfactory way to overcome this is to cover the plate loosely with a sheet of waxed paper so that the heat will be distributed evenly. The plate should also be allowed to stand for 1 or 2 minutes to complete the even distribution of the heat.

Occasionally strange things happen because some foods absorb energy more readily than others. For example, in a sausage roll the pastry wrap is much less dense than the sausage, so you would expect the pastry to become hot first. However, the sausage absorbs microwave energy much more readily because it contains a high percentage of moisture, while the pastry has very little. Therefore, after a few seconds of cooking, the pastry may still feel cool but the sausage inside will be hot.

Most items require a standing time of a few seconds to a few minutes after being removed from the oven. Remember that microwaves heat the outer sections of food. This heat is then conducted towards the center so that food actually continues to cook after leaving the oven. The standing time is necessary in order that the cooking process can finish and the center won't be undercooked. Standing times are given with the recipes.

Because microwaves penetrate the outer portions of food first, it is always best to place the thickest part of a food towards the outside of the dish so that the thinner parts do not overcook. If food can be arranged in a ring or circle this is ideal. Items such as baked potatoes are best placed with about 1″ between them so that the microwaves can penetrate from all sides. Do not set one in the center of a ring.

Stirring

This is necessary with items such as casseroles, puddings, vegetables and scrambled eggs, for as previously explained, food will be cooked first on the outside. By stirring, you can bring the center to the outside and the dish will be evenly cooked throughout.

When you are not certain about the cooking period, it is easy to open the door (which stops the cooking), check the food, then stir or turn the food as necessary and keep on cooking for the extra seconds or minutes needed. The cooking times given in this book can only be approximate, as all the variables, such as food moisture and starting temperature, voltage level in your home or district and the wattage of your particular brand of oven must be taken into consideration when determining the time required for a given recipe. But the problem is not complex, as it is always a matter of seconds or minutes and the food is rarely overcooked.

All of this may seem complicated at first sight, but soon it will become as familiar to you as your present type of cooking. The only difference will be the minimum amount of time spent cooking, no oven cleaning or overheated kitchen, and no problems in serving late-comers or unexpected guests.

3. The Best Utensils to Use in Your Oven

Because microwaves pass through certain materials rather than being absorbed by them, you have a wide choice of cooking utensils and containers that can be used in your oven.

In fact, you can use anything from paper to glass, even a wicker basket for warming rolls, provided it does not contain or have any metal parts. Because of this, there are many advantages in cooking in the microwave oven. It's unlikely you'll get burnt fingers because, for the most part, utensils remain cool unless food has been heated for a long time, thus transferring heat to the utensil. You can often cook in the same utensil in which you mix or prepare a food, defrost food right in the packages or pouches, and use throw-away items such as paper plates, cartons, napkins or towels to cook in or on, therefore doing away with messy washing up or scrubbing burnt or sticky pans. This is because glass, paper or dishwasher-safe plastics are transparent to microwaves, so they *transfer* microwaves without absorbing them, since they do not contain moisture molecules like foods.

Below is a Basic Cooking Kit which will give you an idea of the most popular sizes and shapes of utensils used in a microwave oven and suggested for the recipes throughout this book. It is, however, simple to substitute a similar type of bowl or dish if you do not have the one listed.

Most PYREX® and CORNING WARE® products can be used in the microwave oven with the exception of those with metal trim or parts, such as coffee makers or teapots. These include: CORNING WARE utensils with the * symbol and/or "For range and microwave"; PYREX Ware, whether transparent glass ovenware or decorated opal ware; CORELLE® Livingware, with the exception of the closed-handle cup which should not be used; CENTURA®

Basic Cooking Kit

Utensil	Quantity	Typical Use
6-oz. custard cup	4	eggs, custard, sauces
Covered casseroles:		
10-oz.	2	individual portions vegetables, scrambled eggs, sauces, gravy
32-oz.	1	desserts, vegetables, sauces, casseroles
48-oz.	1	vegetables, casseroles, desserts
64-oz.	1	vegetables, soups, beverages made in quantities, casseroles
8 x 8-in. square cake dish	1	fish and seafoods, desserts, cakes, chops
12 x 8-in. oblong baking dish	1	roasts, meats, poultry
48-oz. loaf dish	1	meat or fish loaf, casseroles
48-oz. round cake dish	1	cakes, appetizers, vegetables
9-in. pie plate	1	appetizers, omelettes, pies
Measuring Cups:		
16-oz. liquid measure	1	sauces, gravy, mixing, sautéeing onions, mushrooms
32-oz. liquid measure	1	as above
Additional items you might like to have:		
96-oz. covered casserole	1	soups, pasta
8-in. and/or 10-in. CORNING WARE Skillet with handle	1	where top-of-the-stove searing is necessary, also for chops, some vegetable dishes
Plastic or glass bulb-type baster		

Cook'n' Serve ware by Corning (available in U.S. only) if it has the * symbol and does not have metallic trim.

Note CENTURA dinnerware is not acceptable in microwave ovens.

Fire-King cookware by Anchor Hocking can be used in microwave ovens unless it has metal trim. Information is given on labels accompanying these products. *Temperware* by Lenox, a cook-and-serve-ware line, can also be used in the microwave oven.

There are other equivalent products on the market that can also be used. If in doubt, test the utensil in the oven for 15-30 seconds. If it does not heat up, it is microwave oven safe. If it gets very hot, it should not be used.

In addition to the above glass and ceramic ware, you can also use most china items, particularly for reheating items such as a meal on a plate or for making drinks, soups or hot cereals in individual cups or bowls. Check first that the cup handle is not glued on. Delicate glassware is not recommended as it may tend to crack when food or liquid is heated in it to a high temperature. When using china, check first to ensure that it does not have any metallic trim or glazing. The presence of metal can cause "arcing" or sparks set up by a static discharge of energy and could take off the trim and damage the china.

Paper Products

Many people find it hard to believe that you can use paper towels, napkins, plates or cups, (be sure that cups are for hot liquids only) in the microwave oven, but these throw-away items are ideal and, of course, lessen dishwashing considerably. Freezer wrap for thawing frozen foods as well as the type of heavy cardboard that comes with your meat packages can also be used. In addition, many frozen foods or take-out foods can be cooked or reheated right in their cardboard cartons.

Plastic Utensils

Plastics that are of rigid materials and are marked or labelled dishwasher-safe can be used in the microwave oven, including dishes, cups, certain freezer containers, picnic-ware and thermal cups and mugs, although it is recommended that they be used only for heating foods to a serving temperature rather than cooking for any length of time. Be particularly careful when heating products with a high fat or sugar content which rise to a high temperature very quickly, as the plastic could become misshapen or pitted.

Plastic baby bottles can be used in the microwave oven without harm.

Plastic pouches such as boil-in-the-bag which are specifically designed for heating or freezing can also be used to defrost or cook foods completely in the microwave oven, but it is necessary to punch several holes in them to release the steam. For simple defrosting this is ideal. However, when cooking food, it's usually much easier to transfer the food first to a regular container as this avoids having to remove hot food from a steaming pouch. Regular plastic storing bags *cannot* be used in a microwave oven as they are likely to melt and contaminate the food.

Note   Most Melamine plastic utensils are not recommended for microwave oven use as they tend to absorb microwaves and retain heat.

Straw and Wicker

Straw or wicker baskets can be used in the microwave oven for a few seconds to heat bread, buns, rolls or potato chips.

Wood

Most wood items such as steak platters or serving boards tend to crack if left in the oven for any length of time because of their high moisture content, and are not recommended. If you accidentally leave a wooden spatula or spoon in for stirring while cooking, there shouldn't be any problem.

Metal

Metal utensils CANNOT BE USED in the microwave oven. In some ovens, metal can actually damage the magnetron, but also, as I have already said, metal reflects microwaves and food will not cook or will be slowed down considerably.

Before putting any quantity of metal in your oven, for any purpose, check the instructions given by the manufacturer of your oven.

In those ovens where some metal can be used:

Foil: Foil can be used in small quantities to cover chicken wings or legs or areas where there is a fairly large bone in meat or where one area of meat is thinner than the whole.

Metal skewers: Although it is not generally recommended, it is possible to use metal skewers where there is a much larger quantity of food than the metal. In this case, the microwaves will be attracted by the large density of the food.

TV trays or foil: It is possible to cook foods in trays that are less than 1/2-inch deep because this is shallow enough to allow the heat to penetrate from the top. However, it is advisable to transfer food from trays deeper than 1/2-inch to an alternative container.

In all cases, ensure that metal is not touching the sides of your oven as it will cause arcing.

Be especially careful not to leave the small metal "ties" that come with plastic bags or frozen food when defrosting, as these will "arc" and cause sparks in the oven as well as melting the plastic which will get onto the food.

Pottery or Earthenware

Some glazed earthenware pots can be used in the oven, but it is best to test the pot first. Some earthenware absorbs microwave energy because of metals in the composition of the clay. To test, place the pot in the oven together with half a cup of water in a measuring cup to protect the oven. If, after one minute, the utensil is hot or quite warm, do not use in the oven.

Covers

In my recipes I have specified whenever a dish should be covered. There are two very good reasons for using covers. The first is to contain moisture which, when heated, will penetrate the food for faster, more even cooking. Second, a cover will prevent spatters.

Casserole lids, waxed paper, plates or saucers can all be used effectively as covers, provided you do not use anything that contains metal. Plastic wrap can be used providing it does not touch the food; it is advisable to punch one or two holes in it after cooking and before removing to let steam escape, or you can burn your hand. If it does touch food, it is likely to melt. Be especially careful when removing this type of wrap because it forms a tighter seal and steam may still be trapped beneath it. Ordinary paper towels can be used to prevent spatters from bacon.

Thermometers

The regular meat or candy thermometers *cannot* be used in food while it is cooking in the oven because they are all made of metal. Where temperature is important, remove food from oven and test while standing.

Be sure to follow the instructions given in my recipes regarding temperature shown on the thermometer, rather than temperatures you would use in cooking conventionally. Because cooking times are shorter in microwave cooking and a standing time is necessary for heat to flow towards the center of the food, you stop cooking when the thermometer indicates 10-20° less than it would in conventional cooking.

Use of the Meat Thermometer This graph may be a little technical, but it shows you what happens when a roast is cooked.

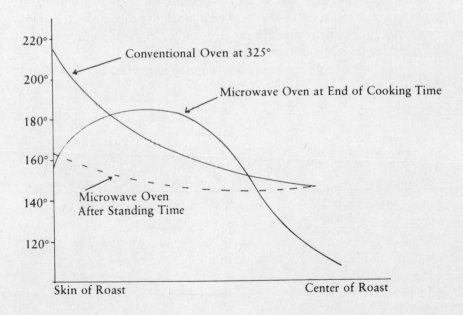

The first line shows what happens when a roast is cooked in a conventional oven at 325°. As might be expected, the roast is hottest at the surface and the temperature becomes cooler as you move towards the center. The internal temperature is about 155 to 160° fahrenheit at the end of the cooking time and this is the reading you would get on the meat thermometer.

The temperature distribution is rather different in a microwave oven. Because the heat is built up below the surface, the hottest temperature is somewhat below the surface. The skin of the roast is cooler because it is losing heat to the air in the oven which, as you remember, is basically at room temperature. Beyond the zone of 1 to 1¼ inches below the surface where the microwaves can penetrate, the temperature falls off very rapidly and the center of the roast is quite cool. Cooking would be complete when the meat thermometer gives a reading that is less than the reading you would look for in a conventional oven.

Now during the standing time, the heat which has built up in the zone just below the surface of the roast flows towards the center. The temperature at the center of the roast increases (you can watch this on your thermometer), and the temperature just below the surface of the roast goes down as heat flows away from this zone. The dotted line shows the temperature after the standing time.

Remember that you cannot cook with the meat thermometer in the oven but must remove the food and place the thermometer in it for a reading. Place the tip of the thermometer in the thickest part of the food. Keep it away from fat or bone.

The following table can be used as a guide in the use of your meat thermometer.

Food	Reading at end of cooking	Final reading after standing
Roast Beef—Rare	120° F.	140° F.
—Medium	140	160
—Well	160	170
Lamb	160	175
Pork	170	185
Ham	130	140
Chicken	180	190
Turkey	175	190

Browning Utensils

The browning utensils now available come in varied shapes, from flat grills to skillet-shaped dishes with sides, cover and detachable handles. There is also a variety of sizes available.

All of these browners are coated with a material that absorbs microwaves. They are preheated in a microwave oven and then the food to be cooked is placed on the hot surface of the browning utensil. The sketch below shows the cooking mechanism.

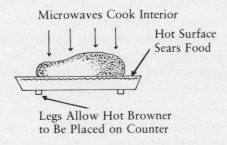

Microwaves Cook Interior

Hot Surface
Sears Food

Legs Allow Hot Browner
to Be Placed on Counter

The hot surface of the browner sears the food but because the cooking times are very short, most of the heat transferred from the browner to the food stays at the surface and does not have time to conduct towards the center of the food. Most of the actual cooking action in the interior of the food comes from the microwaves penetrating the food.

If you had a browning utensil that was 1 square inch in size, it would get hotter the longer you heat it, but you would finally reach a point where no more heating occurs. Now if you had a browner 2 square inches and heated it, it would take longer to become hot because the energy would now be heating 2 square inches of surface. This is exactly the same thing that happens when you place more food in the oven; the cooking time goes up. For this reason, the larger browners require more preheating time than the smaller ones.

It is a mystery to me why some browning utensils come with a lid. This traps steam and moisture in the browner which washes away the browning on the surface of the food. For searing, you should always use the browning utensil uncovered.

You can use butter, oil, fat or a non-stick spray for easier cleaning of the browner after cooking. Preheat your browner first and then apply this just before putting the food in.

Because there is a slight unevenness in the cooking pattern of all microwave ovens, the heat distribution in your browner may be uneven after preheating. Allow 30 to 60 seconds standing time for the heat to equalize, and then preheat for an additional 30 to 40 seconds to bring it back up to temperature. This will give you the most even heat across the surface.

As you can see from the sketch, the side of the food in contact with the browner takes heat out of the browner. When you turn the food to sear the second side, the browner is much cooler than it was when the first side was placed on it and the browning action on the second side of the food will be considerably less. You may wish to reheat the browner for a minute or so between sides on large steaks for example.

You can check for the desired degree of doneness simply by slitting the steak or chop with a knife and checking the interior color.

Because of the different sizes of browners, you are going to have to experiment to find the correct preheating time for a particular food item. I would recommend about 2 minutes for frying eggs; about 3 minutes for items such as pancakes, french toast and grilled cheese sandwiches, and $4^1/2$ to 5 minutes for meat, fish or poultry.

The following table gives approximate cooking times for common items.

Food	Cooking time 1st side	Cooking time 2nd side
2 fried eggs	50-60 seconds	
6-8 sausages	5 min.—turn frequently	
french toast	25 seconds	25 seconds
grilled cheese sandwich	40 seconds	30 seconds
small steak—rare	1 minute	50 seconds
—medium	$1^1/2$ minutes	1 minute
—well-done	2 minutes	$1^1/2$ minutes
2 pork chops	$2^1/2$ minutes	2 minutes
2 lamb chops ($3/4''$)	$2^1/2$ minutes	2 minutes
2 pieces chicken	7 minutes	3 minutes
2 hamburger patties	2 minutes	$1^1/4$ minutes

4. Defrosting Guide

Among the many uses and conveniences of microwave cooking is that of being able to defrost frozen foods right in the oven. This is something that cannot be done in your conventional oven.

The benefits of defrosting in your oven are threefold:
Speed — foods can be defrosted in a few minutes instead of several hours the conventional way
Less moisture loss — valuable juices are retained
No bacteria build-up — usual with conventional thawing

Defrosting is a slightly different process from regular cooking in the microwave oven. The intention is to thaw the food right through to the center with no cooking taking place at the outside or around the edges.

To accomplish this the oven must be slowed down. Ice in food is more like glass to microwaves and absorbs energy poorly. Water, by contrast, absorbs readily. As frozen food begins to absorb microwave energy, a thin layer around the outside of the food is thawed and can quickly reach temperatures where cooking begins. If the oven is turned off before this point is reached, the heat in the outer layer will flow inward, melting the ice as it goes. After a short time the oven can be turned on again to increase the quantity of heat in the food and turned off again before cooking begins.

There are two ways of slowing down the oven for defrosting:
1. To alternate short cooking times and resting times. This can be done either manually or automatically, depending on your brand of oven.
2. To use lower power with continuous cooking. A number of microwave ovens have the low power feature.

When defrosting foods, start them in their packages or freezer wrap, providing they do not contain any metal — remember also to remove metallic tie wraps. You can then turn packages over halfway through defrosting or take the food out of the package or remove the freezer wrap and place in a dish or shallow container. Stir, re-arrange or separate food as it begins to defrost. More specific instructions are given in the following chart and in recipes and charts throughout the book. Most foods require a short standing time to complete thawing throughout.

Some frozen foods are extremely easy to defrost, while others take a little more care and attention, as you will see from the charts.

Easy
Pancakes, bread, rolls, cake
>These items have a very low density and moisture content and microwaves can penetrate right through them.

Frozen fruit juice concentrate, berries in syrup
>These have a high liquid content, small size. Liquid acts as a good heat transfer medium.

Standard size packages of vegetables.
>In this case, microwaves can easily penetrate their low mass, slab shape. Because vegetables are washed before they are frozen, the moisture on them turns to steam and transfers heat to the vegetables when set in a covered utensil. A small quantity of water can be added also. Times are given in the Vegetable chapter.

None of these foods requires special defrost techniques. Refer to individual recipes for instructions.

Moderately Easy
Steak, chops, hamburger patties, fish, chicken pieces
>Although these foods are of a higher density than those listed above, microwaves can easily reach the center from each side because of their basically slab shape. Defrosting is done by using the cycle of cooking and resting times or low power. Be especially careful with fish, where cooking could take place around the edges. It is often best to give a little longer standing time after defrosting, i.e., 5–10 minutes for temperature equalization and complete defrosting.

>The following chart gives instructions for foods within the Moderately Easy category. Times are approximate and will vary according to the quantity of food and with your make of oven. However, it is very easy to assess the progress of defrosting and you can use your judgement. Use a fork, skewer or

Dinner Menu, page 29
Steak, Deep-Browned Potatoes,
Green Peas, Chocolate Rum Mousse, Vanilla-Chocolate Cupcakes

Cold Dinner Menu, page 30
Vichyssoise, Veal Loaf, Creamy Rice Pudding

meat thermometer probe to feel for ice crystals in the center of the food. Stop defrosting in the oven when there are still some ice crystals in the center. These will disappear during the final standing time.

If your oven has a defrost feature of either the cycling or low power type, set the timer for the time shown in the table. If you do not have a defrost feature on your oven, you can cycle it off and on by hand. The oven should be on for about half the time given in the table and off for the other half. You can begin with cooking times of 1-2 minutes. As thawing proceeds, shorten the cooking times to 20-30 seconds to avoid cooking.

Food item	Time	Resting Time
1 lb. ground meat	5 mins.	5 mins.
2 lb. ground meat	8 mins.	8 mins.
16 oz. steak	3 mins.	4 mins.
1 lb. pork chops	3½ mins.	4 mins.
3 lb. spare ribs	8-10 mins.	10 mins.
1 lb. fish	3 mins.	5 mins.
1 lb. cut-up chicken	6 mins.	10 mins.
2 lb. cut-up chicken	10-12 mins.	15 mins.

Hints: Separate chicken pieces, break up ground meat and scrape off pieces already thawed.

More Difficult
Roast, chicken or other poultry, large quantities of ground beef. These are dense and uneven in shape with large mass and relatively small surface area. In this case it is necessary to allow time for the conduction of heat to the center of the foods. This calls for the use of the defrost cycle—heating and resting—or low power, *plus* additional resting periods between defrost cycles and a longer resting period at the end.

Food item	Step 1	Intermediate Rest time	Step 2	Final rest
Roast – 2 lb.	6 mins.	3 mins.	3 mins.	10 mins.
3 lb.	10 mins.	4 mins.	5 mins.	12 mins.
4 lb.	14 mins.	5 mins.	7 mins.	15 mins.
5 lb.	16 mins.	7 mins.	8 mins.	20 mins.
Chicken – 2 lb.	8 mins.	5 mins.	4 mins.	10 mins.
4 lb.	15 mins.	5 mins.	7 mins.	15 mins.

When cycling manually, cooking times can be up to 2-3 minutes to start, decreased as thawing proceeds.

Hints: Turn roast, chicken, etc., over half-way through. In the case of roast beef, it's best to leave some ice in the center so that it is rare after cooking. Test by pushing meat thermometer or skewer through center; there will be some resistance.

Meat or poultry weighing more than the quantities given above are best thawed in the refrigerator overnight. If, however, you are very pressed for time, it is possible to defrost larger items. However, the effort involved is hardly worth the trouble as you will see from the following:
To defrost a 6–7 lb. turkey:

Step	Defrost time	Rest
1.	16 mins.	5 mins.
2.	12 mins.	5 mins.
3.	12 mins.	20 mins.

To defrost a 10-lb. goose:

Step	Defrost time	Rest
1.	20 mins.	5 mins.
2.	16 mins.	5 mins.
3.	12 mins.	20 mins.

Remove plastic wrap covering birds and take out the giblets as defrosting begins to take place. It will also be necessary to turn the bird over onto its back and also onto alternate sides during the defrosting period to ensure even defrosting. If meat begins to gray or change color, cooking is beginning to take place and defrosting cycles should be slowed down. Push a metal skewer through poultry to ensure that it is thawed throughout. You will feel the resistance of the ice if it is not quite thawed.

The items on these charts include foods in most common use. Other foods or larger quantities can be substituted following the basic principles for easy, medium or more difficult defrosting.

Other Uses of Defrost: Since defrost features slow down the oven, you can also use the above mentioned methods to cook tougher cuts of meat—some tenderizing will result. Use approximately twice the normal cooking time. Use the defrost for custards, eggs, etc., where slower cooking gives better results.

5. Meal Planning

Because cooking with microwaves is so totally different from conventional cooking, I have devised some simple rules to help you get the best use out of your oven in the shortest possible time. This will show you how, by organizing your menus and cooking foods in the best sequence, you can have all the foods you need cooked and ready to serve at the same time, with the maximum convenience and savings of time and fuel.

The scope for cooking with microwaves is limited only by your imagination. Once you've read through the examples listed below to understand the underlying principles, it might be an idea to take a pencil and paper and plan a few meals yourself. You will soon reach the point where you do the organizing in your head and automatically apply these principles whenever you prepare a meal.

First it's necessary to consider the other appliances in your kitchen, (principally your regular range) as auxiliary appliances you can use to complement your microwave oven.

Second, remember also that the microwave oven has three basic uses: cooking, reheating and defrosting. In organizing a meal you may use only one or all of these capabilities.

Third, when cooking with microwaves you can interrupt the cooking of any item at any time *without affecting the quality of the food.* This is one of the major differences between microwave cooking and conventional cooking. It means that you can interrupt cooking if you wish, to soften butter, prepare a sauce, warm the baby's bottle, etc.

Fourth you can let most items stand while the others are being cooked, with little loss of heat. Covering a roast or chicken with aluminum foil or keeping the vegetables in covered utensils will help the food retain heat. This means that at the conclusion of cooking the entire meal will still be hot and ready to serve. As mentioned earlier, a standing time after cooking is necessary for many items anyway.

If, on the other hand, some cooling has occurred, the easiest thing to do is to place the meal on the serving plate and return it to the oven for a few seconds. Be careful not to reheat too long, as you will cook the food further.

Cooking an entire meal by microwaves

Here are some sample menus.

Roast Beef

	Cooking time	Standing Time	Page No.
3-4 lb. rolled rib roast with onion gravy	28 mins.	20 mins.	105
Potatoes au Gratin	15 mins.	10 mins.	206
Frozen peas and mushrooms	6 mins.	2 mins.	202
Peach Crumble	6 mins.	4 mins.	246

Method: Cook the beef first because it takes the longest time. Then cook the vegetables while the roast is standing. The Peach Crumble can then be cooking while you are eating the first course.

Each item on the menu has, of course, a preparation time as well as cooking time. Naturally you would use the time available while the first item is cooking to begin preparation of the rest of the menu.

Orange Glazed Ham

	Cooking time	Standing time	Page No.
1³/₄-2 lb. ham slice	20 mins.	5 mins.	134
Baked sweet potatoes (4)	15-18 mins.	3-4 mins.	208
1 lb. spinach, buttered	4-5 mins.	2 mins.	211
Caramel Pudding	15 mins.		230

Method: Make caramel pudding and refrigerate to thicken and cool. Next cook the sweet potatoes, which will retain their heat, followed by the glazed ham. Finally cook the spinach while ham is standing.

Haddock "à la Grecque"

	Cooking time	Standing time	Page No.
1 lb. frozen haddock fillets			
	Defrost—3 mins.	5 mins.	
	Cook —8-10 mins.	5 mins.	158
Confetti Rice	15 mins.	10 mins.	221
Caramel baked apples	8-9 mins.	3-4 mins.	238

Method: First defrost the fish. Leave on kitchen counter to continue thawing while cooking the rice. While rice is cooking, prepare the fish and the apples. When rice is done, cook the fish. Cook the apples while you are eating your first course.

Note All menus are for 4 servings.

Complementary Cooking

This form of cooking combines the use of both the microwave oven and conventional range. Items such as seafood and vegetables should always be cooked in the microwave oven if you appreciate good food. These types of foods are much better in color, texture and flavor when cooked in the microwave oven.

You will probably cook less tender cuts of meat in the conventional range for the best tenderness. The cooking time will be longer but you needn't be in the kitchen once you have placed the meat in the oven. You can then cook the rest of the meal in the microwave just before eating.

Where complementary cooking is appropriate for this reason or for browning of meat, I have mentioned it in the directions with the recipe.

Meals to Freeze or Refrigerate and Reheat

The capabilities of your microwave oven can be most fully enjoyed when you use it to plan meals in conjunction with your freezer. With many dishes the preparation often takes longer than the cooking but preparation time is scarcely increased if you double quantities. You will find it very easy to make two meals when you have time to spend in your kitchen, and then freeze one for later use when you are busy.

In families where everyone cannot take meals at the same time, where the cook has to be away from home for a time — this is certainly so in my family—or when entertaining is often on the spur of the moment, the ability to have a hot meal on the table in minutes, tasting as good or better than if cooked fresh by the conventional methods, is one of the greatest boons offered by a microwave oven. You will also find you can take advantage of seasonal price reductions and supermarket specials by cooking for your freezer whenever you have the time.

I have prepared these menus to show you some ways to start using freezer and oven in combination and also to show how easy it will be for you to use your own favorite recipes in the same way.

Lunch Menu

	Defrosting Time	Heating Time	Page No.
Chinese Fish Fillets	5	2-4	161
Long grain rice	5	5-8	220
Vanilla Ice Cream			
Sauce Jubilée	10	2-3	255

Method: First cook Chinese Fish Fillets using fresh fillets. Cool, cover, freeze. (It will keep 2 to 3 weeks.) Thaw on defrost, turning dish once, then reheat.

Next, cook rice and freeze. (Rice will keep 6 months frozen.) Thaw on defrost, then reheat until hot, stirring twice. Sauce Jubilee will keep 3 to 4 months in freezer and takes only 10 minutes on defrost to thaw out. When ready to serve, just warm it up.

Dinner Menu

	Page No.
Steak	110
Deep-Browned Potatoes	204
Green Peas	200
Chocolate Rum Mousse	234
Vanilla Chocolate Cupcakes	262

Method: Cook Deep-Browned Potatoes in the morning and leave on kitchen counter. Thaw steaks (cooked conventionally and frozen) on kitchen counter for 2 to 4 hours, then reheat 2 to 4 minutes on hot browning utensil. (See full directions on page 110.) Cook fresh or frozen peas as preferred. Reheat potatoes 1 minute, stir to cover with the sauce and heat 30 to 40 seconds. The Chocolate Rum Mousse will keep 3 months frozen—it can be served frozen as ice cream or removed to refrigerator 3 to 5 hours before serving.

Cupcakes will freeze and keep for 2 months. Remove from freezer a few hours before serving.

Cold Dinner for a Summer Evening

	Page No.
Vichyssoise	66
Veal Loaf	125
Salad	
Creamy Rice Pudding	232

Method: The Vichyssoise, Veal Loaf and Creamy Rice Pudding can all be cooked in advance in the microwave oven, then frozen. To serve cold, all that is required is to defrost each item, then let stand for a few minutes to bring to room temperature. The Veal Loaf will take 5 to 6 minutes at defrost plus 10 minutes standing time. The Vichyssoise will take 8 to 10 minutes on defrost and should be stirred once or twice during the defrost cycle. The Creamy Rice Pudding will take 3½ to 5½ minutes on defrost. Test with a fork and remove from oven when a few crystals remain in center and let stand while eating first course.

My chart gives heating times for pre-cooked frozen foods whether store-bought or home-made.

Heating Frozen Pre-cooked Food

Product	Portion	Heating Instructions	Time
Baked Foods			
Bread, thawing baked	4 slices	Arrange in single layer on paper towel, uncovered.	10 seconds; rest 15 seconds; 10 seconds
Buns, hamburger and frankfurter	1 bun	Heat, uncovered, on absorbent paper, paper napkin, or serving dish.	24-26 seconds
	2 buns	Same as above.	45-47 seconds
	4 buns	Same as above.	$1^1/_4$ to $1^1/_2$ minutes
Danish pastries, baked	4 servings (8 oz.)	Heat, uncovered, on paper plate or serving dish.	$1^1/_2$-2 minutes
Dumplings, apple, baked	2 servings	Heat in serving dishes. Let stand 5 minutes before serving.	5-$5^1/_2$ minutes
Pie, fruit, baked	8-inch pie	Remove from foil pan; place in serving plate. Temperature given is for warm pie. Let stand 5 minutes before serving.	$5^1/_2$-$6^1/_2$ minutes
Rolls, dinner, baked	2 medium	Heat, uncovered, on paper plate or serving dish.	20-25 seconds
	4 medium	Same as above.	40-50 seconds
	6 medium	Same as above; arrange in circle.	60-65 seconds
Prepared Foods			
EGGS AND CHEESE Ravioli in Tomato sauce	$12^1/_2$ oz.	Remove from foil container. Place in 1-quart casserole, covered.	5 minutes
Macaroni and cheese sauce mix	$7^1/_4$ oz.	Combine all ingredients as directed on package. Place in 2-quart casserole, covered.	10 minutes; stand 5 minutes

Product	Portion	Heating Instructions	Time
FISH AND SEAFOOD			
Frozen and breaded Fish Sticks	8 oz.	Arrange in a circle on paper plate, uncovered.	Cook 1 minute; rest; cook 2 minutes
Frozen and breaded Scallops, Fish or Shrimp	7 oz.	Arrange in a circle on paper plate or towel, uncovered.	$1^1/_2$ minutes
MEATS AND POULTRY			
Roast beef, turkey, chicken, and other meats	4 oz.	Heat $1^1/_4$ minutes; let stand 2 minutes. Return to oven and complete heating.	4-5 minutes
Chicken in gravy	1 serving	Heat 2 minutes; let stand 2 minutes. Return to oven, cover and complete heating, turning dish several times. Let stand 5 minutes before serving.	8-10 minutes
Chow mein	14 oz.	Heat 2 minutes; let stand 2 minutes. Stir. Cover and complete heating, stirring once again. Let stand 4 minutes before serving.	$7-7^1/_2$ minutes
T.V. Dinner, 1 meat, 2 vegetables	1 serving (10-11 oz.)	Remove from aluminum tray to dinner plate. Heat, uncovered, turning plate frequently. Let stand 2 minutes before serving.	5-6 minutes
Hamburger, cooked	1 4-oz. patty	Heat, uncovered, on serving plate. Do not overcook.	$1-1^1/_2$ minutes
	2 4-oz. patties	Same as above.	$2-2^1/_2$ minutes
Macaroni, beef and tomatoes	$11^1/_2$ oz.	Remove from foil container. Place in 1-quart casserole, covered.	7-8 minutes
Meat loaf	$1^1/_2$ lbs.	Remove from foil pan. Place in $1^1/_2$-quart loaf dish. Cover with waxed paper.	Cook 8 minutes; rest 5 minutes; cook 5 minutes; stand 5 minutes
Ribs, cooked, barbecued	2 lbs.	When edges are softened, transfer from plastic container to serving platter. Cover with waxed paper.	1 minute transfer 6 minutes

Product	Portion	Heating Instructions	Time
Sloppy Joe Sauce with beef	26 oz.	Remove from foil container. Place in 2-quart casserole, covered. Stir twice.	9-10 minutes

VEGETABLES

Product	Portion	Heating Instructions	Time
Frozen Tater Tots or Croquettes	16 oz.	Place on paper plate or towel-lined plate, uncovered.	5-6 minutes
Frozen French fries or Shoestring potatoes	16 oz.	Place on paper plate or towel-lined plate.	5-6 minutes
Frozen Baked Stuffed Potatoes	6 oz. (2 halves)	Place in shallow baking dish. Cover with waxed paper.	7 minutes
Frozen Batter fried Onion Rings	16 oz. (30-32 rings)	Place on paper plate, uncovered.	2 minutes for 8 rings

Refrigerated Temperature

Product	Portion	Heating Instructions	Time
Cooked meat roast beef, turkey, chicken, etc.	4 oz.	Heat, uncovered, on serving plate. If gravy is included or any other sauce, increase time by 1 minute.	$1^{1}/_{2}$-2 minutes
	8 oz.	Same as above	$2^{1}/_{4}$-$3^{1}/_{2}$ minutes
Hamburger, cooked	1 patty	Heat, uncovered, on serving plate. Do not overcook.	45-50 seconds
	2 patties	Same as above	$1^{1}/_{4}$-$1^{1}/_{2}$ minutes
Macaroni and cheese	2 cups	Place in 8-inch glass pie plate. Cover with sheet of waxed paper. Stir half-way through cooking time. Let stand 3 minutes before serving.	3-4 minutes

6. Appetizers

The kind of appetizers you serve can do a lot toward breaking the ice at your party and help guests to feel at ease. As you know, conversation will fly when everyone gathers around your hibachi to barbecue shrimp, meat balls, or whatever savory you provide. Don't be surprised if your microwave oven also becomes a conversation piece! There are many other advantages for the hostess.

Many appetizers can be prepared early in the day and refrigerated until serving time. If they are stored wrapped, they are simply transferred directly to the microwave oven for heating in seconds or minutes. This, of course, gives you much more time to spend with your guests and enjoy your own party instead of spending half the time in the kitchen. Those foods that need to be piping hot always will be because you can cook one batch while serving another. In addition, you never need be caught unprepared if the hockey or football gang suddenly descends on you, for you can walk in with hot crisped chips or freshly toasted peanuts within minutes. A plateful will be hot in 45 seconds to 1 minute, and they become crisp in the time it takes to hand them around. If you prefer a hot dip, it's easy to do and it can be surrounded with crisp crackers, good breads, or very easy do-it-yourself appetizers.

Walnuts Heloise

Unusual and most tasty — also quite a conversation piece.

1	lb. unshelled walnuts	1/2	teaspoon ground
	Grated rind of 1 orange		cardamom
1	teaspoon cinnamon	1/4	teaspoon nutmeg

Crack the nuts, but do not remove from the shells. Place on a pie plate. Mix the remaining ingredients together. Sprinkle over the walnuts. Heat, uncovered, 5 minutes. Stir, cook another 3 minutes. Serve hot with nut picks. These look nice in a basket lined with red or green linen.

Sugared Spiced Nuts

Will keep for 6 to 8 weeks in a metal or airtight container, in a cool place. Nice to serve with sherry or punch.

3/4	cup brown sugar	2 1/2	tablespoons water
3/4	teaspoon salt	1	cup walnut halves
1	teaspoon cinnamon	1	cup pecan halves
1/2	teaspoon ground cloves or coriander	1	cup Brazil nuts or replace variety of nuts
1/4	teaspoon allspice		with 3 cups of one
1/4	teaspoon nutmeg or cardamom		type

In a 1-quart glass casserole, combine brown sugar, salt, spices and water. Cook, uncovered, 2 minutes, stirring once. Add 1/2 cup nuts to syrup mixture, stir with a fork until coated. Then lift out nuts with fork to drain excess syrup, and place in a single layer in oblong glass dish. Prepare another 1/2 cup nuts as before, add to those in the dish. Cook, uncovered, 4 minutes or until syrup on nuts begins to harden slightly. Transfer nuts to waxed paper to cool until crisp. Finish the remaining nuts in the same manner. These are also delicious used as a topping for ice cream.

Hot Savory Pretzels

These will also keep well in an airtight glass jar or plastic container at room temperature.

<table>
<tr><td>1/4</td><td>cup margarine</td><td>1/4</td><td>teaspoon garlic powder</td></tr>
<tr><td>4</td><td>cups small pretzels</td><td>1/4</td><td>teaspoon each celery salt and plain salt</td></tr>
<tr><td>1</td><td>teaspoon crumbled tarragon</td><td></td><td></td></tr>
<tr><td>2</td><td>teaspoons parsley flakes</td><td></td><td></td></tr>
</table>

Melt margarine in a 2-quart casserole, uncovered, 1 minute. Add the remaining ingredients, toss well to coat pretzels. Heat 3 minutes, tossing thoroughly after each minute. Serve.

Toasted Hot Nuts

Everyone enjoys these crisped and delicious hot appetizers. Use any type of shelled nuts of one variety or a mixture.

Spread salted or unsalted nuts on a glass pie plate. Toast $1^1/_4$ to $1^1/_2$ cups (about $^1/_2$ lb.) at a time, uncovered, $1^1/_2$ minutes, stirring once. Serve hot.

Chutney Sardines

Prepare as many narrow strips of toasted bread as you wish. Keep in plastic box with a piece of waxed paper between each layer. With the help of the microwave oven, the hot canape is ready in seconds.

<table>
<tr><td>12</td><td>smoked Norwegian sardines</td><td>2</td><td>tablespoons melted butter</td></tr>
<tr><td>4</td><td>teaspoons chutney</td><td>4</td><td>tablespoons grated cheese</td></tr>
<tr><td>12</td><td>toasted bread strips</td><td></td><td></td></tr>
</table>

Spread chutney generously over the toasted bread strips. Place a sardine on each. Pour a little melted butter over each sardine. Sprinkle with grated cheese. Set in a circle on paper plate or towel and place in oven. Cook, uncovered, 1 minute. Serve.

Sweet and Sour Wieners

The cocktail wieners can be replaced by 1 pound of ground beef or pork or lamb, shaped into little sausages. No seasoning added.

1	lb. cocktail wieners	1	can (10 ounces) tomato
1	small onion, chopped fine		soup
			grated rind and juice
1/2	teaspoon salt		of 1 lemon
1/4	teaspoon pepper	1/4	cup brown sugar
1	teaspoon paprika	1	cup pineapple chunks,
1/2	teaspoon ground coriander (optional)		well drained (optional)

In an 8 × 8 × 2″ glass dish, combine the onion, salt, pepper, and paprika, coriander, tomato soup, lemon juice and rind, and brown sugar. Cook, uncovered, 7 to 8 minutes, stirring twice. Place wieners (or meat balls) into the sauce, stirring gently until they are coated. Cook another 7 minutes, turning dish once during cooking period. Add drained pineapple chunks, heat 1 minute. Serve hot with picks.

Cold Cocktail Sausages

These can be prepared in advance on the day of a party. Do not refrigerate as they must be served at room temperature.

1/2	cup chili sauce	2	green onions, chopped fine
1	tablespoon prepared horseradish	1/4	cup sherry or dry Madeira
1	teaspoon Worcestershire sauce	1 to 2 lbs. cocktail sausages	

In an 8-inch glass cake dish, mix all the ingredients, except the sausages. Heat, uncovered, 2 minutes, stir and set aside. Brown sausages in batches on a hot browning utensil, uncovered, 2 to 3 minutes, turning once or twice. As they are cooked, add quickly to cooled sauce. When sausages are all cooked, cover bowl and let stand 3 to 6 hours before serving. Serve with picks.

Hot Crabmeat or Shrimp Canapes

Very elegant, easy to put together, cooks in 1¹/₂ to 2 minutes, and one plate can be served while the next is cooking. Still easier if you keep on hand 2-inch squares of thinly sliced toasted bread.

6	*ounces frozen crabmeat or ready-to-heat shrimps*	¹/₂	*teaspoon curry powder*
1	*cup mayonnaise*	1	*egg white, beaten stiff*
1	*teaspoon lemon juice*		*2-inch squares of thinly toasted bread or melba rounds*

Defrost crabmeat or shrimp, still in box, for 6 minutes, turning once. Remove from box and shred crabmeat with a fork, removing any shells. Cut shrimp into small pieces.

Stir mayonnaise into chosen fish. Mix lemon juice and curry powder together and add to mixture. Then fold in beaten egg white. Pile about 1 teaspoon of the mixture on each toasted square or melba round. Arrange 12 canapes on serving dish or other plate and cook 1¹/₂ to 2 minutes or until hot and puffy. Repeat until all the mixture is used. Serve as soon as ready.

Hot Shrimp Canapes, page 38
Devilled Cocktail Sausages, page 40
Cheese Crisps, page 42

New England Chowder, page 69
Health Vegetable Soup, page 65

Baked Golden Shrimp

This can only be made with fresh or frozen uncooked, unshelled shrimp.

1	lb. raw shrimp, unshelled	1	tablespoon dry sherry
1	tablespoon soy sauce	1	tablespoon brown sugar
2	teaspoons Worcestershire sauce		

Wash the unshelled shrimp in cold water and spread them on absorbent paper to dry. Mix the remaining ingredients together in a bowl.

Place the shrimp on a 9-inch pie plate. Pour the sauce over. Stir to mix. Let stand 30 minutes to 1 hour.

Cook 10 to 15 minutes, stirring twice. When shrimp are pink, cool and shell. Serve with the sauce, using picks.

Curried Smoked Oysters

Quick and delicious.

1	tin undrained smoked oysters
1/4	teaspoon curry powder
1	tablespoon brandy
1	tablespoon butter
	melba toast

Pour the smoked oysters into a small glass dish, cut each oyster in half. Add the curry and brandy mixed together. Dot the butter over the oysters. When ready to serve, heat 2 minutes. Serve with a basket of melba toast or thinly sliced rye bread.

Devilled Cocktail Sausages

Cook in serving dish. Serve piping hot with picks and cocktail paper napkins.

1 to	2 lbs. cocktail sausages	1	clove garlic, chopped fine
1	cup chili sauce		grated rind of 1/2 lemon
1/4	cup dry sherry		

Place the sausages on hot browning utensil,* uncovered, and brown 2 to 3 minutes, turning once.

Place in an 8 × 8-inch glass dish, add remaining ingredients, stir to mix. Heat, covered, 5 minutes, stirring once or twice. Let stand a few hours at room temperature to marinate. When ready to serve, heat, uncovered, 2 minutes.

*If you do not have a browning utensil, brown on a surface range.

Angels on Horseback

Use canned or fresh oysters. The canned variety is easier to prepare and readily available.

5	slices of bacon	1/2	cup very fine breadcrumbs
1	can (8 ounces) oysters, drained	1/4	teaspoon each paprika, salt and curry powder
1/4	cup cream		

Cut bacon slices in half (one half for each oyster). Arrange in two layers on paper towel with paper between layers and on top. Cook 3 minutes or until partially cooked.

Drain oysters, dip each one in cream, then roll in fine breadcrumbs mixed with seasoning.

Wrap each coated oyster with a piece of bacon and hold together with a pick. Roll again in coating. Arrange on paper plate on a double thickness of paper towelling. Lay paper towel on top. Cook 2 minutes or until bacon is crisp. Serve hot.

Dark Angels on Horseback

This is one of my favorites in spite of its funny name.

12	medium size pitted prunes	2	green onions, chopped fine
2	cups hot tea	1/4	cup chopped parsley.
		12	bacon slices

Place prunes in a 1 1/2-quart casserole. Pour hot tea on top. Cook, covered, 5 minutes. Let stand until cooled. Remove prunes from tea and drain on paper towelling. (If unpitted prunes are used, pit when cool enough to handle.) Mix the chopped onions and parsley and fill cavity of each prune.

Cook bacon in two batches of 6 slices, 4 minutes each. Wrap each prune with a slice of precooked bacon. Place pick through each to hold together. Arrange on plate on a double thickness of paper towelling. Lay paper towel on top. Cook 2 minutes or until bacon is crisp. Serve hot.

Plum Sauce Meat Balls

It's useful to have small meat balls in your freezer for unexpected guests. Separate rows with a sheet of waxed paper before freezing, so you can take just what you need without thawing the whole lot.

1 to	2 lbs. minced pork grated rind and juice of 1 lemon	1/4	cup soy sauce
		1	clove garlic, minced
1/4	cup water	1/3	cup Oriental plum sauce

Shape meat into miniature balls. In a 1 1/2-quart casserole, combine the lemon rind and juice, water, soy, garlic and plum sauce. Stir until well blended. Heat, uncovered, 3 minutes, or until bubbling hot. Add the meat balls, stir until well coated with sauce. Heat, uncovered, 3 minutes. Serve hot with picks.

Hot Cheese Appetizers

These can be prepared in advance as the mixture is dry enough to prevent the toast getting soggy. Heat when ready to serve.

12	slices of bacon	1	teaspoon caraway
1	cup grated cheddar cheese		seeds
2	teaspoons sesame seeds or		about 30 melba rounds

Cook bacon on a plate between layers of paper towelling about 8 to 10 minutes, or until crisp. Cool and crumble in a bowl. Add grated cheese, sesame or caraway seeds. Mix thoroughly. Top each round of melba with a teaspoon of this mixture, spreading to the edges. Cook a plate at a time (about 10) uncovered, 20 to 25 seconds or until cheese is melted.

Cheese Crisps

Quick and easy to put together when unexpected company comes. The mayonnaise melts into the cracker and makes it almost like pastry.

1	cup grated cheddar cheese	1	teaspoon prepared mustard
1/2	cup mayonnaise	24	crackers
1/4	teaspoon Worcestershire sauce		sesame seeds

Blend cheese, mayonnaise, Worcestershire sauce and mustard and spread on crackers, spreading to the edges. Sprinkle with sesame seeds. Set on plate in rows. Cook, uncovered, 30 to 35 seconds. Serve warm.

Curry Nibbles

These nippy, tasty bits will keep for weeks in an airtight glass jar or plastic container, at room temperature.

2	cups bite-size shredded wheat cereal	$^1/_2$	teaspoon curry powder
$^1/_4$	cup butter	$^1/_4$	teaspoon marjoram
$^1/_4$	teaspoon garlic powder	3	tablespoons grated Parmesan cheese

Place cereal on an 8 × 8 × 2″ glass dish. Mix butter, garlic, curry powder and marjoram in small dish. Heat to melt, 30 seconds. Stir well. Pour over cereal, stir together. Heat, uncovered, 5 minutes, stirring twice. Remove from oven. Sprinkle cheese on top. Stir and toss until cereal is well coated with the cheese. Cool and serve.

Chicken Liver Rumaki

A world famous chicken liver hors d'oeuvre.

1	lb. chicken livers	2	teaspoons brown sugar
1	can small white onions, drained	1	teaspoon ground ginger
3	slices bacon, cut in 4	1	tablespoon soy sauce
1	small can water chestnuts, drained, cut in half		

Cut chicken livers in half. Line an 8 × 12-inch glass dish with a double thickness of absorbent paper.

Use 6 wooden skewers or *brochettes* (I like to use wooden chopsticks, sold tied together in packages of 12). On each one thread an onion, bacon pieces, water chestnuts and chicken livers, ending with an onion.

Combine brown sugar, ground ginger and soy sauce. Brush each brochette generously with the mixture. Place one next to the other in prepared dish. Cover with waxed paper. Bake 9 to 10 minutes or until bacon and liver are browned. 4 to 6 servings.

Chopped Chicken Liver

A perfect hors d'oeuvre or main course for a light lunch. Heap in a lettuce nest and serve with crisp, toasted rye bread.

2	tablespoons butter	1/4	teaspoon dried
2	tablespoons chicken		tarragon or thyme
	fat or	1/2	lb. chicken livers
3	tablespoons butter	2	hard-cooked eggs
2	medium size onions,	1/4	cup chopped parsley
	chopped fine		salt and pepper to taste

Place the 2 tablespoons butter and finely chopped fat or butter in a glass pie plate. Melt, uncovered, 2 minutes. Add onions and cook, uncovered, 3 minutes, stirring once.

Add the tarragon or thyme and the cleaned chicken livers. Cook, covered with waxed paper, 5 minutes. Pour into a bowl. Add the hard-cooked eggs (cooked the conventional way). Chop with a sharp knife, then with a fork until mixture is fine and everything is well mixed. Add the parsley, season to taste. Mix and place in bowl. Cover and refrigerate until ready to serve. 4 servings.

Sweet and Sour Pigs

One of the best of all hot sausages.

1	lb. cocktail sausages	1/2	cup red or black
1/2	cup prepared mustard		currant jelly
	Dijon Style		

Place sausages in 8 × 8 × 2" baking dish. Cook, uncovered, 4 minutes, stirring twice. Mix the mustard and jelly, pour over the hot sausages. Stir well. Heat, uncovered, 2 minutes. Serve hot with picks.

Dips

Curried Clam Dip

To make ahead, mix ingredients as given and refrigerate. Heat when ready to serve.

1	8-ounce package cream cheese	2	green onions, chopped fine
1 1/2	teaspoons curry powder	1/4	teaspoon garlic salt
		1/4	teaspoon salt
1	8-ounce can minced clams, drained	3	tablespoons milk or cream

Place cream cheese in a 1-quart mixing bowl or serving dish, sprinkle curry powder on top. Heat, covered with waxed paper, 30 seconds. Mash cheese and add remaining ingredients. To serve, cook, uncovered, 2 minutes, stirring twice. Sprinkle top with parsley. Serve with melba or sesame crackers. Yields about 2 1/4 cups.

Dip for Meatballs

Prepare and cook miniature meatballs ahead of time. Keep at room temperature. The very hot dip is sufficient to warm them up.

	grated rind and juice of 1 lemon	1/4	cup soy sauce
		1	clove garlic, minced
1/4	cup water or Sake wine	1/3	cup bitter orange marmalade

Combine in a bowl the lemon juice and rind, water or Sake wine and soy sauce. Stir until blended. Add garlic and marmalade. Stir.

Heat, uncovered, 2 minutes or until very hot.

Serve hot, surrounded with small meatballs on wooden picks. Yields about 1 cup.

Dip for Raw Vegetables

Place cold dip in middle of a large oval dish. Surround with raw vegetable sticks, celery, turnip, carrots, parsnip, cauliflowers, etc.

3	slices bacon one 8-ounce package cream cheese	1	tablespoon fresh lemon juice
1	small onion, grated	1½	tablespoons milk
2	tablespoons salad dressing of your choice	1	clove garlic paprika

Place bacon in a glass pie plate and cook, covered with paper napkin or towel, until crisp, about 3½-4 minutes. Remove bacon from fat with a slotted spoon and put on one side. Add the rest of the ingredients to the remaining fat. Heat, uncovered, 45 seconds. Mash and mix thoroughly. Crumble bacon and add to mixture. Cover and refrigerate. Yields 1 cup.

Bean Cheddar Dip

Use different varieties of bean for a different flavor. Good with all types of chips.

2	cans (16 ounces each) kidney beans	¼	teaspoon salt half an onion, grated
¼	cup peanut oil	1	teaspoon ground cumin
1	cup grated, strong cheddar cheese	1	teaspoon paprika

Drain beans, reserve liquid. Combine beans, oil and ⅓ cup bean liquid in glass bowl. Heat, uncovered, 4 minutes. Stir twice.

Remove from oven. Mash beans with large fork, then blend until smooth.

Stir in remaining ingredients. Heat, uncovered, 3 minutes, stir thoroughly. Serve with chips. Yields about 2 cups.

Egg and Bacon Dip

Always on hand, egg and bacon make a delicious dip for chips or to spread on rye bread.

4	slices bacon	2	green onions, chopped fine
4	hard cooked eggs		
1/2	teaspoon dry mustard or *curry powder*	3	tablespoons mayonnaise
1	teaspoon grated onion or		salt and pepper to taste

Cook bacon according to directions in previous recipe. When cool, crumble coarsely.

Hard cook eggs the conventional way, or poach in the microwave oven until hard (see p. 90). Mash the eggs, and add all the ingredients, including the crumbled bacon. Serve. Yields about 2/3 cup.

7. Beverages

You may wonder if there are any advantages in preparing beverages in the microwave oven, for boiling fairly large quantities of water for tea or coffee is faster on your conventional range top or in your electric kettle. But there are very definite advantages in terms of variety, for preparation and heating are so fast that you can easily suit the special and often individual tastes of your family or friends. Not only can each member choose his own, but he can also prepare it. Offering hospitality presents no problem whether you're serving a beverage with a meal, after the late-late show or when friends pop in unexpectedly. Tea, coffee, mulled cider, plain or fancy chocolate and many other delights can be served within seconds. You can heat beverages in a pitcher, mugs, a heat-resistant juice jar, brandy snifters (very elegant), or everyday coffee or tea cups. And instead of leaving your filtered coffee to simmer on the stove for hours to become bitter, use what you need, cool and refrigerate the rest. Just reheat the quantity you need in minutes in the microwave oven.

Instant Coffee or Tea

The temperature of the water when you start will affect the heating time, and the cooking time necessary to heat water will increase with the size of the cup and the number of cups. It is important to stir after the coffee or tea is added to distribute the heat.

Very important — heat water first then add tea or coffee, otherwise it will taste bitter or like boiled coffee.

Fill mug or coffee cup with cold tap water. Cook, uncovered, until steam appears. Add desired amount of coffee or a tea bag. Stir and serve or heat 30 seconds.

48

Mug or Cup	Time for water to heat
1	2 to 2^1/$_2$ minutes
2	3 to 3^1/$_2$ minutes
3	4 to 4^1/$_2$ minutes
4	5^1/$_2$ to 6 minutes
5	7 to 8 minutes

Defrosting Fruit Juice Concentrate

Remove the top from a 6-oz. can frozen juice concentrate, ensuring that there isn't any foil sticking up around the edge. Place can in oven, heat 15 seconds. Empty concentrate into a glass or other jug and heat another 15 seconds or until melted. Add water as directed on can and serve.

A 12-oz. can will need 30 seconds cooking time instead of 15.

Tomato Mary

A mild hot form of Bloody Mary. The following is enough for 10 small mugs. It can easily be reduced by half.

1	can (46 ounces) tomato juice	1	unpeeled lemon, sliced vodka
2	cans (10 ounces each) beef broth		

Fill mugs ^{2}/$_3$ full with tomato juice. Add beef broth to fill, leaving 1^1/$_2$-inch head space. Heat, following chart for heating beverages (see above). Add a lemon slice to each and 2 tablespoons or more of vodka.

Hot Buttered Rum

Another winter warm-up. Also made in individual mugs, leaving each one to his taste where rum quantity is concerned.

1 tablespoon brown sugar	2 tablespoons rum
water or apple cider	1 teaspoon butter

Place brown sugar in each mug, then fill mug ³/₄ full with water or apple cider. Heat, following chart for heating beverages (see p. 49). Add rum and butter. Stir well and serve.

Lemony Fresh Lemonade

An interesting lemon syrup base from which you can make a cooling lemonade in seconds.

1 tablespoon grated lemon peel	¹/₂ cup water
1¹/₂ cups sugar	1¹/₂ cups fresh squeezed lemon juice

In a 2-quart casserole place the lemon peel, sugar and water. Cook, uncovered, 6 minutes, stirring twice. Add lemon juice and stir for a few seconds. Cool. Pour into glass jar, keep refrigerated.
Yield: about 2²/₃ cups syrup base.

Lemonade by the glass: Pour ¹/₄ to ¹/₃ cup syrup base into a tall glass, add ³/₄ cup cold water and ice cubes to taste, stir briskly.

Lemonade by the jug: Combine full recipe of syrup base and about 5 cups cold water in a large pitcher, add ice cubes and stir. Makes 7 to 8 glasses.

Mulled Cider

Make individual servings. An ideal apres-ski drink.

1/2	cinnamon stick	2	teaspoons brown
1	or 2 whole allspice		sugar
2	whole cloves	1	slice each unpeeled
			lemon and orange
			apple cider or juice

Place all the ingredients except the cider in a mug. Fill ³/₄ full with cider. Heat to taste, following chart for heating beverages (see p. 49). Stir, remove spice if preferred.

Tom and Jerrys

Keep Tom and Jerry base covered, in your refrigerator. Then it takes only a few minutes to make in the microwave oven. The cream will keep 3 to 5 weeks.

2	egg whites	dash nutmeg
1	cup fine fruit sugar	rum
2	egg yolks	brandy
1/2	teaspoon vanilla	

Beat egg whites with ¹/₂ cup of the sugar until it forms soft peaks. Beat yolks with remaining ¹/₂ cup sugar, until thick and creamy, about 5 minutes. Both can be done in electric mixer or with rotary beater. Blend the vanilla and nutmeg into yolk mixture. Fold in the egg whites, until well blended. Refrigerate until ready to use.

To make Tom and Jerrys, fill mug ³/₄ full with water and heat, following chart for heating beverages (p. 49). Add 1 generous tablespoon mixture and 1 or 2 tablespoons each of rum and brandy. Stir to mix. If necessary, heat 30 seconds. Sprinkle with a dash of nutmeg to taste.

Thomas and Jeremiahs

The Southern U.S.A. version of Tom and Jerrys, with strong black coffee, rum and Bourbon whisky which can be replaced to taste by Irish Whiskey or Canadian Rye. Serve as after-dinner coffee in a demi-tasse.

3	egg yolks	1/4	cup light rum
1	tablespoon sugar	2	cups Bourbon or
1/2	teaspoon each ground		other alcohol of your
	cloves and cinnamon		choice
3	egg whites	2	cups hot, strong
			coffee

Beat egg yolks until thick and pale. Stir in sugar and spices.

Beat egg whites until stiff. Fold in yolk mixture. Stir in rum. Pour into glass jar. Refrigerate overnight (will keep 6 to 8 days refrigerated).

To serve, put 1 tablespoon of mixture in a 4-ounce demi-tasse. To each cup, add a jigger (1 1/2 ounces) Bourbon and the same amount of hot coffee.* Stir and serve. Yield: 10 to 12 demi-tasses.

*To heat coffee in microwave oven, follow chart for heating beverages (see p. 49).

Old-Fashioned Base

Another practical one to have on hand. Keep refrigerated as long as you need to.

2	oranges, unpeeled	2	cups water
2	cups sugar	1	8-ounce bottle Maraschino cherries

Slice oranges thinly (do not use ends), then cut each slice in half.

Place sugar and water in a 2-quart casserole. Heat 6 minutes, uncovered, stirring twice. Add orange slices. Cook, uncovered, 4 minutes. Add well-drained Maraschino cherries. Stir to mix. Pour into glass jar. Keep refrigerated.

To make Old-Fashioned: Fill Old-Fashioned glass with crushed ice. Add 2 teaspoons of base. Pass a pick through a slice of orange and a cherry and place on ice. Fill glass to top with whisky of your choice.

Mint Tea

Serve hot, serve cold, vary the mints, the flavor will change. In Algeria, they serve hot mint tea after dinner with a rose petal floating on top.

1	bunch fresh mint leaves or	2	cups water
4	tablespoons dried mint	1	unpeeled lemon, thinly sliced a bowl of honey

Clean and cut fresh mint leaves and place in a 2-quart casserole with the water. Cover and let stand 20 minutes. Then place in oven and heat, uncovered, 15 minutes. Let stand 30 minutes. Strain the mint leaves. Heat if serving hot or leave at room temperature.

Serve in small cups along with a plate of lemon slices and a bowl of honey. Let each person use to taste.

To serve cold, add 1 more cup of water to the drained mixture. Stir in the lemon slices and sweeten to taste with honey or sugar. Stir well, pour over ice in glass.

Fruit Tea

Equally good hot or cold.

4	cups water	1	unpeeled orange,
5	tea bags		sliced
1	unpeeled lemon, sliced	1	bunch fresh mint
			lemon-sugar to taste

In a 2-quart casserole place water and heat, uncovered, 6 to 8 minutes, or until boiling. Add tea bags, lemon, orange, and mint. Cover and cook 2 minutes. Let stand 10 minutes. Strain, sweeten to taste. Serve hot with a bowl of lemon-sugar.

Lemon-sugar: $1/2$ cup sugar mixed with the grated rind of 1 lemon.

To serve cold: Pour strained mixture over the ice cubes and add sugar to taste.

English Barley Water

Will keep a month refrigerated. Surprisingly refreshing in summer.

3	tablespoons barley,		grated rind of $1/2$ lemon
	pearl or pot type	$2 1/2$	cups boiling water
3	teaspoons sugar		

In a 2-quart casserole cover barley with cold water. Cook, covered, 15 minutes. Strain through a fine sieve. Discard the liquid and place the barley in a glass jar. Add sugar, lemon rind and boiling water. Cover. Cool, then refrigerate until cold.

To serve, pour into small glasses through a tea strainer for individual portions or strain the whole into a jug. Add a half slice of lemon to each glass or a whole lemon slice to the jug. Sweeten to taste.

This drink should not be served with ice.

English Lemonade

A memory of my youth in London!

2   cups lemon juice   1   cup sugar
    grated rind of 2 lemons   ginger beer or ginger ale

In a 1-quart bowl, place the juice, rind and sugar. Heat, uncovered, 4 minutes, stirring twice. When sugar is all dissolved, cool and refrigerate.

To serve, place ¼ cup lemon syrup in tall glass, fill with cold ginger beer. Ice to taste, but this is not English style.

Hot Cocoa Mix

Fill cups or mugs with milk, heat until steam appears. Do not boil.
Stir in cocoa, mixed as directed on package. Stir and serve.
    To heat milk:
        1 cup – 1 minute 15 seconds
        2 cups – 2 minutes 25 seconds
        3 cups – 3 minutes 35 seconds
        4 cups – 5 minutes
    Stir before serving to distribute heat.

Cocoa Syrup

1¹/₂ to 2 tablespoons of this syrup added to ³/₄ or 1 cup of milk,
heated together for the time in above chart, gives quite a special cup
of cocoa.

1¹/₄ *cups pure cocoa*	1¹/₂ *cups boiling water*
1 *cup sugar*	¹/₂ *cup honey*
¹/₂ *teaspoon salt*	2 *teaspoons vanilla*
a pinch cinnamon	

Mix together in a 2-quart casserole the cocoa, sugar, salt and
cinnamon. Add boiling water. Stir until well mixed.
    Cook, uncovered, 3 minutes. Add honey and vanilla. Cook 1
minute. Beat thoroughly. Cool. Pour into a glass jar. Cover. Keep
refrigerated. Yield: 2¹/₄ cups cocoa syrup.

Chocolate Around the World

There are so many delectable ways to make a cup of chocolate, all of them easy to prepare and heat with the help of the microwave oven.

French Chocolate

Another basic cocoa mix, one that will keep 5 to 6 weeks refrigerated. Makes superb chocolate.

1	cup sugar	1	cup boiling water
3/4	cup cocoa	1	cup whipping cream
	pinch of salt		

Mix together in a 2-quart casserole the sugar, cocoa and salt. Add the boiling water. Stir to mix. Cook, uncovered, 5 minutes. Cool and refrigerate for 1 hour. Whip cream. Mix in cold chocolate. Pour into glass jar. Cover. Refrigerate.

To serve, place 3 or 4 tablespoons of mixture in 1 cup of hot milk.* Stir to blend and serve.

*Follow heating chart given in Hot Cocoa Mix to heat the milk.

Swiss Milk Chocolate

When ready to serve, beat with whisk to make the chocolate become foamy.

2	squares (1 ounce each) unsweetened chocolate	1/4	cup honey
			pinch of salt
1	cup water	3	cups milk

Place chocolate and water in a 2-quart casserole. Cook, uncovered, 5 minutes. Stir well, add honey, salt and milk. Cook, uncovered, 3 to 5 minutes or until hot to taste, stirring during cooking period.

Mexican Chocolate

A spicy, tasty chocolate.

2	squares (1 ounce each) semi-sweet chocolate	1/4	teaspoon ground cinnamon
1/4	cup water	1/8	teaspoon nutmeg
2	tablespoons sugar		pinch of salt
		4	cups milk

In a 2-quart casserole, combine chocolate, water, sugar, cinnamon, nutmeg and salt. Cook 4 minutes, uncovered, stirring twice. Stir in milk. Cook, uncovered, 6 to 7 minutes. Whisk and serve.

For a light and foamy chocolate, add 4 large marshmallows to chocolate when ready to be served. Beat with rotary beater until marshmallows are soft. Heat 2 minutes and serve.

Spanish Chocolate

Very creamy, very rich. Serve with hot brioches.

2	cups milk	6	squares (1 ounce each) semi-sweet chocolate
2	cups light cream		
1/4	teaspoon nutmeg		
1	tablespoon butter	3	tablespoons sugar
		1/2	teaspoon salt

In a 2-quart casserole combine milk, cream, nutmeg, butter, chocolate, sugar and salt. Cook, uncovered, 8 minutes. Then beat with rotary beater until foamy. Heat, uncovered, 4 minutes. Beat again until foamy. Heat 2 minutes more. Serve. The beating is necessary to give this chocolate its foamy, light texture.

Acapulco Chocolate

Cocoa syrup and instant coffee are combined to give a special flavor to this chocolate. Serve with small sugary doughnuts.

4	cups milk	2	teaspoons instant
1/4	cup cocoa syrup		coffee
	(page 56)		pinch mace

Pour milk into a 2-quart casserole. Add syrup, instant coffee and mace. Stir to blend. Heat, uncovered, 10 minutes or until milk is just scalded but not boiling. Whisk for a minute and pour into small cups.

8. Soups

The old way of simmering soups on the stove is a thing of the past with the microwave oven. With microwave cooking there is very rapid penetration of flavor and seasonings giving the same results as simmering. The vegetable flavors will also be much fresher than when simmered on the stove for hours.

Convenience soups in cans or dry mixes can be made speedily in individual bowls and to suit individual tastes.

In both cases an individual serving or a whole recipe of soup can be prepared easily and quickly. A bowl of cold soup can be heated in a minute, rather than warming up the same soup two or three times.

I've divided this chapter up into three parts: the basic stocks, soups made from scratch, and canned or dehydrated soups. The speed with which you can make fresh soups in the microwave oven will make you think twice before using the canned variety. In fact, a cook with good instincts and a bright imagination need never repeat the same soup from one year's end to the next. All it needs is a little change here and there and you've a new flavor.

Soup tureens are back in fashion. Use them for your family, for parties, indoors or even out in the garden or on the patio. You can always make quite a show just with soup, a salad and good hot bread. Try it!

Chicken Bouillon

In the microwave oven chicken bouillon can be made with the gizzard, ends of wings, back, and neck skin—the parts we too often discard. Twenty minutes of cooking and 5 minutes of preparation is all that is needed: the result is 4 cups of tasty bouillon. You can also use roasted chicken or turkey carcass.

	chicken pieces or carcass as above	$1/2$	teaspoon thyme
4	cups hot water (from tap)	$1/2$	teaspoon salt
1	stick of celery or a few tops	$1/4$	teaspoon pepper
1	small, unpeeled onion, cut in four	1	or 2 chicken bouillon cubes or
		1	tablespoon chicken bouillon concentrate

Place all the ingredients in a 2-quart glass casserole. Cook, covered, 20 minutes. Let stand 1 hour. Strain. Taste for salt. Cool, keep refrigerated.

Beef Stock

Like the chicken broth, bones from a roast, $1/2$ lb. minced beef or accumulated bones or 1 lb. of beef shank will give a very tasty stock.

	bones or meat as above	2	bay leaves
4	cups hot water	$1/4$	teaspoon thyme
1	scrubbed unpeeled carrot, sliced		a few celery leaves
2	onions, unpeeled, cut in four	1	beef bouillon cube (optional)
			salt and pepper to taste

Place all the ingredients in a 2-quart glass casserole. Cook, covered, 20 minutes. Let stand 1 hour. Strain. Taste for salt. Cool. Keep refrigerated.

Celery Bouillon

To be used with either chicken or beef stock.

5	stalks celery with leaves	2	tablespoons rich cream
4	cups chicken or beef stock	1	tablespoon chopped fresh chervil or parsley

Wash and cut up celery into large pieces. Place in a 2-quart glass casserole. Cook, covered, 10 minutes. Strain. Warm up 2 minutes if necessary. Add cream and parsley or chervil. Stir and serve.

Tomato Bouillon

To be used with beef stock.

2	medium tomatoes	1	teaspoon dried basil
4	cups beef stock		salt and pepper to taste
3	tablespoons chopped fresh dill or	1/2	cup buttered croutons (optional)

Peel tomatoes, remove seeds and cut into small pieces. Place in a 2-quart glass casserole. Add beef stock. Cook, covered, 10 minutes. Add dill or basil, salt and pepper to taste and serve piping hot. To garnish with croutons, dice 1 cup of crustless bread, place in glass pie plate with 1 tablespoon butter. Cook, covered, 2 minutes. Stir well and cook, uncovered, another minute. Add a spoonful of the croutons to each cup of bouillon.

Springtime Vegetable Soup

The vegetables are warmed up in chicken bouillon, but they must not cook. They should also be sliced paper-thin.

4	radishes	1	small stalk of celery
1/2	small cucumber	1/2	small carrot
1/2	zucchini	4	cups chicken bouillon

Clean radishes, peel cucumber, wash zucchini and celery, scrape carrots. Cut each vegetable into paper-thin rounds.

In a 2-quart covered glass casserole heat chicken bouillon, 15 minutes. When piping hot, add vegetables. Let stand, covered, 5 minutes, or until ready to serve. Do not refrigerate. To reheat, heat 3 to 4 minutes or until hot to taste. Serve with bowls of chopped parsley and chopped fresh mint to taste.

Consommé Faubonne

A French cuisine classic, preferably made with beef stock, although chicken bouillon can be used.

4	cups beef stock	1	medium sized raw
2	tablespoons ground rice		beet
	or quick-cooking tapioca		dill weed

Place beef stock in a 2-quart glass casserole. Stir in the ground rice or quick-cooking tapioca. Peel raw beet and grate on fine grater. Add to stock. Cook, covered, 20 minutes. Add dill. Taste for seasoning. Serve hot.

Curried Consommé

Equally good with chicken or beef stock.

2	slices bacon, diced	1	tablespoon flour
1	medium onion, chopped fine	4	cups hot chicken or beef stock
1	tablespoon butter	1	tablespoon instant rice
1	teaspoon curry powder		

Place the bacon in a 2-quart glass casserole. Cook, covered, 4 minutes, stirring once. Remove pieces with a perforated spoon and drain on paper towelling. Leave 2 tablespoons of bacon fat in dish, add onion and butter, stir well. Cook, covered, 3 to 4 minutes. Add curry powder and flour. Stir until well mixed. Add stock and rice. Cook, covered, 10 to 12 minutes or until hot. Add bacon pieces and serve.

Beef Extract Onion Soup

After testing a number of ways to make onion soup in the microwave oven, I found this one the very best. To gratinée the soup, it must be done under the broiler. I suggest making cheese toast in the conventional oven ahead of time and serving one on top of each bowl of soup when serving, or serve the old-fashioned way with a dish of grated cheese on the table.

2	tablespoons bacon or pork fat	3	tablespoons concentrated beef extract
2	tablespoons butter		
4	large onions, peeled and thinly sliced	4	cups hot water
		1/4	teaspoon thyme salt, pepper to taste

In a 2-quart glass casserole place the bacon fat, butter and onions. Cook, uncovered, 15 minutes, stirring twice. Add the beef extract, stir until onions are well coated with it. Add hot water and thyme. Cook, covered, 15 minutes. Let stand 15 to 20 minutes. Salt and pepper to taste and serve.

Diplomat Consommé

Very good, and quite elegant served before a roast, when you have guests for dinner.

4	cups chicken bouillon	1/4	teaspoon basil
2	eggs	1/4	cup chopped parsley
2	tablespoons flour	3	tablespoons dry sherry
1	cup light cream or milk		salt and pepper to taste

In a 2-quart glass casserole heat the chicken bouillon, uncovered, 15 minutes. Beat the eggs with a whisk, add the flour, cream or milk, basil and parsley. Add to hot bouillon. Whisk for a second. Cook, uncovered, 3 to 4 minutes, stirring each minute. Add sherry. Taste for seasoning and serve.

Health Vegetable Soup

This is a complementary recipe started on top of the stove and finished in the microwave oven.

1/2	lb. beef or lamb liver	2	cups hot water
2	tablespoons butter	1	tablespoon sugar
4	small carrots, diced	1	cup fresh or frozen spinach, chopped
1/2	cup celery, diced		
1	large onion, thinly sliced	1	can (20 ounces) tomatoes salt and pepper to taste

Chop the liver very fine with a sharp knife or put through meat chopper. Heat a CORNING WARE skillet on top of range and when hot, add liver, stir until sizzling. Add butter and stir, scraping liver from bottom of pan. Add remaining ingredients. Stir well. Place pan in the oven, cook, covered, 25 minutes, and serve. This soup freezes and reheats very well.

Note If you do not have a CORNING WARE skillet, liver can be cooked in a 2-quart casserole, $1^{1}/_{2}$ minutes in the microwave oven. Add butter and proceed as above.

Vichyssoise

A microwave oven, a blender or whisk, and 25 minutes—and the Vichyssoise is ready to be served hot or cooled in the refrigerator.

2	medium size leeks	2	cups instant potato
1	medium size onion		flakes
2	tablespoons butter	1	cup cream
4	cups chicken broth		salt, pepper to taste

In a 2-quart glass casserole place cleaned and chopped leeks and onion and the butter. Cook, uncovered, 4 minutes, stirring once.

Add chicken broth or chicken bouillon cubes and 4 cups hot water. Cook, uncovered, 15 minutes, stirring once. Add instant potatoes. Stir well with a whisk or hand beater or put through blender, add cream. Heat 1 minute, salt and pepper to taste. Serve hot or cool and refrigerate.

Mayorquine Soup

A Spanish vegetable soup, colorful and very tasty.

4	tablespoons olive or salad oil	3	tomatoes, peeled and diced
3	cloves garlic, chopped fine	1	cup cabbage, shredded
		$1/2$	teaspoon thyme
2	large onions, diced	1	bay leaf
1	leek, thinly sliced (optional)	2	whole cloves
		5	cups boiling water
2	red pimientos, diced		salt, pepper to taste
1	green pepper, diced		

In a 3-quart glass casserole heat the olive or salad oil, uncovered, 3 minutes. Add the garlic, onions and leek. Stir to coat with oil. Cook, uncovered, 5 minutes, stirring once. Add the remaining ingredients. Stir well, cook, covered, 10 minutes. Let stand 10 minutes. Taste for seasoning. Serve.

Pumpkin Soup

A delicate, delicious soup of the French cuisine.

3   tablespoons butter or margarine
4   cups peeled and diced pumpkin
1/4 teaspoon nutmeg
1   cup hot water
1   cup milk
1/2 cup cream
1/2 cup small bread croutons
    salt and pepper to taste

In a 3-quart glass casserole melt the butter or margarine. Add the diced pumpkin and nutmeg. Cook, covered, 10 minutes, stirring once or twice. Add water and milk. Cook, covered, 8 minutes. Force through a sieve or blend 40 seconds in blender. Return to cooking dish. Add the cream. Heat 1 minute and serve with buttered croutons and/or a sprinkling of fresh parsley or chives.

Celery Soup

I like this soup made with chicken bouillon, although cubes and water or beef stock can be used. For a variation, the bouillon can be replaced by 4 cups canned tomatoes, adding 1 teaspoon sugar to the tomatoes.

2   full cups diced celery stalks and leaves
2   medium sized potatoes, peeled and grated
4   cups chicken bouillon
1/2 teaspoon pepper
1   teaspoon salt
1/4 cup parsley, chopped fine
3   tablespoons butter
1   cup milk (optional)

In a 3-quart glass casserole place all the ingredients, except the milk. Cook, covered, 20 minutes. Let stand 20 minutes. Add the milk, taste for seasoning. Warm up 1 minute and serve.

Summer Fresh Tomato Cream Soup

Very simple but delectable and rich.

8	large ripe tomatoes	1	teaspoon salt
2	cups boiling water	1/4	lb. unsalted butter
1	tablespoon sugar	1 1/4 to 1 1/2 cups rich cream	

Cut tomatoes into large pieces. Place them in a 3-quart glass casserole with the boiling water, sugar and salt. Cook, uncovered, 15 minutes. Pass through a sieve to remove skin and seeds, pressing the dry mixture in sieve to remove all the tomato possible.

Return to the cooking dish. Add butter in thin slivers, stirring well. Heat, covered, 1 minute. Add the cream gradually, stirring all the time with a whisk until soup has reached the consistency you prefer. Heat 1 minute and serve, thickly sprinkled with parsley or chives.

To serve cold, proceed the same way, but serve cool at room temperature, not refrigerated as the butter would harden into globules.

Oyster Soup

The microwave oven makes an exceptional oyster soup, as you will discover.

3	cups milk	1/4	cup cream or white wine
2	celery sticks		
1	small onion	1 to 1 1/2 cups fresh oysters, undrained	
1	bay leaf	1	tablespoon paprika

Place in a 3-quart glass casserole the milk, celery, onion, bay leaf, cream or white wine. Heat, uncovered, 9 to 10 minutes, watching carefully to see that milk doesn't boil over. When milk is boiling hot pour in the oysters. Cook 1 minute. Let stand 5 to 10 minutes as convenient. Sprinkle each plateful with paprika and serve.

New England Chowder

Fresh or canned clams make an equally good chowder, providing the canned type is used with bottled clam juice.

4	tablespoons butter	1	teaspoon salt
2	medium onions, chopped fine	4	cups boiling water
1½	cups fresh steamed and shucked clams with their juice or	1	large potato, grated
		2	cups cream or half and half
1	can (6 ounces) minced clams, drained, and 1 bottle (8 ounces) clam juice		paprika

In a 3-quart glass casserole place the butter and onions. Cook, uncovered, 5 minutes. Stir well, add the fresh or canned clams and the juice. Add the remaining ingredients except the paprika. Cook, covered, 12 minutes. Salt and pepper to taste. Sprinkle each serving with paprika.

Canned Soups

Canned soups and dehydrated soup mixes are so easy to prepare that a cup of soup is ready to be served in no time.

You can heat the canned soup right in your individual soup bowls, thus saving washing a pan. For soup with vegetables or noodles, first divide the liquid portion equally, then divide the solid.

To prepare canned, condensed soup
   Directions are for standard 10-ounce cans.
   Divide contents between 3 or 4 soup bowls. Add an equal amount of water or milk to each. Cover with a small plate or waxed paper. Cook, 3 to 4 minutes or until steaming hot, stirring once during the cooking. Stir, let stand 1 minute. For 4 to 6 servings, use 2 cans of soup; cook 6 to 7 minutes.

To prepare dry soup mixes
   Dry soup mixes need time to rehydrate after coming to a boil, so it is better not to prepare them in individual bowls.
   Prepare 1 envelope of soup mix in a 4-cup measure or in a 1-quart casserole, using amount of water or milk called for on package. Cook, covered, 6 to 8 minutes or until mixture comes to a boil, stirring twice. Let stand, covered, 5 to 10 minutes. Serve.
   Mix your canned soups for some excellent taste treats. The directions are the same as for canned soups, although it is better to prepare them in a 2-quart glass casserole so they can be well stirred. Place all the ingredients in the dish. Beat with a whisk until well mixed. Heat, covered, 6 to 7 minutes, stirring once or twice, or until boiling hot. Serve.
   The recipes have been tested with 10-ounce cans of condensed soup.

Crème Verte

   1   *can cream of green pea soup*
   1   *can cream of mushroom soup*
       Half can of milk
       Half can of cream

Mongole Cream Soup

1   *can cream of tomato soup*
1   *can cream of green pea soup*
     Half can of milk
     Half can of cream

Farmer's Cream Soup

1   *can vegetable soup*
1   *can cream of tomato soup*
     Half can of milk
     Half can of cream

Tomato Consommé

1   *can consommé*
     Equal quantity of tomato juice

Du Barry Cream

1   *can cream of celery soup*
1   *can cream of chicken soup*
     Half can of milk
     Half can of cream

Italian Consommé

1   *can consommé*
1   *cup tomato juice*
3   *unpeeled slices lemon*
1   *slice onion*
$1/2$ *teaspoon sugar*

Quick St. Germain Cream

1   can consommé
1   can cream of green pea soup
     Half can of milk
     Half can of cream

Easy Lobster Bisque

1   can cream of mushroom soup
1   cup canned lobster
1/4   cup dry sherry
1   can cream

Chicken Cream Parisienne

1   can cream of chicken soup
1   can cream of mushroom soup
1   can cream

Lobster Cream Rosé

1   can cream of mushroom soup
1   can tomato soup
1   8-oz. can lobster
1   tablespoon sherry
     A pinch curry
2   cans of cream

Cream Louisiana

1   can cream of mushroom soup
1   can creamed corn
1   can milk

Curried Cream Tomato

1   *can old-fashioned tomato soup*
¹/₂ *teaspoon curry*
1   *can milk*

Tomato Cream Voisin

1   *can cream of tomato soup*
1   *can cream of celery soup*
      Half can of milk
      Half can of cream

9. Sauces: For Fish, Meat and Vegetables

If, because of time involved, you have never bothered much with sauces to finish a dish of meat, vegetables, etc., you will soon change your mind with a microwave oven since it has completely eliminated the difficulty, extra care and work required to prepare a sauce on the conventional range. Lumps, burning, constant stirring, all are eliminated.

It is also an idea to keep some ready made in the refrigerator for quick reheating when needed.

You will quickly learn how to adapt your own favorite sauce to microwave cooking. Even making a Hollandaise or Béarnaise sauce is very simple. Learn to stir your sauce, and do not be afraid to open the oven door to check the cooking as, depending on the ingredients used, the time can sometimes vary, and seconds and minutes make a difference in microwave cooking.

Throughout the book you will find recipes with their own sauces, which will show you how to proceed when you wish to adapt one of your own recipes.

Sauces are important in good cooking, since they garnish, extend or bind together the food with which they are served.

Basic White Sauce

Light Sauce

> 1 tablespoon butter or other fat
> 1 tablespoon flour
> 1 cup milk or other liquid

Medium Sauce

> 2 tablespoons butter or other fat
> 2 tablespoons flour
> 1 cup milk or other liquid

Thick Sauce

> 3 tablespoons butter or other fat
> 4 tablespoons flour
> 1 cup milk or other liquid

Choose fat, flour and liquid to suit your need. Depending on what you are preparing the sauce for, you could use margarine, bacon or beef fat or a variety of liquids including wine, tomato juice, broth, vegetable water, etc.

Place butter in a 1-quart casserole or measuring cup. Heat, uncovered, 1 minute. To melted butter, add the flour, mix thoroughly; add milk, whisk or beat with rotary beater until well mixed. Cook, uncovered, 1 minute. Stir well. Cook 2 minutes to 2 minutes 30 seconds, or until creamy and bubbly, stirring twice during that period. Salt and pepper to taste.
Yield: 1 cup.

Basic White Sauce with Roux

White sauce can have a white or light brown color, depending on the roux. A roux is made by heating fat and flour together until it goes from pale golden color to light brown. It not only changes the color of the sauce, but also the flavor. A brown roux sauce is excellent with meats, whereas a white sauce goes better with vegetables.

How to Make Roux

In a 1-quart glass casserole melt fat and flour required by your recipe, uncovered, for 1 minute. Stir thoroughly. Cook 4 to 5 minutes, uncovered, or until the mixture has changed color, stirring twice during that period. Then add liquid and finish as for Basic White Sauce.

White Sauce Mix

This is very useful to have in your refrigerator. When you want to use it, just add water and two minutes later you will have a very nice white sauce with a few less calories.

2	*cups instant powdered skim milk*	1 *cup (¹/₂ lb.) butter or margarine*
1	*cup flour*	

Mix together in a bowl the dry milk powder and the flour. Add the butter, cut with two knives as for pie dough until it is blended into a coarse texture.

Empty mixture into a glass jar. Cover and refrigerate.

To make 1 cup of white sauce:

Light: Measure ¹/₂ cup prepared mix, add 1 cup water (or 1 cup milk or ¹/₂ milk – ¹/₂ cream, if you prefer a richer sauce.) Place in a 1-quart casserole or 4-cup measure. Cook, uncovered, 1 minute. Stir, cook another minute or until creamy and bubbly. Stir well. Season to taste.

Medium: Measure ³/₄ cup prepared mix. Mix with 1 cup water (or milk or ¹/₂ milk – ¹/₂ cream). Cook as for the light white sauce.

Thick: Measure 1 cup of prepared mix. Mix with 1 cup water (or milk or ¹/₂ milk – ¹/₂ cream). Cook as for the light white sauce.

Béchamel or Velouté Sauce

Béchamel is a rich white sauce made with chicken stock (or use chicken bouillon cubes) and light cream. Part white wine can replace chicken stock, when used with fish.

2	tablespoons butter	1	teaspoon grated onion
2	tablespoons flour	1	cup chicken stock
1	teaspoon salt	1	cup light cream
1/8	teaspoon thyme		

Melt butter in a 1-quart casserole or 4-cup measure, 30 seconds. Stir in flour, salt, thyme and grated onion. Blend to a smooth paste. Add chicken stock and cream, whisk together or beat with a rotary beater. Cook, uncovered, 2 minutes, stir well. Cook about 3 minutes more, stirring twice or until sauce is light and creamy. This is a light Béchamel. Double flour and butter with the same amount of liquid if you need a thicker sauce. Yield: 2 cups.

Sauce Mornay

French cheese sauce.

2	egg yolks	1/2	cup grated cheese of
1/2	cup cream		your choice
1	cup Medium White Sauce (see p. 76)		

Beat the egg yolks and cream together. Cook White Sauce according to basic recipe. Add egg mixture to hot sauce, beating well. Beat in the cheese. Cook, uncovered, 1 minute. Stir and serve.

Chef's Brown Sauce

Usually prepared from long simmering concentrated beef stock. The same results can be achieved with canned beef broth and it takes only minutes in the microwave oven.

$1/2$	teaspoon sugar	1	bay leaf
1	small onion, diced	$1/4$	cup milk
3	tablespoons butter	$1/2$	cup dry skim milk
2	tablespoons flour	$1/4$	cup water
1	can (10 ounces) beef broth (bouillon)	2	teaspoons tomato paste
$1/8$	teaspoon thyme		

Place the sugar and onion in a 1-quart casserole or 4-cup measure. Cook, uncovered, 5 minutes, or until sugar is partially browned.

Add butter. Cook, uncovered, 1 minute. Mix well. Stir in flour, blend well, add beef broth, thyme, bay leaf and the $1/4$ cup milk. Mix well, then cook, uncovered, 1 minute. Stir well, add dry milk, water and tomato paste, blend well. Cook, uncovered, 2 to 3 minutes more, or until sauce is creamy. Stir twice during that period.

For a Madeira Sauce, add 3 tablespoons dry Madeira to the cooked sauce. Will keep 3 weeks, covered and refrigerated. Also freezes well. Yield: 2 cups.

Sauce Soubise

A Soubise always indicates an onion sauce.

2	medium onions	2	cups Medium White Sauce (see p. 76)
1	tablespoon butter	$1/8$	teaspoon nutmeg

Slice onions thinly or dice. In a 1-quart casserole or 4-cup measure, melt butter, 30 seconds. Add onions. Stir well. Cook 8 minutes, stirring twice. Add to hot White Sauce without draining. Add the nutmeg. Season to taste with salt and pepper. Serve.

Caper Sauce

Excellent on fish and veal.

1	cup Medium White Sauce (p. 76)	1/8	teaspoon curry powder
2	tablespoons capers	1	teaspoon butter
1	green onion, chopped fine		

Make White Sauce. Add all remaining ingredients. Stir until butter is melted. Season to taste. Serve.

Parsley Sauce

1	cup Medium White Sauce (p. 76)	1	green onion, chopped fine
2	tablespoons chopped parsley	1	teaspoon butter

Make White Sauce. Add all remaining ingredients. Stir until butter is melted. Season to taste. Serve.

Provençale Sauce

This sauce is good on fish, on meat, on noodles, or on boiled new potatoes. All taste equally good.

3	tablespoons salad or olive oil	2	tomatoes, unpeeled and diced
1	medium onion, chopped fine	2	tablespoons chopped parsley
2	cloves garlic, chopped fine	1 to 2	cups Medium White Sauce (p. 76)

Place in a 1-quart casserole or 4-cup measure, the oil, onion and garlic. Heat, uncovered, 5 minutes, stirring once. Add the tomatoes and parsley. Heat 1 minute. Pour this mixture into the hot White Sauce. Mix well. Season to taste with salt and pepper. Serve.

Mushroom Sauce

Soy sauce can replace Kitchen Bouquet, but the flavor is not as delicate. Half a teaspoon of "Marmite" vegetable concentrate can replace Kitchen Bouquet with success.

3	tablespoons butter	1/4	teaspoon salt
1½	tablespoons flour	1/8	teaspoon basil or
1	teaspoon Kitchen		tarragon
	Bouquet	1	can (4 ounces) undrained
3/4	cup light cream		sliced mushrooms

Place butter in a 1-quart casserole or 4-cup measure, heat, uncovered, 1 minute, to melt. Stir in the flour and Kitchen Bouquet, blend to a smooth paste. Add cream, salt, basil or tarragon. Whisk until smooth. Add undrained mushrooms, mix well. Cook, uncovered, 2 minutes, stirring twice. The sauce should be creamy and bubbly. Taste for seasoning. Yield: about 1½ cups.

Variation: For Madeira Mushroom Sauce, add 3 tablespoons dry Madeira and replace cream with undiluted canned consommé.

True Hollandaise

A sheer delight to make in 30 seconds. Never fails.

1/3 to 1/2	cup unsalted		juice of 1 small lemon
	butter	2	egg yolks

Place butter (unsalted when possible) in a medium size CORNING Petite Pan or 2-cup measure and heat uncovered, 1 minute. Add lemon juice and egg yolks. Beat with small whisk for 20 seconds or until well mixed. Cook, uncovered, 30 seconds. Whisk for a few seconds. Salt to taste (about 1/4 teaspoon) and serve. To reheat, place, uncovered, in oven for 20 seconds. Whisk and serve.

Mousseline Sauce

Make True Hollandaise sauce. When ready to serve, fold in the 2 beaten egg whites. If you have to reheat the Hollandaise, fold in the egg whites after reheating.

Dijon Hollandaise

Can be served hot or cold. Superb cold with thinly sliced roast beef.
   Replace the fresh lemon juice in the True Hollandaise sauce with 2 tablespoons cold water blended with 1 tablespoon Dijon mustard.

Chantilly Hollandaise

An ideal sauce to serve with cold fish, asparagus or chicken breasts.

1 recipe True Hollandaise	$^1/_2$ cup whipping cream

Make sauce. Cool 15 minutes. Whip cream until stiff and fold into sauce. Salt to taste.

Mock Hollandaise Sauce

Not as rich as the True Hollandaise but also very good. Perfect with poached cod or other white fish, rolled in chopped parsley or chives.

2	tablespoons butter	2	slightly beaten egg
2	tablespoons flour		yolks
1/2	teaspoon salt	1 to 2	tablespoons fresh
1	cup milk		lemon juice, to taste
		2	tablespoons margarine

Make a White Sauce with the 2 tablespoons butter, flour, salt, and milk, following directions for Basic White Sauce (p. 75).

When hot, whisk in the egg yolks, lemon juice and margarine. Heat 1 minute. Whisk again, taste for seasoning. Serve.

English Bread Sauce

I found out that only the microwave oven could do a creamy, light, perfect bread sauce. It's delicious with roasted partridge, pheasant or Cornish hen.

1	cup milk	1	tablespoon butter
2	whole cloves	1	tablespoon cream
1	small onion		salt, pepper to taste
	a dash of sage		
1 1/4	cups fresh breadcrumbs without crust		

Place the milk in a 1 1/2-quart casserole. Stick the cloves into the onion and add to the milk. Add sage. Cook, uncovered, 3 minutes. Add the breadcrumbs. Mix well. Cook, uncovered, 2 minutes. Remove onion. Add butter and cream, whisk sauce for a few seconds. Salt and pepper to taste. Cook, 30 seconds, whisk again and serve.

Sauce Vaucluse

Another creation of a French chef. Serve with roasted or poached chicken or turkey, white fish, cauliflower and steamed celery.

2	tablespoons butter	1	recipe True
2	tablespoons flour		Hollandaise Sauce (see
1½	cups light cream		p. 80)
	salt, pepper to taste		

Make a White Sauce with the butter, flour and cream, salt and pepper to taste following directions for Basic White Sauce. Make a Hollandaise. Add to White Sauce. Whisk together. Season to taste. Both sauces can be made ahead of time and kept covered at room temperature. Mix when ready to serve and heat, uncovered, 40 seconds or until hot. Stir and serve.

Sauce Béarnaise

A Béarnaise is a Hollandaise flavored with tarragon and white wine vinegar. A connoisseur's sauce to top a broiled steak or to top poached eggs on a bed of asparagus or with artichoke hearts.

3	tablespoons wine or	4	peppercorns, crushed
	cider vinegar	⅓	cup butter
1	green onion, chopped	2	egg yolks
1	teaspoon tarragon		

Place in a 1-cup measure, the vinegar, onion and tarragon. Heat, uncovered, 3 minutes. Strain into a medium size CORNING Petite Pan or serving dish, pressing juice from onion. Add peppercorns and butter. Melt 50 seconds. Add egg yolks. Whisk until well blended. Cook, uncovered, 30 seconds. Whisk again for a few seconds. Taste for seasoning. Serve.

Curry Sauce

Can be served over eggs, meat, chicken, fish or rice.

1/4	cup butter	1	clove garlic, minced
1	to 2 teaspoons curry powder	3	tablespoons flour
1/2	teaspoon turmeric	1 1/4	cups chicken broth
1	onion, chopped fine	1	cup light cream or milk
1	unpeeled grated apple	1	teaspoon salt

Place butter in a 1-quart casserole or 4-cup measure, heat, uncovered, 1 minute. Add the curry powder and turmeric, mix well. Cook, uncovered, 2 minutes, stir well. Add onion, apple and garlic. Cook 1 minute. Add flour, mix well. Add chicken broth (chicken bouillon cubes can be used), cream and salt. Stir until well mixed. Heat 2 to 3 minutes, stirring twice, until sauce is creamy and bubbly.

My Favorite Tomato Sauce

Perfect when prepared with fully ripened summer tomatoes.

3	slices bacon	1/2	teaspoon thyme
1	large onion, minced	1/2	teaspoon salt
1	tablespoon flour	1/2	cup tomato paste
4	large fresh tomatoes	1	teaspoon sugar
1/8	teaspoon nutmeg		

Place bacon in a 1-quart casserole, cover with a double layer of paper towelling. Cook 4 to 5 minutes. Remove from fat and drain; let cool. To the fat remaining in the casserole, add the onion, stir well and cook, uncovered, 3 to 4 minutes. Stir in the flour. When well mixed, add the remaining ingredients. Stir to blend. Cook, covered, 10 minutes, stirring 3 times. Taste for seasoning. Crumble bacon and add to sauce. If you wish to remove tomato seeds from the sauce, pass through a strainer before serving (then add bacon). Keep refrigerated. To reheat, cook 2 to 3 minutes.

Sour Cream Sauce

Creamy, tasty, and easy to prepare. This sauce goes well with vegetables, seafood, veal and poultry.

1	cup commercial sour cream	$1/8$	teaspoon pepper
$1/2$	teaspoon salt	1	tablespoon lemon juice
$1/2$	teaspoon curry powder		the grated rind of 1 lemon

In a 2-cup measure combine all ingredients. Cook, uncovered, 2 minutes or until bubbling hot, stirring twice during cooking period. Yield: 1 cup.

Barbecue Sauce

This sauce will keep 10 days refrigerated or two months frozen. So easy to defrost in the microwave oven.

3	tablespoons salad oil or olive oil	$1/4$	teaspoon celery seeds
1	envelope onion soup mix	$1/4$	cup cider vinegar
$1/2$	cup diced celery	$1/4$	cup well-packed brown sugar
$3/4$	cup chili sauce or ketchup	1	tablespoon French Dijon mustard grated rind of 1 orange, 1 lemon
$1/4$	cup tomato juice, red wine or water		

Place oil and onion soup mix in a $1^{1}/2$-quart casserole. Stir well and cook, uncovered, 2 minutes.

Add all the remaining ingredients, stir well. Cook 3 minutes, uncovered, or until sauce bubbles. Stir well. If you wish to refrigerate or freeze sauce, cool first.

Note For a hotter sauce, add a few drops of Tabasco or a pinch of red pepper.

Raisin Sauce

A sweet sauce traditionally served with ham or tongue.

1/2	cup brown sugar		rind of half a lemon,
1	tablespoon cornstarch		not grated
1	teaspoon dry mustard	1 1/2	cups water
2	tablespoons cider	1/3	cup seedless raisins
	vinegar	1	tablespoon butter
2	tablespoons lemon		
	juice		

In a 4-cup measure, combine all ingredients, stirring until thoroughly mixed. Cook, uncovered, 4 to 5 minutes or until mixture is creamy and bubbly, stirring 3 times during cooking period. Yield: about 1 1/2 cups.

Old-Fashioned Cooked Salad Dressing

This will keep 3 to 4 months, refrigerated. Fine with all types of vegetable salads.

3	tablespoons butter		pinch of mace
2	tablespoons flour	1 1/4	cups milk
1 1/2	teaspoons salt	2	egg yolks
1	teaspoon dry mustard	1/3	cup cider vinegar
1	tablespoon sugar	1	thick slice of onion

In a 1-quart casserole or 4-cup measure, melt the butter for 40 seconds. Mix in the flour, salt, mustard, sugar and mace. Add 1 cup of the milk. Mix well. Cook, uncovered, 2 minutes, stirring once. Cook another minute, stir again.

Beat the egg yolks with the remaining 1/4 cup milk, add to sauce and whisk for a second. Add the cider vinegar, mix well, add slice of onion. Cook, uncovered, 2 minutes or until creamy and bubbly, stirring twice. Remove onion. Stir. Taste for seasoning. Yield: 1 1/2 cups.

All-purpose Basting Sauce

This basting sauce can be used with all meats and poultry roasted in the microwave oven.

1	tablespoon salad oil or *melted, unsalted butter* or *unsalted margarine*	1	teaspoon Kitchen Bouquet
1	teaspoon paprika	1/4	teaspoon *thyme* or *tarragon, basil, marjoram, cumin* or *curry powder*

Stir all ingredients together and brush mixture all over meat or poultry.

Brown Gravy for Roast Meat

The gravy is made while meat is standing and the variations give a different flavor according to your own personal taste.

When meat is cooked, remove to a platter and add any of the following variations to the juices in the dish:

For Beef: 2 tablespoons Madeira wine *or* whisky *or* cold tea *or* 1 teaspoon tomato paste with 3 teaspoons water *or* 4 tablespoons undiluted canned consommé. Stir well. Cook, uncovered, 8 to 10 minutes. Stir 1 minute. Serve separately.

For Pork: Grated rind and juice of ¹/₂ orange *or* ¹/₄ cup cranberry juice, stirred with 1 teaspoon cornstarch *or* 3 tablespoons dry vermouth *or* 3 tablespoons water with 2 teaspoons instant coffee (dry). Stir well. Cook, uncovered, 8 to 10 minutes, stirring during cooking period. Stir 1 minute. Serve separately.

For Veal: 3 tablespoons white wine *or* dry sherry *or* 1 tablespoon soy sauce (preferably the Japanese type) *or* 2 tablespoons Teriaki Sauce (sold in bottles) *or* 2 teaspoons Worcestershire Sauce *or* 2 tablespoons sour cream or 1 cup fried onions. Cook, uncovered, 8 to 10 minutes. Stir 1 minute. Serve separately.

For Lamb: 2 to 3 tablespoons dry Madeira, *or* 1 tablespoon mint sauce (not jelly), *or* 1 tablespoon chutney, *or* 2 teaspoons instant coffee (dry) with 3 tablespoons water, *or* juice and rind of ¹/₂ lemon and ¹/₂ teaspoon grated fresh ginger. Cook, uncovered, 8 to 10 minutes. Stir 1 minute. Serve separately.

10. Eggs and Cheese

Eggs

A delicate touch should be used when cooking eggs in the microwave oven, but you will be surprised at the ease and convenience, even though cooking eggs the conventional way is comparatively quick compared to many other foods.

Never try to boil an egg in the microwave oven, because microwave cooking is so fast that pressure will build up inside the shell and cause it to explode. However, poached, scrambled, baked and even fried eggs can be cooked successfully.

The exact time for cooking eggs in the microwave oven will vary from $1/2$ to 1 minute according to the size and temperature as well as the number of eggs prepared at one time. As with all foods cooked in the microwave oven, it is necessary to remember that eggs continue to cook after they have been taken from the oven and, for this reason, they should be removed while still slightly underdone.

One thing you will find when cooking eggs with butter is that the butter flavor is much better and that a small quantity goes further. When you cook butter in a conventional frying pan the heat breaks down the different fats. This does not happen in the microwave oven because of the speed of cooking. Care should, however, be taken when you cook omelettes. You might need to experiment until they become perfect. If you have a slow speed setting on your oven, then this is a good time to use it. The cooking times should be doubled.

Fried Eggs

The composition of an egg is such that the yolk has the highest fat content so microwave energy tends to cook the yolk before the white. This is why a fried egg must be covered with waxed paper during cooking. The egg can be taken out before the white is completely set. The trapped steam will finish cooking the white during the minute of standing.

To cook, melt $1/4$ to $1/2$ teaspoon butter in a 10-ounce glass custard cup for 25 seconds. Break 1 egg into dish. With the point of a small knife, make two to three incisions gently in the yolk; it will not break the egg. Cover with waxed paper, cook 30 seconds. You may hear a cracking sound, like an egg frying in a pan on the stove, but if the egg has been pierced it will not explode. Let stand, covered, 1 minute before serving. This will give you an egg with a soft yolk and cooked white.

> For 2 eggs: Cook 1 minute, 5 seconds; let stand 1 minute.
> For 3 eggs: Cook 1 minute, 35 seconds; let stand 1 minute.
> For 4 eggs: Cook 2 minutes; let stand 1 minute.

Always remember to pierce each yolk and cover the dish with waxed paper. Even when cooking more than one egg it is best to cook each separately in its own dish.

Poached Eggs

The vinegar used helps to set the white of the egg.

In a 10-ounce glass custard cup, heat $1/2$ cup water and $1/4$ teaspoon white or cider vinegar to boiling, 1 minute. Carefully break an egg into dish, pierce yolk gently with the point of a knife 3 times. Cook, covered with waxed paper 20 to 25 seconds. Let stand, covered, 1 minute before serving. Remove from water with a perforated spoon.

> 2 eggs will cook in 1 minute.
> 3 eggs will cook in 1 minute, 30 seconds.

Cook each egg individually in its dish. Pierce each yolk.

Scrambled Eggs

Scrambled eggs can be cooked individually in glass custard cups but I prefer to use a glass pie plate so that 2 to 4 eggs can be scrambled at one time. They need lots of stirring and should be removed from the oven while eggs are still slightly softer than desired. If cooked individually, or only two are cooked, it is necessary to stir only once. With very little practice you will have soft, creamy, fluffy scrambled eggs.

4	eggs	$1/2$	teaspoon salt
$1/4$	cup light cream or milk	2	tablespoons butter

Combine eggs, cream and salt. Beat with a fork just enough to mix and break the eggs. Melt butter in a glass pie plate for 30 seconds. Pour in egg mixture. Cook $1^1/2$ minutes covered with waxed paper, stir well. Cook another minute, stirring twice. Remove from oven while eggs are still slightly softer than when ready to eat.

For 1 egg: Place in a 6-ounce custard cup, add 1 teaspoon butter, 1 tablespoon cream or milk. Cook 30 seconds, stir, cook 15 seconds.

For 2 eggs: Place in a 10-ounce glass custard cup, add 2 teaspoons butter, 2 tablespoons cream or milk. Cook, 45 seconds, stir, cook 30 seconds.

For 3 eggs: Place in pie plate, add 1 tablespoon butter, 3 tablespoons cream or milk. Cook 1 minute, stir, cook 40 to 50 seconds.

Note If you want to add tomato, chopped left-over meat, ham, etc., this should be heated first then added after eggs are stirred for the first time. Grated cheese, cottage cheese, etc., should be added at beginning of cooking and a few seconds added to cooking time.

Omelettes

Cooking, stirring and waiting times are all important in achieving success with an omelette in the microwave oven. Once understood it is surprisingly easy and it becomes interesting to make many types of omelette.

3	eggs	$^1/_2$	teaspoon salt
3	tablespoons milk or		pinch of pepper
	cream	1	tablespoon butter

Beat in a bowl the eggs, milk, salt and pepper. In a 9-inch glass pie plate, melt butter for 40 seconds. Pour in egg mixture. Cook, covered with waxed paper, 1 minute, 30 seconds. Then stir with a fork to move cooked eggs around the edges, toward the center. Cook, covered, another minute. If at that point the center is still too moist, stir lightly with a fork, cook covered, 20 to 30 seconds. Let stand covered, 1 minute. Loosen all around with a rubber spatula, fold over in two or three folds. If at that point the underside is softer than you prefer, return omelette, on serving plate, to oven, uncovered and cook for 30 seconds.

For 2-egg omelette use 2 tablespoons milk or cream, some salt and pepper and 2 teaspoons butter. Cook 45 seconds, stir cooked part to middle, cook 1 minute, let stand 1 minute.

For a 4-egg omelette use 4 tablespoons milk or cream, only $^1/_4$ teaspoon salt, pinch pepper and 1 tablespoon butter. Cook 1 minute, 40 seconds. Stir, cook 1 minute, 20 seconds. Let stand 2 minutes.

Bacon Omelette

    3 to 4 slices of bacon
       a 3- to 4-egg omelette
       mixture

Place bacon slices between paper towels set on a glass or paper plate. Cook 3 to 4 minutes. Let stand until ready to use.

Cook omelette as in basic recipe. Crumble bacon on top before folding.

Mushroom Omelette

2 tablespoons butter	$1/2$ teaspoon basil or
1 $4^{1}/2$-ounce jar	tarragon
well-drained sliced	a 3- to 4-egg omelette
mushrooms	mixture

In a 9-inch glass pie plate, melt the butter for 1 minute. Add the mushrooms, stir until partially coated with butter. Add basil or tarragon. Cook, covered, 3 minutes, stirring once.

Prepare eggs as in basic omelette recipe, pour over mushrooms and cook as directed. Serve with chutney.

Spanish Omelette

1 tablespoon olive or salad oil	2 fresh tomatoes, diced
	1 teaspoon sugar
$1/2$ green pepper, chopped fine	$1/2$ teaspoon salt
	a pinch of thyme
2 green onions or 1 small onion, chopped	a 3- to 4-egg omelette mixture
$1/4$ cup diced celery	

In a 9-inch glass pie plate, heat oil, uncovered, 3 minutes. Add the green pepper, onion and celery. Stir well. Cook, covered, 5 minutes, stirring twice. Add tomatoes, sugar, salt and thyme. Mix well. Cook, covered, 2 minutes. Let stand 5 minutes. Meanwhile, make omelette according to basic recipe. Top with tomato mixture. Do not fold. Serve with bowl of grated cheese.

Cheese Omelette

A 3- to 4-egg omelette mixture

$^1/_2$ cup strong or mild cheddar cheese, grated or 5 to 6 thin slices of Swiss cheese

Make plain omelette as in basic recipe. Sprinkle with grated cheese or cover with sliced cheese. Heat 30 seconds. Then let stand as indicated in the basic recipe.

Fines-Herbes Omelette

Sprinkle herbs of your choice on the cooked omelette before the standing period. For a 3- or 4-egg omelette take your choice of the following:

1 teaspoon fresh basil or $^1/_2$ teaspoon dried

1 teaspoon fresh tarragon or $^1/_4$ teaspoon dried

2 tablespoons fresh parsley

4 tablespoons fresh chives

1 teaspoon fresh mint combined with $^1/_2$ teaspoon fresh basil or parsley

1 tablespoon chopped chervil mixed chives and parsley to taste

Baked Eggs, page 95
English Bacon and Cheese Pie, page 100

Sukiyaki, page 111

Baked Eggs

This is the famous French dish "Oeufs en cocotte". Nice to serve for lunch with a salad or a bowl of watercress.

2	eggs		parsley or chives
2	tablespoons cream		salt and pepper to taste
1	teaspoon butter		

Break eggs into 2 10-ounce glass custard cups or into French ramekins.

Carefully pierce each egg 3 times with the point of a small knife. Spoon 1 tablespoon cream over each egg. Dot each one with $1/2$ teaspoon butter. Cook, covered, 45 seconds. Sprinkle with parsley or chives, salt and pepper. Let stand, covered, 1 minute.

Variation: Sprinkle top of cooked eggs with 1 tablespoon grated cheese. Let stand, covered, 1 minute. Sprinkle with parsley to serve.

Baked Eggs Bercy

4	cocktail sausages	$1/2$	teaspoon curry powder
	a pinch of marjoram		
2	baked eggs	1	tablespoon dry sherry
$1/2$	cup chili sauce		chopped chives or parsley

Place 3 thicknesses of paper towels on plate. Place sausages on towels, cover with another towel. Heat 1 to 2 minutes, turning once. Sprinkle with marjoram and keep warm. Bake eggs according to previous recipe. While eggs are standing, place the chili sauce, curry powder and dry sherry in a bowl. Heat, covered, 40 seconds. Place sausages on eggs and top with 1 teaspoon of the sauce. Serve remaining sauce in dish.

Variations: Place a thin slice of cheese in bottom of dish, break egg on top. Omit sausages. Serve with sauce.
— Replace sausages with cooked bacon cut in 2-inch pieces.
— Replace sausages with a small buttered tomato (see Vegetables). Omit sauce.

Golden Bacon and Egg Casserole

A good brunch or luncheon dish which takes only 20 minutes to prepare and can be done ahead of time if preferred. It can then be heated, covered with waxed paper, about 5 minutes before serving.

6	hard cooked eggs	1	teaspoon curry powder or turmeric
6	slices bacon		
2	tablespoons margarine	1 1/2	cups milk
2	tablespoons flour	1/8	teaspoon dry mustard
1/2	teaspoon salt	2 to 4	green onions, chopped fine

Hard boil eggs the ordinary way or have them in readiness in the refrigerator. Cook bacon between sheets of paper toweling in baking dish 6 minutes or until crisp. Remove bacon, paper towels and any excess dripping from the dish.

Melt the margarine for 30 seconds in the same baking dish. Stir in the flour, salt, curry powder or turmeric, until smoothly blended. Add milk and stir until well mixed. Cook, uncovered, 4 minutes, stirring once after 2 minutes. Stir in the mustard.

Peel and quarter the eggs, mix into the sauce. Crumble the bacon and sprinkle over all. Cook, uncovered, 2 minutes or until hot. Sprinkle green onions on top and cook, uncovered, 1 minute. 4 servings.

Cheese

Cheese is cooked so quickly in the microwave oven that even seconds can make quite a difference so it requires careful watching. You know cheese is overcooked if it has become rubbery.

Different types of cheese often can be interchanged, according to personal taste.

Swiss Fondue is even easier than cooked the conventional way, as it does not have to be made by the slow gradual process of stirring the cheese. All the ingredients are heated together until warm enough to melt the cheese, then blended together. If the fondue cools off while eating it, just put it back in the oven, covered, for 30 seconds.

It is sometimes possible to use the glazed earthenware type of fondue pots in the microwave oven (see p. 16). Just cover with waxed paper.

Melted grated cheese can be a nice topping to many a casserole dish. Simply top cooked ingredients with a generous coating of grated cheese of your choice. Heat, uncovered, 40 seconds to 1 minute.

Bread and Cheese Casserole

Serve for lunch with coleslaw or hot carrots of your choice. Any leftover can be sliced and browned in butter over medium heat on surface range.

4	slices bread	1	cup milk
1	teaspoon each butter and prepared mustard	1/4	teaspoon salt
		1/4	teaspoon pepper
1/2	lb. grated cheese of your choice	1/2	teaspoon sage or marjoram
2	eggs		paprika

Butter each slice of bread with a mixture of the butter and mustard.

In the middle of an 8 × 8-inch cake dish, place a small custard cup open side up. Cut bread in fingers and place around custard cup.

Sprinkle cheese over the bread. Beat remaining ingredients together and pour over the cheese. Sprinkle top generously with paprika.

Cook, uncovered, 10 minutes, turning dish 4 times during that period. Let stand 8 to 9 minutes and serve. Serves 4.

Italian Cheese and Rice Loaf

Serve hot, or cold at room temperature.

1	cup uncooked short grain rice	1	teaspoon salt
3	eggs	1/2	cup chili sauce
6	tablespoons salad oil	1/4	cup finely chopped walnuts
1	teaspoon basil	1	tablespoon dry Madeira (optional)
1/4	cup chopped parsley		
1	cup strong cheddar cheese, grated		

Cook the rice as given for Regular Rice (see p. 221).

Beat the eggs with rotary beater, add the salad oil and basil and beat again. To this add the minced parsley, grated cheese, salt and rice.

Place in an 8½ × 4½-inch glass loaf pan and press to make top even. Mix the remaining ingredients and pour on top.

Bake, covered, 10 minutes, turning dish twice. Let stand 5 to 8 minutes before serving. 6 servings.

American Cheese Rarebit

Serve quite hot over toast. Reheats very well in the microwave oven.

1	10-ounce can tomato soup	$^1/_2$	teaspoon paprika
1	lb. (4 cups) grated cheddar cheese	1	teaspoon brown sugar chopped chives or parsley
2	eggs, separated		

Pour tomato soup into a 2-quart casserole dish. Stir in the cheese. Cook, covered, 2 minutes. Stir and cook another $1^1/_2$ minutes. Beat egg yolks with paprika and brown sugar. Stir into cheese mixture. Cook 1 minute, stirring once. Whip egg whites until stiff, fold gently into tomato mixture. Serve over toast, sprinkled with chives or parsley.

Cheese and Bacon Casserole

A creamy, custardy, tasty casserole.

4	slices of bacon		medium cheddar cheese
3	eggs		
1	cup milk	$^1/_2$	cup canned french fried onions or
2	cups grated Swiss or	4	diced green onions

Cook bacon following directions on p. 138. Cool and crumble.

Beat together the eggs and milk. Add cheese, fried or green onions and bacon pieces. Pour into an 8-inch pie plate.

Cook, uncovered, 8 minutes, stirring once. Let stand 6 to 10 minutes or until set in middle. 4 to 5 servings.

Welsh Rarebit

For an English version, serve the cooked rarebit over thin slices of cooked chicken, placed on top of or over a thin slice of ham rolled around 2 or 3 stems of cooked asparagus.

2	eggs	1	teaspoon dry mustard
1	cup lager beer	1	teaspoon
2	cups cubed mild or		Worcestershire sauce
	medium cheddar		a pinch cayenne pepper
2	tablespoons margarine		

Beat the eggs with rotary beater in a 1-quart bowl or casserole. Stir in the remaining ingredients.

Cook, uncovered, 4 to 5 minutes or until cheese is melted and mixture is creamy, stirring 4 to 5 times during the cooking period. Beat 1 minute with rotary beater or whisk. Serve over unbuttered toast or as above.

English Bacon and Cheese Pie

Good hot, or when served at room temperature with draft beer and sliced tomato. English pub special.

	9-inch baked pastry shell (see p. 269)	3	green onions, chopped
4	slices of bacon	1/4	teaspoon sage
3	eggs, slightly beaten	1	tablespoon chutney or
1	cup milk		chopped mustard
2	cups grated strong cheddar cheese		pickles

Bake pastry shell and let cool. Cook bacon between paper towels set on glass or paper plate, 3 to 4 minutes or until crisp. Remove paper and cool on plate.

Beat together the eggs and milk, add the cheese, green onions and sage. Stir until well mixed.

Crumble bacon into cooled pie shell, spread with chutney. Pour egg mixture on top. Cook, uncovered, 8 to 9 minutes or until custard is almost set. Let stand 20 minutes before serving. 6 servings.

Quiche Lorraine

Even if the crust is omitted you will have the taste of quiche, with its custardy texture. Nice when served over toasted English muffins or unmolded over a thick slice of tomato, then heated 1 minute in the microwave oven.

	one 8-inch baked pastry shell or	¹/₄	teaspoon nutmeg
		¹/₂	teaspoon basil
	six 6-ounce custard cups	2	cups grated Swiss cheese
3	eggs	¹/₂	cup grated Parmesan cheese
1	cup light cream		
¹/₂	teaspoon salt	2	slices cooked ham, diced (approximately ²/₃ cup)

Beat in a bowl the eggs, cream, salt, nutmeg and basil. Stir in grated cheeses and diced ham.

To serve in a cooked pastry shell, prepare, cook and cool shell (see p. 269).

Cook quiche mixture, covered with waxed paper, in an 8-inch pie plate for 1 minute, 30 seconds. Stir with a fork to move cooked mixture around edges to the center. Cook, covered, another 2 minutes. Let stand 10 minutes. Slip into cooked shell. 6 servings.

To cook in custard cups: pour mixture into the cups. Place cups in a circle in the microwave oven, leaving a small space between each one. Cook, uncovered, 10 minutes, stirring each one after 4 minutes to move cooked edges to the center. Cook until knife inserted in center comes out clean. Let stand, covered, 4 minutes, before unmolding.

11. Meat and Poultry

Most meats will cook well in the microwave oven and it's just as easy to obtain the required rareness as it is in the conventional way. I've given a number of suggestions with each recipe to help with individual types and cuts of meat, but there are some points which apply to cooking meat generally.

First there is the misconception that meat will not brown in the microwave oven. This is only true of the small, individual cuts, such as small steaks or chops. Anything that takes more than 10–12 minutes to cook will indeed be brown.

One of the major benefits of cooking meat in the microwave oven is that there is a lot less shrinkage than when cooked conventionally. In fact, shrinkage is only about 10–12% of the volume of the meat instead of 25–35%, depending on how the meat is cooked the regular way. When you consider that you're paying for this shrinkage, this is certainly nice to know. Even with less shrinkage there is still enough juice to make gravy. To preserve the juices without the meat sitting in them, place an inverted saucer or casserole cover at the bottom of the baking dish and sit the roast on top. If your oven allows use of metal (see manufacturer's instructions), it is also possible to use the metal rack that comes with the CORNING WARE Dutch Oven.

Usually it is recommended that only the better cuts of meat are cooked in the microwave oven. For those less tender cuts that need hours of cooking, it's best to cook the conventional way. As you will see, I have included one or two recipes for these less tender cuts, but they are either marinated to tenderize beforehand or cooked in sufficient moisture (gravy) to slow down the cooking enough for the meat to become tender.

It is always wise to check meats with a thermometer. This should be placed in the thickest part of the meat *after the cooking time is up* and should never be left in while the oven is in operation unless you have a thermometer that is specifically designed for use in a microwave oven.

If you prefer to defrost in the microwave oven before cooking rather than letting the meat stand in your refrigerator overnight, let it sit at room temperature for at least an hour for the larger cuts and half an hour for smaller cuts, after defrosting and before cooking.

Beef

There are a few pointers to remember when roasting beef in a microwave oven. The best cut to use is a rolled rib or standing rib of 3 to 4 lbs. Do not salt the meat before cooking.

The following factors should be taken into consideration for they will affect the cooking time:

1. The temperature of the meat before cooking; room temperature is the very best; for meat just out of refrigerator allow additional cooking time.
2. The shape and size of meat.
3. Tenderness of the cut and degree of cooking desired.
4. Use a shallow glass or CORNING WARE dish of a suitable size — 10" × 6", 12" × 8", or 8" × 8" are the best. Place an inverted saucer or casserole cover in dish to hold meat out of the juices. Place roast, fat side down, on saucer. Turn roast over half way through cooking time, also turn dish around. Lay a sheet of waxed paper loosely on top of roast.

   As juices accumulate in the dish, remove with a spoon or gravy baster and keep to make the gravy. This is important as excessive juices absorb energy and take some away from the meat. If the roast has a tendency to tip over, prop it with a small custard cup.

Attention Meat continues to cook after being taken out of the oven as heat flows to the center. Wrap roast with foil, let stand 15 to 20 minutes. Then test with meat thermometer placed in the thickest part of the meat. If after checking roast, it is not cooked to your taste, remove foil, cover with waxed paper and return to the oven for required time.

Roasting Guide for Beef

For Rolled Rib

- Rare: 6 to 7 minutes per pound
  Internal temperature on thermometer: 120°F. It will increase to 140°F. during standing.
- Medium: 7 to 8 minutes per pound
  Internal temperature on thermometer: 140°F. It will increase to 160°F. during standing.
- Well done: 8 to 10 minutes per pound
  Internal temperature on the thermometer: 160°F. It will increase to 170°F. during standing.

For Standing Rib

Same as above, reducing cooking time by 1 to 2 minutes per pound.

Note These times are for meat which is at room temperature before cooking. If meat is just out of the refrigerator, add 1 to 2 minutes per pound.

Always thaw frozen meat before roasting in the microwave oven. The best way is to refrigerate the unopened package 12 to 24 hours before cooking.

For occasions when this is not possible proceed as follows: place meat in same type of dish as recommended for roast. Defrost in microwave oven 2 minutes per pound. Let stand 20 minutes, then defrost for an additional 1 minute per pound. Turn meat over several times during thawing period.

A Good Tip
You may want to cook your roast until it is just rare. Then, in order to suit individual preferences, you can slice and place each portion on a hot plate, cover with waxed paper and return to the oven for 1 to 3 minutes according to chosen doneness.

To keep roast for serving 6 to 24 hours after cooking, set roast on a plate, wrap with plastic wrap and refrigerate. To serve, slice roast and warm up as above.

Rolled Rib Roast

3 to 4 lb. rolled rib roast
1   clove garlic or 2 bay
    leaves (optional)

Kitchen Bouquet
Paprika

Place clove of garlic, cut in half, or two bay leaves under string holding meat together. Brush roast all over with Kitchen Bouquet. Sprinkle generously with paprika. Place fat side down on inverted saucer or casserole cover placed in bottom of chosen dish. Place waxed paper loosely on top. Cook for half the given time (see meat roasting chart). Turn fat side up, baste and cook, still covered with waxed paper, for the remainder of the time. Remove from oven, wrap in foil and let stand 20 minutes. Test doneness with thermometer. Make gravy while roast is standing (see p. 87). Carve and enjoy.

Standing Rib Roast

Follow directions for rolled rib roast, pushing garlic or bay leaves into the fat. Cook fat side down with bone side up for the first half of the cooking.
Important: Cover the bone with a piece of foil during this first half of cooking time because the bone absorbs energy faster than the meat.

Then remove foil, turn meat over and finish cooking. Wrap in foil and let stand 20 minutes. Test doneness with thermometer and make brown gravy as for the rolled roast (see p. 87).

Note For a different type of gravy, dilute an envelope of dried onion soup in ³/₄ cup hot water and baste the roast two or three times after it has been turned. When the cooking is finished, you will have a nice onion gravy that does not need thickening.

Tender Pot Roast

It will take an hour in all to cook a pot roast in the microwave oven, which is quite a difference from the usual 3 hours. The flavour is something quite special.

2 1/2 to 3 lbs. beef pot roast of your choice*
2 tablespoons fat removed from meat
1 teaspoon salt
2 large onions, sliced
6 peppercorns
1 teaspoon thyme

1/2 cup hot water or consommé or red wine
4 medium carrots, sliced 1/4-inch thick
6 small potatoes, peeled
2 stalks celery, cut in 1-inch pieces

Remove fat from meat, cut into small pieces and melt in a large frying pan until browned. Sear meat all over, over medium heat until a nice brown color. Sprinkle with the salt. Place meat in a 10 × 6-inch baking dish. Lay onion slices on top. Place peppercorns around the meat. Sprinkle thyme over the onion. Cover meat with waxed paper. Cook in oven 20 minutes, turn roast over. Pour hot liquid of your choice on top. Cover and cook another 20 minutes.

Remove meat, wrap in foil and set aside. The temperature after 20 minutes should be 170°F. Add the vegetables to juices in the pan and cook, covered, 15 minutes, stirring the vegetables, and turning potatoes once. Check meat for tenderness.

If you wish to thicken the gravy, remove vegetables with a perforated spoon to a hot platter. Mix 1 tablespoon flour with 2 tablespoons cold water and pour into cooking liquid. Cook 1 minute, stirring well after 30 seconds.

* The cuts I prefer are point sirloin or rolled blade or chuck or cross-rib — 1 1/2 to 3 inches thick is the best.

Beef Noodle Casserole

Even the noodles get cooked in the pot with the other ingredients. A true one-dish meal. Do not use elbow macaroni.

1	lb. ground beef or combination of meats	2	cups tomato or V-8 juice
1 1/2	cups dry noodles	1	teaspoon sugar
1	small onion, chopped fine	1	teaspoon basil
		1	teaspoon salt
1	cup diced celery	1/2	teaspoon pepper

Place ground beef in a 2-quart casserole. Sprinkle with broken up noodles and onion. Next add the celery. Stir the sugar and basil into the tomato juice. Pour over the meat and vegetables. Cover with waxed paper. Cook 10 minutes. Stir well, cook another 10 minutes, season with salt and pepper. Stir and let stand 10 minutes, stirring once. Serve with a bowl of grated cheese. 6 servings.

Mushroom Beef Timbales

An elegant word for a simple idea nicely presented. A timbale is always a small mold of meat or other ingredients topped with a sauce. When true ceramic timbales are not available, use 6-ounce custard cups.

1	lb. ground lean beef	2	green onions, chopped fine
1/2	cup light cream		
1	slightly beaten egg	1/2	teaspoon salt
1/2	cup quick cooking oatmeal	1/4	teaspoon pepper
2	tablespoons finely diced celery	1/2	teaspoon thyme or tarragon

Combine all the ingredients in a bowl. Mix lightly but thoroughly. Divide equally into 6 well-buttered 6-ounce custard cups. Arrange in a circle in the middle of the oven. Cover with waxed paper. Cook 10 minutes. Remove from oven. Let stand 5 minutes, while making sauce. Invert cups onto hot platter or plates. Pour a spoonful of the timbale sauce over each. 6 servings.

Beef and Vegetable Stew

Use red wine, consommé or water as liquid; each one will give a different color and flavor to the stew. The vegetables can also be varied to suit yourself. This stew is an example of complementary cooking, using the surface range and the microwave oven.

3/4 to 1	lb. beef stew meat	1	cup water or consommé or dry red wine
1	tablespoon flour		
1/2	teaspoon salt	2	teaspoons cider vinegar or fresh lemon juice
1	teaspoon paprika		
1/2	teaspoon thyme		
1	tablespoon bacon fat or beef drippings	1	cup diced potatoes
		3/4	cup sliced carrots
1	can (8 ounces) tomato sauce	1	stalk celery, diced
		6	whole small onions
1	clove garlic, chopped fine	1	cup frozen green peas (optional)
2	bay leaves		

Cut beef in 2-inch pieces. Mix the flour, salt, paprika, and thyme. Coat meat with mixture. In a large frying pan or 10″ CORNING WARE skillet heat bacon fat or drippings on surface range, add meat and brown all over using a high heat. Keep in skillet or place in a 3-quart casserole.

Add tomato sauce, garlic, bay leaves, liquid of your choice, vinegar or lemon juice. Cover with waxed paper. Cook 25 minutes or until beef is tender.

Then arrange potatoes, carrots, celery and onions around the dish. Cover and cook 10 minutes. Sprinkle frozen green peas on top. Cook 4 minutes. Stir well and serve. 4 to 5 servings.

Timbale Mushroom Sauce

A recipe to use whenever you wish to serve a mushroom sauce. The color will vary from light beige to golden brown depending on whether you use dry Madeira or soy sauce, and the flavor will also vary. Both are good.

3	tablespoons butter or	milk
	margarine	1/4 teaspoon salt
1 1/2	tablespoons flour	1 can (4 ounce)
1	teaspoon soy sauce or	chopped mushrooms,
	1 tablespoon dry	undrained
	Madeira	1/4 teaspoon tarragon or
3/4	cup light cream or	curry powder

Place butter in 1-quart glass bowl. Heat 1 minute. To the melted butter, add the flour, soy sauce, or dry Madeira. Blend to a smooth paste. Add cream or milk, stir until smooth. Add salt, mushrooms, tarragon or curry powder. Cook, uncovered, 2 minutes. Stir well. Cook another 2 minutes. Stir well. By this time sauce should be thick and creamy. If it gets cold before you are ready to serve, stir well, heat 1 minute, uncovered. Makes 1 1/2 cups.

Marinated Steak

The marinating mixture flavors and tenderizes the meat. This method is used for less tender types of steak, such as round or minute steaks, and resembles Swiss Steak.

1	medium onion, sliced	2	lbs. round steak cut in
2	tablespoons ketchup		6 steaks or 6
1/4	cup fresh lemon juice		medium-size minute
	grated rind of half		steaks
	a lemon	1/2	cup water or
1/4	cup soy sauce		consommé or red
1/2	teaspoon thyme		wine
1	bay leaf	1	teaspoon cornstarch

In a 12 × 8-inch baking dish, combine onion, ketchup, lemon juice and rind, soy sauce, thyme and bay leaf. Add meat, turning in marinating mixture until well coated all over. Cover and marinate 1 hour or overnight in refrigerator.

Place in oven and cook, uncovered, 20 minutes. Add liquid of your choice, cover with waxed paper and cook 15 minutes, turning meat once. Remove meat to a hot platter. Mix cornstarch with 1 tablespoon cold water. Stir into juices. Return to oven for 2 minutes. Stir well and pour over steak. 6 servings.

T-Bone or Porterhouse Steak

Some meats are better enjoyed when browned under direct heat or on the surface of the range, then finished or reheated in the microwave oven. Steak is definitely one of those.

There are three different methods and each is successful:

1. Sear steak in hot butter in cast iron frying pan over high heat, just enough to give it a good color. Then place on a hot browning dish (see p.19) and cook 1 minute on each side for rare.
2. Sear steak as above on one side only, brush other side with Kitchen Bouquet and sprinkle with seasoned salt. While searing steak, heat a browning utensil (see p. 19). Place steak on it, seared side touching bottom of dish. Cook 2 minutes and serve.
3. Cook a steak of your choice to your taste the conventional way. Cool, wrap individually. Label. Freeze. To serve, thaw out without unwrapping for 2 hours, then unwrap. Heat browning utensil. Cook 2 to 4 minutes or until hot to your taste.

Note This is for a 1-inch thick steak. Add 2 minutes per inch of steak. Remember that it is always wise to undertime meat cooked in the microwave oven because it keeps on cooking for another minute or so after being taken out of the oven. Should you wish the meat to be cooked more thoroughly, you just have to return it to the oven for seconds or minutes as needed, even if it has been taken out for 5 minutes.

Green Pepper Steak

This favorite can serve five with only 1 pound of round steak.

1	lb. round steak	1	teaspoon fresh ginger
3	tablespoons salad oil		root grated or
1	clove garlic	1/2	teaspoon ground ginger
1	large onion chopped	1	tablespoon cornstarch
2	large green peppers,	1	cup consommé
	cut in thin slivers	1	tablespoon soy sauce
1/2	teaspoon salt	1	teaspoon sugar
1/4	teaspoon pepper		

Cut steak across the grain in thin slices. Heat salad oil with garlic in a 10-inch CORNING WARE skillet, uncovered, 1 minute. Remove garlic. Add the meat, stir until coated with oil. Cook, uncovered, 3 minutes, stirring after 2 minutes. Add onion, green peppers, salt, pepper and ginger. Stir to mix. Cook, covered with waxed paper, for 5 minutes. Stir thoroughly. Cook, covered, another minute. Combine cornstarch with consommé and soy sauce, add sugar. Stir into meat mixture. Cook, uncovered, for 3 to 4 minutes, stirring once after 2 minutes. When sauce is creamy and transparent, it is ready. Serve with boiled rice. 4 to 5 servings.

Sukiyaki

A perfect example of complementary cooking, using surface range and microwave oven. Cook in front of your guests for a special party.

1	(8-ounce) can bamboo shoots	1	tablespoon salad oil
1	(3½-ounce) can water chestnuts	⅓	cup soy sauce
		2	tablespoons white sugar
1	lb. fresh bean sprouts	1	tablespoon brown sugar
4	green onions		
½	lb. fresh mushrooms	1	teaspoon fresh ginger root, grated (optional)
3	stalks celery		
1	lb. top round steak	½	cup consommé

Drain bamboo shoots and water chestnuts. Slice thinly. Rinse bean sprouts. Drain well. Slice thinly on the bias the onions, mushrooms and celery. Slice steak on the bias, as thinly as possible, across the grain.

Heat the salad oil in a 10-inch CORNING WARE skillet on surface range. Add meat, stir quickly with a fork, just until rawness disappears. Remove from heat. Arrange meat in center of skillet to form a strip. Arrange vegetables on either side of the meat.

Combine the soy sauce, white and brown sugar, fresh ginger and consommé. Pour over all. Cook in oven, uncovered, 8 minutes. Cover with waxed paper and let stand for 5 to 10 minutes. Taste for salt, or let each one salt to taste. Serve with plain, boiled rice. 4 to 6 servings.

Hamburgers

Hamburger is a tender, economical meat that cooks quickly and well in a microwave oven, so make sure you always have some on hand in the refrigerator or the freezer.

There is no need to pre-brown hamburgers because Kitchen Bouquet, soy sauce or All-purpose basting sauce (see p. 87) will do the work. If you have a browning utensil, it is better still, although they can be equally successful done on a glass pie plate.

For each pound of ground beef *or* a mixture of veal, beef and pork, or veal and beef or minced lamb use:

1	*teaspoon salt*	1	*tablespoon instant*
1/4	*teaspoon pepper*		*potato flakes*
2	*tablespoons cold*		
	water		

Blend together. Divide into 4 equal patties of 1/4 lb. each or make 6 smaller ones. Do not pack tightly, as this never makes a good patty no matter how it is cooked.

Coat each patty with Kitchen Bouquet, soy sauce, or basting sauce and arrange in shallow baking dish such as a glass pie plate, loosely covered with a sheet of waxed paper. For patties made with 1/4 lb. of meat each, cook as follows, without turning for medium rare. Add 1 minute for well done.

1 patty:	3 minutes
2 patties:	4 minutes 30 seconds
3 patties:	5 to 6 minutes
4 patties:	6 to 8 minutes
5 patties:	8 to 10 minutes
6 patties:	10 to 12 minutes

To cook frozen patties: do not thaw out, place on plate as above, cover loosely with waxed paper, cook:

1 patty:	4 minutes defrost, turn, cook 2 to 3 minutes
2 patties:	4 minutes defrost, turn, cook 5 minutes
3 patties:	8 minutes defrost, turn, cook 8 to 10 minutes
4 patties:	8 minutes defrost, turn, cook 12 minutes

Note Hamburgers should not be overcooked as they continue to cook after being removed from oven.

To vary the flavor, add one of the following to basic meat mixture:
1   tablespoon A-1 sauce (*mild, fruity flavor*)
1   tablespoon Worcestershire sauce (*peppery flavor*)
1   tablespoon toasted dried onion (*a favorite*)
4   fresh green onions, both green and white parts (*pleasant*)
1/2 teaspoon garlic powder or 1 clove crushed (*interesting*)
1   tablespoon ketchup or chili sauce (*chili is the best*)
2   teaspoons French Dijon mustard (*Gourmet*)
1   teaspoon curry powder (*spicy*)
1   teaspoon each ground cumin and lemon rind (*Egyptian*)
2   tablespoons lemon juice, instead of water, 1/4 teaspoon thyme
     (*Greek*)
1   teaspoon thyme, 1/8 teaspoon ground bay leaf (*French*)
1   teaspoon oregano, 2 tablespoons red wine, instead of water
     (*Italian*)
1   teaspoon basil, 1 clove garlic, 1 teaspoon coriander
     (*Rumanian*)

Another variation is to top each patty with one of the following, during the last minute of cooking.

1   slice of precut cheese
1   tablespoon grated cheddar or Parmesan cheese
2   teaspoons commercial sour cream, sprinkled with paprika
1   teaspoon dry onion soup mix
2   tablespoons undiluted cream of mushroom or celery soup
     A pat of butter flavored with fresh herbs to choice

Have patties in your freezer for quick meals. Patties can be seasoned, plain or with any of the variations, shaped and coated with Kitchen Bouquet or basting sauce. Place in container with a square of waxed paper between each patty so they will not stick together.

   It makes life so easy to have patties in the freezer, ready to be cooked, that I strongly advise it. Be sure to label type of seasoning or variation, so each member of the family can have what he or she prefers.

Meat Loaf with Hamburger

Add to basic formula of the 1 pound ground beef, 1 egg slightly beaten and any of the variations or toppings you prefer. Place mixture in an 8½ × 4½-inch loaf dish. Cook, covered with waxed paper, 10 to 12 minutes. Let stand 10 minutes before slicing. An additional topping can be made with 2 tablespoons brown sugar, ½ teaspoon dry mustard and 2 tablespoons ketchup or tomato paste. Spread on top of loaf before cooking.

Ring Meat Loaf

Place a custard cup open side up in middle of an 8-inch round cake dish. Shape meat in circle around it. Cook as for basic meat loaf.

Notes on Freezing Meat Loaf

Meat loaf can be frozen before cooking, but should be used within 1 month.
   Defrost for 10 minutes. Cook 10 to 15 minutes. Let stand 10 minutes, before serving.

Meat Loaf à la Mode

Choose any combination of flavorings for the hamburger mixture. (Do not use topping.) Press mixture lightly and evenly in a 9-inch glass pie plate. Pour ½ cup canned tomato sauce on top, spreading it evenly. Cover with clear plastic wrap. Puncture wrap here and there with the point of a knife. Bake 6 minutes, remove cover, bake another 6 minutes. Remove from oven, let stand another 6 minutes. Cut in wedges to serve and top with a mound of hot mashed potatoes.

Italian Casserole

Vegetables, meat and noodles are combined in a tasty and colorful dish.

8	ounces noodles, cooked	1	cup canned creamed corn
2	tablespoons margarine or salad oil	1	teaspoon curry powder
1	large onion, chopped	1	teaspoon salt
1	clove garlic, minced	1/4	teaspoon pepper
1	lb. ground beef	1/2	cup grated cheese of your choice
1	10-ounce can tomato soup		

Cook noodles according to directions on p.224.

Place margarine or salad oil in a 1½-quart glass casserole dish and melt 1 minute. Add onion and garlic and cook, uncovered, 2 minutes, stirring once. Add the meat and cook, uncovered, another 4 minutes, stirring twice. Stir in undiluted tomato soup and corn, season with curry powder, salt and pepper. In a 2-quart casserole make alternate rows of the meat mixture, noodles and cheese, ending with cheese.

Cover with waxed paper. Cook 6 minutes. 4 servings.

Another recipe for a hamburger casserole is Rice and Beef Casserole on p. 223.

Quick Chili Casserole

The 2-hour chili reduced to 25 minutes!

3	slices bacon	1/3	cup diced green
1	lb. ground beef (or		pepper or celery
	pork)	1	16-ounce can red kidney
2	cups water		beans, drained
1	envelope onion soup	1	8 1/2-ounce can whole
	mix		kernel corn, drained
1/4 to 1/2	teaspoon chili powder		
1	cup cubed raw		
	potatoes		

Dice bacon, place in an 8 × 8-inch glass dish. Cook, uncovered, 3 minutes, stirring once. Remove bacon pieces with perforated spoon and set aside. Stir ground beef or pork in remaining fat. Cook 4 minutes, stirring thoroughly once.

Combine water, onion soup mix and chili powder. Pour over meat. Stir in the potatoes. Cook, covered with waxed paper, 10 minutes, stirring twice. Add remaining ingredients and reserved bacon. Cover and cook 10 minutes, stirring once. 4 to 5 servings.

Speedy Frank 'n' Beans Casserole

Canned beans and frankfurters, ready for lunch in 5 minutes.

1	can or glass jar of	1	teaspoon prepared
	baked beans (16 or 20		mustard
	ounces)	2	tablespoons brown
1	small onion, diced		sugar
3	tablespoons ketchup	6 to 8	frankfurters
			grated cheese (optional)

Place all the ingredients, except frankfurters, in a 1 1/2-quart glass casserole dish. Mix well. Cut frankfurters in two and bury in the beans or place on top.

If desired, spread a tablespoon or two of grated strong cheddar cheese on top of beans.

Cook, uncovered, 5 minutes or until hot. Serves 4 to 6.

Lamb

When buying lamb, look for meat that is firm, fine-grained and smooth, with color varying from a light to a darker pink. The fat has a light creamy color.

Darker meat with yellowish fat is mutton, not successfully cooked in the microwave oven, but lamb is very tasty and easier to brown than beef or veal.

Seasonings for Lamb

You may wish to vary the seasonings given in the recipes. Here are some that I find to be the most successful with lamb.

Sprinkle meat before roasting with basil, rosemary, thyme, oregano, mint, parsley, ground ginger or curry powder. The quantity can vary from ¼ to 1 teaspoon.

The French method is to make several slits in top of roast before cooking and insert slivers of garlic, rolled in the chosen seasoning.

Before serving roast, steak or cutlets, sprinkle with fresh lemon juice, brandy, dry Madeira or Crème de Menthe—just a dash over each cutlet and steak, about 2 tablespoons over a roast. Do this as soon as it is taken out of the oven.

Cooking a Roast of Lamb

A boneless lamb roast is easier to cook in a microwave oven than a roast with bone; the shoulder or leg can be rolled.

The shank end of the leg with just a small bone can be cooked successfully without being rolled, but the bone end should be covered with a piece of foil during the first half of the cooking.

Lamb takes 8 to 9 minutes per pound; like other meats, it is much better to rely on a meat thermometer. This should be inserted when roast is taken out of the oven—temperature should then read 150° to 160°, which is from rare to medium rare—then roast is wrapped in foil, to stand for 20 to 30 minutes. Temperature should rise to between 160° to 175° during this standing time.

Marinated Roast Leg of Lamb

While roast is standing there is plenty of time to cook the vegetables and finish dinner preparations, and the meat will still be very hot.

1	leg of lamb or half leg, from 2 to 3 lbs.	2	cups dry red wine
1	clove garlic, slivered (optional)	3	medium onions, sliced
		2	teaspoons salt
1/2	cup salad oil	1	teaspoon basil
			a few celery leaves

Make several small pockets in flesh of lamb with small pointed knife. Insert slivers of garlic. Place meat in glass dish or bowl. Mix remaining ingredients and pour over the meat. Cover, refrigerate in this marinade for 12 to 48 hours, turning lamb a few times in the liquid.

To cook, remove roast from marinade. Place on an inverted saucer or cover set in a 12 × 8-inch baking dish, fat side down. If any bones show, cover with foil. Roast, uncovered, 8 to 9 minutes per pound, turning meat 4 times during cooking period, basting each time with a few spoonfuls of the marinating liquid. When done, wrap in foil, insert meat thermometer, and let stand 10 to 20 minutes, until thermometer registers desired doneness.

To make gravy, add a few more spoonfuls of marinating mixture to juices in the dish. Let stand until ready to serve, then heat gravy, uncovered, 2 minutes, or until bubbling hot.

Glazed Lamb Roast

A glaze enhances the flavor of the lamb and gives it a pleasing brown color when done.

1/4	cup dry sherry or dry Madeira wine	2	tablespoons salad oil
1	tablespoon paprika	2	cloves garlic, minced
1	tablespoon Kitchen Bouquet		grated rind 1 lemon
		4	lbs. boned leg of lamb roast

In a 1-cup measure combine first six ingredients and cook, uncovered, 1 minute. Place roast on an inverted saucer in 12 x 8-inch baking dish. Baste with hot mixture and cook, uncovered, 8 minutes. Turn roast, baste again with glaze, cook 24 minutes, basting 4 times. Wrap roast in foil, insert meat thermometer, let stand until thermometer registers desired doneness. When ready to serve, heat gravy remaining in the dish for 2 minutes.

English Shoulder Roast

To roast a lamb shoulder successfully in the microwave oven it must be rolled. This is a very tasty roast with its vegetables and sauce all cooked in the same dish.

2	teaspoons grated lemon peel	1	tablespoon Kitchen Bouquet
1	teaspoon basil	4 to 6	carrots, peeled and thinly sliced
1/4	teaspoon garlic powder	2	tablespoons dry Madeira
1/8	teaspoon pepper	1	teaspoon cornstarch
1	tablespoon butter	2	green onions, chopped fine
1	onion, thinly sliced a 3 to 4-lb. rolled shoulder of lamb		

Combine lemon peel, basil, garlic powder and pepper. Mix well and rub all over the meat. Put butter in a 12 × 8-inch baking dish and melt in oven for 1 minute. Stir in onion, cook 2 minutes. Roll lamb roast in this mixture. If tied with string, cover string with foil for the first part of the cooking. Place lamb on inverted saucer. Cook 8 to 9 minutes per pound, turning roast twice during cooking period. Remove roast and saucer from dish when time is up, wrap roast in foil, insert thermometer, let stand until it registers between 160° and 175°, according to how rare you like it.

To gravy in the dish, add carrots, Madeira and cornstarch. Stir well, cover with waxed paper. Cook 7 to 8 minutes, stirring twice. Pour around meat when ready to serve and sprinkle with green onions.

Glazed Shoulder of Lamb

Lamb takes as well as ham to all types of glazes. When possible use Bitter Orange Marmalade. Apricot jam can also be used in same quantity as marmalade.

3	to 4-lb. rolled shoulder of lamb		grated rind of 1 orange and 1 lemon
2	tablespoons flour	1/4	cup lemon juice
1	teaspoon salt	3	tablespoons chopped parsley
1/2	teaspoon pepper		
1/2	cup orange marmalade		

Place meat in a 12 × 8-inch baking dish, set on inverted saucer. (If roast is tied with string, cover string with foil.) Cook 9 minutes to the pound, turning 4 times during the cooking period. Remove foil when half the cooking is done.

While roast is cooking, combine flour, salt, pepper, marmalade, rind of orange and lemon and lemon juice. Blend to a smooth paste. When roast is turned for the second time with fat side up, spread marmalade mixture all over meat. Continue cooking, basting twice. When cooking is completed wrap roast in foil, insert meat thermometer and let stand until thermometer indicates that it is cooked.

To serve, place meat on a hot platter. Heat remaining glaze in dish, 30 seconds. Pour over meat. Sprinkle parsley on top and serve.

Finnish Boiled Lamb

Serve with rice buttered and flavored with fresh dill. Lamb cooked this way is good hot or cold.

	a small 2 1/2 to 3-lb. boned and rolled shoulder of lamb boiling water	1	bay leaf
		2	slices unpeeled lemon
		1/2	teaspoon ground ginger
2	teaspoons salt	4 to 5	sprigs of dill
4	peppercorns		Caper Sauce (see p.79)

Place meat in a bowl and pour boiling water over until meat is completely covered. Let stand 5 minutes. Drain. Place meat in a 2-quart dish and add more boiling water to barely cover the meat. Add salt, peppercorns, bay leaf, lemon, ground ginger and dill. Cover top of dish with plastic wrap. Puncture here and there to allow steam to escape.

Cook, 10 minutes per pound, rotating dish 3 times and turning meat over once. Remove meat from water, place on warm service platter. Let stand 15 minutes. Thermometer should register 170°F. Make sauce. Serve separately.

Lamb Loaf

Minced lamb makes very good meat loaf. This can also be combined with veal or pork in the proportions you prefer.

1½	lbs. ground lamb	1	teaspoon sugar
2	well-beaten eggs	1	cup fine cracker
1	can (8 ounce) tomato		crumbs
	sauce	1	tablespoon soy sauce
⅓	cup currants	¼	teaspoon garlic
½	teaspoon salt		powder
1	teaspoon curry		Kitchen Bouquet
	powder		

Combine all the ingredients, except Kitchen Bouquet, in a bowl until thoroughly mixed. Pack mixture into an 8½ × 4½-inch (48 ounce) loaf dish. Smooth top. Brush with Kitchen Bouquet. Cover with plastic wrap, punctured in center to allow steam to escape.

Cook, 20 minutes. Insert thermometer in middle of loaf. Let stand 20 minutes. It should then read 140° to 150°. Serve hot or cold.

Lamb Shanks Française

Lamb shanks are dainty, but make hearty servings if served one to a person. They are also economical to buy.

4	lamb shanks — approx. 1/2 lb. each	2	tablespoons flour
1	onion, sliced	1/2	cup water
1	teaspoon salt	1/2	cup red wine or tomato juice
1	clove garlic, minced	4	medium carrots, sliced
1	bay leaf	2	stalks celery, chopped
1/2	teaspoon thyme		

In a 3-quart casserole, combine lamb shanks, onion, salt, garlic, bay leaf and thyme. Add water gradually to flour and stir to make a smooth paste. Pour over shanks, add remaining ingredients. Cook, covered with waxed paper, 18 minutes, or until meat is tender, turning meat about 4 times to coat with sauce. Then let stand, covered, 10 to 20 minutes. Serve with noodles or potatoes.

Lamb Patties Oriental

Serve with rice and peas. Cook frozen green peas first, then cook lamb patties. When patties are cooked, add peas to gravy and heat 1 minute.

1	lb. ground lamb	1/2	teaspoon thyme
1/2	teaspoon salt		Kitchen Bouquet
1/8	teaspoon pepper	1/2	cup plum sauce
1/2	teaspoon ground cumin	2	tablespoons lemon juice

Mix lamb, salt, pepper, cumin and thyme. Shape into 4 patties. Arrange in an 8 × 8-inch baking dish. Brush each one with Kitchen Bouquet or All-purpose basting sauce (p. 87).

Cook, uncovered, 4 minutes, drain gravy and reserve. Turn patties. Top with plum sauce mixed with lemon juice. Cook 4 minutes. Let stand 2 minutes. Spoon sauce in baking dish on top of patties before serving.

Veal

Roast Veal

Veal is properly cooked when the thermometer registers 170°. The best cuts are rolled shoulder or rump roast of about 3 pounds.

Garlic and tarragon are veal's best friends. Madeira Mushroom sauce is the most interesting to serve with veal (see p. 80).

3	lbs. veal shoulder or rump roast	1	tablespoon Kitchen Bouquet
1	clove garlic, sliced	2	tablespoons soft butter or peanut oil
1	teaspoon tarragon		
1/2	teaspoon salt		

Mix together the slivers of garlic, tarragon and salt. Make slits in meat with the point of a knife and insert garlic mixture. Spread Kitchen Bouquet or All-purpose basting sauce (p. 87) all over the roast. Spread cut side with the butter or oil.

Place in a glass baking dish, bone side down. Cover with waxed paper. Cook 30 to 35 minutes or about 10 minutes per pound. Remove from oven, wrap in foil, let stand 20 minutes. Insert thermometer. It should register 170°F. If not at this temperature, remove foil, cover with waxed paper and put back in the oven for a few minutes until done.

Serve with Deep-browned Potatoes (see p. 204). Add gravy in the pan to the mushroom sauce. 4 servings.

Veal Scallop Florentine

This is a good recipe to make in advance as it will keep well refrigerated or frozen.

1/4	cup salad oil	2	tablespoons flour
1	clove garlic	1/2	teaspoon salt
1	lb. thinly sliced veal	1/4	teaspoon pepper
	cutlets, cut in 4	1/4	teaspoon savory or
	servings		marjoram
1/2	teaspoon paprika	1	can (8 ounce) tomato
2	medium size onions,		sauce
	thinly sliced	1/2	cup water
1	can (6 ounces)		
	mushrooms, drained		

In a 10-inch CORNING WARE skillet heat the oil and garlic together on surface unit of your range, until garlic starts to brown. Sprinkle veal on one side with the paprika. Place that side down in the hot oil and sear quickly over high heat. Turn, sear second side. Remove pan from heat. Remove veal from skillet. Discard garlic. Add the onions and mushrooms to the fat in skillet, stir until coated. Transfer skillet to oven and cook, uncovered, 4 minutes. Stir in flour, salt, pepper, savory or marjoram, until blended. Cook, uncovered, 2 minutes, stir. Add tomato sauce and water. Cook 4 minutes, stirring once after 3 minutes. Add veal, cook another 5 to 6 minutes. Serve with parsleyed noodles. 4 servings.

Both veal and noodles can be cooked, cooled, refrigerated for 3 to 4 days or frozen for 1 month. If frozen, thaw the veal scallops, wrapped, for 4 hours, on kitchen counter. Place on serving platter or glass dish, cover with waxed paper and reheat 8 minutes or until hot. Defrost noodles, 4 minutes. Cover with waxed paper. Cook 2 minutes.

Veal Loaf

More like a "pâté maison" than a meat loaf. Usually served cold, thinly sliced.

1	egg	2	tablespoons margarine
1/2	cup milk	1	large onion, chopped fine
1/2	cup seasoned bread stuffing mix	1	lb. ground veal
1/2	teaspoon pepper	1	(8 ounce) can tomato sauce
1/2	teaspoon thyme		
1/4	teaspoon oregano	2	tablespoons brown sugar
1/4	cup fresh parsley, chopped fine		

Combine egg and milk in bowl. Add stuffing mix, pepper, thyme, oregano and parsley. Mix well, let stand 5 minutes. Meanwhile, melt margarine in an 8-inch round glass cake dish, 1 minute. Add the onion. Stir well. Cook, uncovered, 5 minutes, stirring once during the cooking period. Mix meat with the bread mixture, stir into the onion until well mixed. Form meat into a round loaf. Cook 8 to 9 minutes, uncovered, rotating dish twice during the cooking period. Pour tomato sauce and sugar mixed together on top of meat. Cook, uncovered, 4 minutes. Remove from oven, cool 20 minutes. Place double fold of waxed paper on top. Place a weight on top so that surface will be flat when cold. Refrigerate until cold. If you prefer to serve hot, let stand 10 minutes, covered, after removing from oven. Unmold and serve. 4 servings.

Pork

Roast Loin of Pork

The 3 to 4-lb. boneless pork loin is the most attractive in shape when roasted, but a bone-in pork loin is equally tasty. Like other meats, with pork it is best to cover the bone with foil for the first half of the cooking.

To have a crisp brown top, the roast can be placed 4 inches away from the direct heat (in the oven broiler) and broiled until browned to taste. I do not do this, as I find the browning sufficient and the meat perfect when done in the microwave oven.

Pork takes 10 to 14 minutes per pound. It must stand 20 minutes wrapped in foil, after cooking in the oven. At this stage it should be checked with a meat thermometer which should register between 175°F. to 185°F. Push the thermometer through the foil. The roast will remain hot for another 20 minutes if kept in a warm place.

3	to 4-lb. loin of pork	1/2	teaspoon savory or
1	clove garlic, chopped		sage
	fine	1	teaspoon coarse salt
			paprika

Mash together the garlic, savory or sage and coarse salt. Make incisions in the fat with the point of a knife. Stuff in the flavoring mixture until all is used. Sprinkle fat top of roast generously with paprika. In the bottom of a 10 × 6-inch glass dish place roast, fat side down on an inverted saucer. Cover with waxed paper, cook, 20 minutes, turn fat side up, cover again and cook another 20 minutes. Remove paper and continue to cook for remaining time, according to size of roast.

Remove roast from oven, wrap tightly in foil. Set on a plate, let stand 15 to 20 minutes. Check with thermometer. If the temperature has not reached the proper 175°F., remove foil, cover with waxed paper and put back in the oven for a few minutes until thermometer registers the correct temperature. Make onion gravy while roast is standing.

Glazed Lamb Roast, page 118
Veal Scallop Florentine, page 124

Duck à l'orange, 152

Onion Gravy

Add 1 medium chopped onion to the fat in the roasting dish. Cook 3 to 5 minutes to brown the onion. Remove half the fat (keep to make Deep-browned Potatoes — see p.206). Add 2 tablespoons flour to remaining fat and onion, mix well, add ⅛ teaspoon caraway seed, ½ teaspoon ground cumin, ¼ teaspoon Kitchen Bouquet, 1½ cups hot water. Stir until well mixed. Cook, uncovered, 4 minutes, stirring once during that period. When creamy and bubbly, the sauce is ready. Serve separately. 6 servings.

Glazed Spareribs

The ribs will take on a rich brown color during the cooking period. Nice served with rice.

2	lbs. spareribs, cut into 1-inch pieces	3	tablespoons soy sauce
¼	cup brown sugar	¼	cup dry sherry
1	tablespoon cornstarch	½	cup fresh orange juice
			grated rind of 1 orange

Arrange ribs in a 12 × 8-inch glass baking dish. Cook, covered with waxed paper, 10 minutes. Drain accumulated juices and stir the ribs.

Combine the remaining ingredients. Pour over the ribs, cook, covered with waxed paper, for 15 minutes, turning and stirring ribs in the sauce 2 to 3 times. Let stand 15 minutes. 4 servings.

Pork Chops

Use your browning utensil for this recipe.

4   1-inch thick loin or rib pork chops
    Kitchen Bouquet or soy sauce.
    Seasoned salt or paprika

Heat browning utensil for 4 minutes. Brush chops on each side with Kitchen Bouquet or soy sauce, sprinkle with seasoned salt or paprika. Place in hot browning utensil, cover loosely with waxed paper, cook 4 minutes. Turn over, cover, cook 4 minutes.

Let stand, covered, for 3 to 5 minutes and then press the chops into the bottom of a dish. This will release the juices and give you a gravy in the bottom of the dish. Place the meat on heated plates and pour the gravy on top.

When browning only two chops, cook for 2 minutes on each side and let stand for 3 minutes.

Sweet and Sour Pork Chops

Serve with rice and marinated green peppers.

2   tablespoons
        cornstarch
6 to 8 thin pork chops
3   tablespoons soy sauce
1/4   cup brown sugar
1/2   teaspoon finely grated
        fresh ginger or

1/4   teaspoon ground
        ginger
1/4   cup cider vinegar
1/2   cup water
1 1/2   cups (14-ounce can)
        undrained, pineapple
        tidbits
1   medium onion, sliced

Toss pork chops in cornstarch in a 2-quart casserole until coated. Add remaining ingredients and toss together. Cook, covered with waxed paper, 8 to 11 minutes, stirring twice. Let stand 3 minutes. Stir well. 6 servings.

Breaded Pork Chops

Make your own breading mixture. It will keep 1 month refrigerated in a glass jar or 6 months in the freezer. It makes tasty, juicy chops. The same mixture can be used to coat hamburgers.

2	cups fine dry breadcrumbs	1	teaspoon salt
1	teaspoon sage or oregano	1/2	teaspoon pepper
1/2	teaspoon thyme	1	teaspoon powdered garlic
1	teaspoon ground coriander	1	tablespoon dried onion, crushed fine
1/2	teaspoon curry powder	1	tablespoon paprika
		4	pork chops — 1 to 1 1/4-inch thick

Place all the seasonings in a bowl and mash with a wooden mallet until thoroughly blended.

To prepare pork chops, dip each one in cold water, then in mixture until well coated. For a variation, I sometimes brush the chops on both sides with a bottled sweet and sour or barbecue sauce, then I roll in mix.

In a 10 × 6-inch baking dish or CORNING WARE skillet, place prepared chops. Cook, uncovered, 5 minutes. Turn chops, cook another 3 minutes. Let stand 2 minutes before serving.

New England Pork Chops

Cranberries and oranges add a special flavor to these pork chops which are first browned on top of your surface range. If you prefer, the meat can be removed from the bones which makes an attractive tenderloin per serving.

4	pork chops, 1-inch thick	2	tablespoons brown sugar
1/2	teaspoon salt	3	slices bread, diced
1/4	teaspoon pepper	1/2	cup chopped fresh cranberries
1	teaspoon white sugar		
2	large oranges	1/4	cup diced celery
		3	tablespoons water

Trim fat from chops, dice and melt in frying pan. Salt and pepper chops and sprinkle with white sugar. Brown on both sides quickly over high heat of surface range. When browned, place in a 12 × 8-inch baking dish.

Cut 2 equal slices, about 1/2 inch thick, from middle of each orange. Squeeze juice from remaining pieces and add water, if necessary, to make 1/4 cup liquid. Stir in the brown sugar and pour over the chops. Bake, covered with waxed paper, 8 to 10 minutes.

Meanwhile, mix diced bread, cranberries, celery and the 3 tablespoons water in a bowl. Stir together to form a mass. Divide evenly into mounds on orange slices. Set one on top of each chop when they are baked. Spoon juices from pan over oranges. Cover with waxed paper. Bake 1 minute, 30 seconds. Let stand 2 minutes. 4 servings.

Pork Chops Monique

This is another way to make sweet and sour pork chops. Very good served with Confetti Rice (see p.221).

6	thinly sliced pork chops	2	tablespoons honey or brown sugar
1/2	cup ketchup	6	thin slices unpeeled lemon

Place chops in a 12 × 8-inch baking dish or 10-inch CORNING WARE skillet. Mix together the ketchup and honey or brown sugar. Spread each chop with this mixture. Place a slice of lemon on each chop.

Cook, covered, 12 minutes, remove from oven, let stand covered for 10 minutes. 6 servings.

Bavarian Pork Chops

Pork, sauerkraut and apples or prunes are always a winning combination.

2	cups well-drained sauerkraut	1	tablespoon brown sugar
1	medium onion, chopped	1/8	teaspoon caraway seeds
2	apples, peeled and sliced or	6	juniper berries (optional)
8	prunes, pitted or unpitted	4	to 6 pork chops, cut 1/2-inch thick
		1/4	cup water

Mix in an 8 × 8-inch glass baking dish half of the sauerkraut, onion, apples or prunes, sugar, caraway seeds and juniper berries. Place chops on the top, cover with the remaining sauerkraut, onion, apples or prunes, sugar, caraway seeds and juniper berries. Mix lightly to distribute ingredients. Pour water over all.

Cook, covered with waxed paper, 11 to 14 minutes or until meat is tender. Taste for seasoning. Serves 4.

Baked Pork Shoulder Steak

Tender steak in a celery sauce. Serve with baked potatoes cooked in the microwave oven before the meat. Let them stand covered or wrapped in foil, until meat is ready.

1	pork steak, about 1 lb.	1/4	cup water
2	tablespoons margarine	1	teaspoon soy sauce
1	can (10 ounces) cream of celery soup		

Remove excess fat on meat, cut into 4 portions. Melt margarine in a 10 × 6-inch glass baking dish or a 10-inch CORNING WARE skillet, 1 minute. Roll meat in margarine, cook, covered with waxed paper, 2 minutes, turn meat and dish, cook another 2 minutes. Turn meat and dish again and cook another 2 minutes.

Blend remaining ingredients together. Pour over pork. Cover with waxed paper. Cook 5 minutes, stirring and turning dish once. 4 to 5 servings.

Ham

Ham is a versatile and tender meat, with very little waste. Whatever the type chosen—half a precooked or tenderized ham, slices, cubes or the more expensive smoked loin or Canadian bacon — all are very successfully cooked in a microwave oven and need no browning.

Ham requires a very short cooking time because it is precooked and also because its high sugar content attracts microwave energy.

When cooking a 1 to 2-inch thick ham steak, the bone in the middle (if any) should be removed, as bones absorb too much of the heat.

Precooked ham should register 130°F when removed from the oven and between 140°F. and 150°F. when it has been left to stand wrapped in foil for 20 minutes.

Baked Ham

To cook a 3 to 4 lb. ready-to-eat or tenderized ham, set ham on a saucer, fat side down in an 8 × 8-inch baking dish. Cook, covered with waxed paper, 10 minutes per pound, turning ham and dish 4 times. For example, if the ham is 4 lbs., multiply 4 × 10 = 40 minutes, so the ham and dish must be turned every 10 minutes.

When ham is cooked, wrap in foil. Let stand 20 to 30 minutes. Temperature on thermometer after standing should read 140°F. to 150°F.

Note When one end of the ham is smaller than the other, cover with foil during first half of cooking time.

To glaze: Remove hard skin from ham and brush top with currant or grape jelly or orange marmalade or a combination of ⅓ cup brown sugar and ⅓ cup drained, crushed pineapple, during the last 5 minutes of cooking.

Ham Steak à l'Anglaise

Serve hot with baked potatoes and coleslaw for an interesting lunch. Cook potatoes while meat is standing.

a 1½-inch thick slice of ham (approx. 3 lbs.)
⅓ cup brown sugar
1 cup apple juice
½ cup chutney or A-1 Sauce

½ cup corn or maple syrup
1 tablespoon fresh lemon juice

Place ham in a glass baking dish to fit. Spread top with the brown sugar. Pour ½ cup of the apple juice around ham. Cover with waxed paper. Cook 15 minutes, turn ham, cook another 10 minutes, still covered. Place ham on platter and let stand while making glaze.

To juices in the baking dish, add all the remaining ingredients. Cook, uncovered, 5 minutes. Return ham to dish, coat with glaze by turning it over 2 to 3 times. Cook, uncovered, 5 minutes.

Let stand 10 minutes before serving. To serve cold, turn meat over, cover dish with foil and let stand until cold.

Orange Glazed Ham Slice

Make this with a 1-inch thick slice of ham cut from boned, ready-cooked ham.

½ cup brown sugar
1 tablespoon cornstarch
¼ teaspoon curry powder

1 cup fresh orange juice
1 ham slice 1 inch thick (1¾-2 lbs.)
8 whole cloves

In a 10 × 6-inch baking dish, combine brown sugar, cornstarch and curry powder. Stir in the orange juice and rind. Add ham slice, turn around in the sauce 2 to 3 times to coat both sides.

Push cloves into the fat around the ham.

Cook, uncovered, 10 minutes, stirring twice and spooning sauce over ham. Cook, covered, another 10 minutes. Let stand, covered, 5 minutes. Stir and serve. 4 servings.

Honey Ham Steak

Serve cold. Very good with potato salad and sliced tomatoes.

1 1/2	to 2 lb. slice of tenderized or precooked ham	1	tablespoon prepared horseradish, well drained
1/2	cup pickle relish, well drained	3	tablespoons honey grated rind of 1 lemon

Place ham in a 10 × 6-inch glass baking dish. Combine relish, horseradish, honey and lemon rind. Spoon on top of ham. Cook, covered with waxed paper, 10 minutes. Turn meat and dish, spoon sauce over. Cook, covered, another 10 minutes. 6 servings.

Ham and Sweet Potatoes

Wondering what to do with leftover ham? Try this casserole. The grapefruit gives it a very interesting tang.

2	grapefruit	1/4	cup lemon juice
1 1/2 to	2 cups cooked ham	1/2	teaspoon prepared mustard
1	can sweet potatoes		
1/2	cup honey	1/4	teaspoon allspice

Peel and section grapefruit. Cut ham in small strips. Drain sweet potatoes and slice lengthwise. Reserve 1/2 cup grapefruit and combine remainder with ham and sweet potatoes in a 10 × 6-inch baking dish. Mix together 1/4 cup of the honey, the lemon juice, the prepared mustard and 1/8 teaspoon of the allspice. Pour over ham mixture. Cook, covered, 15 minutes, turning dish and stirring lightly every 5 minutes. When ready, let stand while preparing topping.

Meanwhile combine reserved 1/2 cup grapefruit sections, remaining 1/4 cup honey and 1/8 teaspoon allspice in a measuring cup or bowl. Cook, uncovered, 2 minutes. Stir thoroughly after 1 minute. Pour over cooked casserole. 4 to 5 servings.

Scalloped Ham and Cabbage

You can make this with leftover or precooked ham. I find the cabbage has a delicious flavor and attractive green color when cooked this way.

4	cups shredded cabbage	1/2	teaspoon caraway seeds
1	medium size onion, finely chopped	1	cup milk
3	tablespoons flour	2 1/2 to 3	cups diced cooked ham

In a 3-quart glass casserole mix cabbage, onion, flour and caraway seeds. Stir in milk and ham. Cook, covered with waxed paper, 10 to 13 minutes or until cabbage is done, stirring and turning dish twice during the cooking period. 4 servings.

Ham Loaf

I sometimes use 1 pound ground lean pork with 1 pound ground ham — or make it all ham. Use ready-to-cook ham or leftover cooked ham.

1 3/4	cups soft breadcrumbs	2	lbs. ground ham or half pork, half ham
1/2	cup milk		
1	slightly beaten egg	1	teaspoon salt
1	small onion, minced	1/4	teaspoon pepper
1	tablespoon chopped celery leaves	1/4	teaspoon thyme
1/2	teaspoon cinnamon	1	(8 ounce) can tomato sauce
		1	teaspoon sugar

Pour milk over breadcrumbs in a mixing bowl. Let stand 5 minutes. Add egg, onion, celery leaves and cinnamon. Stir untill well blended. Add meat, salt, pepper and thyme. Mix thoroughly. Pack mixture into a 9 × 5 × 3-inch glass loaf dish.

Combine tomato sauce and sugar. Pour 1/2 cup evenly over top of loaf.

Cook, covered, 18 minutes. Let stand 10 minutes before serving. Remove excess fat. Heat remaining tomato sauce, uncovered, 2 minutes. Serve with meat loaf. 6 servings.

Scalloped Ham and Potatoes

Always a family favorite. Cook at your convenience and keep refrigerated to warm up in minutes when ready to serve.

6	medium size potatoes	2¹/₂	cups milk
¹/₄	cup margarine	2	cups diced cooked
1	large onion, chopped		ham
	fine		salt and pepper to taste
¹/₄	cup flour	3	slices processed cheese

Peel and dice the potatoes into a 2-quart glass casserole, add ¹/₂ teaspoon salt and ¹/₄ cup water. Cover with waxed paper and cook 11 to 14 minutes, stirring once during the cooking period. The potatoes should be tender-crisp. Let stand 5 minutes on the kitchen counter, then drain in sieve.

Measure margarine in a 2-quart casserole. Melt 30 seconds, add onion and stir until well coated. Cook, uncovered, 2 minutes, stir, cook another minute. Blend in the flour, then stir in the milk. Return to oven. Cook 5 to 6 minutes, stirring well after 2 minutes. When sauce is creamy, remove from oven. Add the potatoes and ham. Salt and pepper to taste. Mix well. Top with slices of cheese cut into triangles. Cook, uncovered, 5 minutes. Let stand 5 minutes.

When the casserole has been refrigerated, reheat, uncovered, for 10 to 15 minutes, or until bubbly and cheese has melted. Turn dish halfway through cooking time. 6 to 8 servings.

Bacon

What a pleasure to cook bacon the microwave way! The flavor is decidedly better and one big advantage is that there is much less shrinkage than when cooked conventionally.

Timing for bacon will depend on thickness and different brands. The slight difference in cooking time is due to the varying sugar, salt and fat content of each brand of bacon.

Bacon can be stacked in layers if paper towels are used in between, making sure that the layers are of even thickness for even cooking results. The paper towels absorb the fat as the bacon cooks. It can also be cooked in a shallow baking dish with sides, such as a pie plate, with a paper in the bottom to absorb the fat, or the bacon placed directly in the plate, in which case, the fat must be drained from the bacon when cooking is done.

Cover with a paper towel to prevent spattering.

The Easy Way to Cook Bacon

Place 1 or 2 layers of paper towels in a shallow dish or on a paper plate (do not use a plastic coated type). Lay strips of bacon on towel. If you wish to have another layer, then top bacon with another layer of paper towel and another layer of bacon. Top the whole loosely with a paper towel, to prevent spattering.

Then cook to desired crispness, approximately as follows:

1 slice —	1 to $1^1/_4$ minutes
2 slices —	$1^3/_4$ to $2^1/_2$ minutes
3 slices —	$2^1/_2$ to $3^1/_2$ minutes
4 slices —	3 to 4 minutes
6 slices —	6 to 7 minutes
8 slices —	(stacked) 8 to 10 minutes

The approximate time is determined by your personal taste and how crisp you like your bacon. In addition you will find there is quite a difference between the different brands. If you cook bacon regularly, you will soon find the exact time for your own personal requirements.

Bacon Butter

Use the bacon butter as an appetizer spread on crisped crackers or on toasted English muffins topped with a poached egg. You could also use it to fry an egg instead of butter, or use as you fancy.

4	slices bacon	¾	teaspoon Dijon
½	cup soft butter or margarine		prepared mustard

Cook bacon between paper towels 4 to 5 minutes, or until crisp. Crumble bacon and add to remaining ingredients. Cream together until well mixed. Cover and keep refrigerated. Yield: About ⅔ cup.

Poultry

Microwave cooking preserves the natural tenderness and juiciness of chicken, turkey, duck and Cornish hen. All poultry is even easier to cook the microwave way than other meats, since it requires less attention and less time.

At times the microwave oven can be used to partially cook a chicken; this is especially useful in barbecuing. By partially cooking the chicken in your microwave oven, you prevent the barbecued chicken from getting too brown on the outside before the centre is done. This method works especially well when the chicken is cut into individual pieces.

If you reverse the principle, when you would like to have a microwave roasted chicken with a crisper chicken skin, just place a dish of cooked chicken under the broiler for a few minutes.

A 4½ to 5-lb. chicken will take 40 to 55 minutes to cook, plus the needed 15 minutes standing time; it will be nicely browned and the meat will be tender and especially juicy.

When you cook your first chicken the microwave way, you may overcook it, not believing that it can be cooked in such a short period, so maybe it is not wise to invite guests for your first effort. If you have overcooked a chicken, you will probably notice a hard spot. Although you will not be able to eat it immediately, you can "rescue" the chicken by letting it stand in the refrigerator overnight. In this way the moisture of the bird tends to equalize and the dry spots will become moist after standing.

A few golden rules for cooking poultry the microwave oven way:

A. Chicken may be stuffed — but loosely. I prefer to cook my stuffing separately while the cooked chicken stands.
B. Do not use metal skewers to hold stuffing in place. Instead, use the old time trick of tucking a slice of bread in the opening of the cavity.
C. Turkey should not be stuffed.
D. Tuck legs of poultry in opening or tie legs to tail with wet string.
E. Fold wings under body.
F. Do not use salted butter or margarine because the salt toughens the skin and will cause it to split. Use a basting sauce.
G. Always lay a sheet of waxed paper loosely across top of bird to

prevent spattering oven. It does not prevent browning of chicken. All whole birds should be turned over once during the cooking period to assure even cooking.

H. During the first half of the cooking time when roasting a bird, cover wing tips and end of legs with foil to prevent overcooking. Make sure the foil-wrapped legs do not touch the wall of the oven, as this might cause pitting of the walls.

I. It is advisable to rest all roasted poultry on either a casserole cover or an inverted saucer or something that will keep it out of the drippings. When arranging chicken pieces on a dish, always place the larger part of each piece toward the outside of the cooking dish and the smaller part toward the center to aid even cooking.

J. Defrost poultry the usual way for constantly perfect results when roasting in the microwave oven. It should be defrosted 24 hours in the refrigerator, still wrapped. Turkey may take 2 to 3 days. If you prefer to defrost in the microwave oven, it is advisable to let poultry stand for half an hour to one hour after defrosting to ensure that it is evenly thawed. For defrosting times see pages 23 and 24.

K. Chicken giblets should be cooked the conventional way because they need long slow cooking to become tender and also because they tend to pop in the microwave oven.

Basting Sauce for Chicken

Brush chicken all over with the following sauce before cooking. Different herbs will give different flavor.

1	tablespoon salad oil or *unsalted butter* or *unsalted margarine* or *melted meat fat*	1^1/$_2$	teaspoons *paprika*
		^{1}/$_4$	teaspoon *tarragon* or *thyme* or *basil* or *marjoram* or *cumin*

Melt fat in oven 1 minute. Stir in paprika and herb of your choice. Brush chicken with mixture.

I make different types in larger quantities and keep them refrigerated in a covered container. To use, I take what I need and melt it for 1 minute before brushing on chicken.

Roast Chicken

Chicken takes about 8 minutes cooking time per pound.* To this you add the 15-minute standing period, after the cooking is over.

4 1/2 to 5-lb. roasting chicken	1 thick slice of unpeeled
1 teaspoon salt	lemon
1 thick slice of onion	Basting sauce
	(see previous recipe)

Wash chicken. Dry with paper towel. Sprinkle inside of cavity with salt, put in the onion and lemon. Secure opening with wooden picks or close cavity with a slice of bread. Tie. Cover end of legs, tail and wings with foil. Place chicken breast side down on saucer or cover in a glass baking dish. Brush all over with basting sauce.

Cook, loosely covered with waxed paper, for 20 minutes. Turn chicken breast side up, brush again with basting sauce or with drippings in bottom of pan. Continue cooking another 20 minutes. Remove chicken from oven, wrap in foil and insert thermometer. Chicken will be cooked when temperature reaches 180°F to 190°F. Serves 6.

* This time will vary slightly according to the fat content of the chicken. If chicken is very fat, reduce time to 6 minutes per pound.

Stuffing for Chicken

Prepare and cook the stuffing in the microwave oven while bird is standing. Pour a few spoonfuls of the gravy on top just before serving.

1/4 cup butter or margarine	1/2 teaspoon salt
1 medium size onion, chopped	1/2 teaspoon savory
1/2 cup diced celery	1/4 teaspoon sage
1/4 cup chopped celery leaves	1/4 cup consommé or cider or water
4 cups crustless soft bread cubes	Basting Sauce (see p. 87)

In a 2-quart mixing bowl combine butter, onion, celery and leaves. Cook, uncovered, for 3 minutes, stirring once. Stir in the next five ingredients. Pat into a 1-quart casserole dish. Brush basting sauce on top. Cook, covered with waxed paper, for 5 minutes. Turn dish. Cook another minute. When ready to serve, pour a few spoonfuls of the chicken gravy on top. Yield 4-5 cups.

Microwave Fried Chicken Pieces

A crisped, tasty golden topping makes this cut up chicken an interesting meal.

3-lb.	chicken, cut up	¹/₄	teaspoon garlic powder
1	cup fine dry breadcrumbs	1	egg white
1	teaspoon paprika	1	tablespoon water
¹/₄	teaspoon thyme	3	tablespoons melted butter or margarine
¹/₈	teaspoon powdered bay leaf		

Make sure chicken is cut into equal size pieces. Blend together the breadcrumbs, paprika, thyme, bay leaf and garlic powder. Beat the egg white with the water.

Dip each piece of chicken into the egg white, then coat with the crumb mixture. Place in glass baking dish with the larger pieces on the outside, the smaller in the center. Dribble butter or margarine over chicken. Cook, uncovered, 10 minutes, turn dish around and cover with waxed paper. Cook another 10 minutes or until fork tender. Let stand 10 minutes before serving. 4 servings.

Chicken Wings Oriental

An elegant dinner served on a bed of hot, fluffy rice.

2	lbs. chicken wings		pepper to taste
1/2	cup flour	1/2	teaspoon oregano or
1/2	cup grated Parmesan		basil
	or cheddar cheese	3/4	cup milk or
1	teaspoon salt		buttermilk
1	teaspoon paprika	2	tablespoons butter

Two pounds of chicken wings should give you 11 to 12 wings. Cut each one in half. Use drumstick half and small ends to make a soup for another meal.

Blend together the flour, cheese, salt, paprika, pepper, oregano or basil.

Dip chicken pieces in milk or buttermilk, then roll in mixture of dry ingredients.

Heat butter in an 8 × 8-inch glass baking dish, uncovered, 1 minute.

Place chicken pieces one next to the other in dish.

Bake, uncovered, 10 minutes, turning dish twice. Let stand 5 minutes. 4 servings.

Speedy Crisped Baked Chicken

This recipe shows how to use complementary cooking. It is quickly cooked in the microwave oven, then browned and crisped under broiler element of your stove. Remember to preheat broiler while chicken is cooking in the microwave oven. Pieces of chicken (wings, legs, etc.) can replace the cut up chicken.

3 to 3¹/₂-lb. broiler, cut up   ¹/₂   teaspoon curry
     paprika   powder (optional)
                                 ¹/₄   cup butter

In a 12 × 8-inch baking dish, arrange the cut up broiler, skin side down. Sprinkle with paprika and curry powder. Cook, uncovered, 14 minutes. Turn chicken, cover with waxed paper, cook 10 to 12 minutes or until fork tender. Melt butter in oven for 1 minute. Dribble over cooked chicken. Place under broiler element for 3 to 4 minutes or until nicely browned. Sprinkle with salt and pepper.
To make gravy, remove chicken from dish, add 1 tablespoon of flour to drippings, mix well and add 1 cup consommé or water or tomato juice or ¹/₂ cup water, ¹/₂ cup red or white wine, stir until well mixed. Cook for 2 to 3 minutes, stirring twice. Season to taste. 4 servings.

Creamed Chicken

An easy way to make creamed chicken using a convenience food. Serve with rice or noodles.

3-lb. broiler, cut up   1   can (10-ounce)
  ¹/₂   cup diced celery   mushroom soup,
  4   green onions, chopped   undiluted
  ¹/₂   teaspoon basil or
     marjoram

In a 12 × 8-inch baking dish, arrange broiler, skin side up. Sprinkle chicken with the celery, green onions and basil or marjoram mixed together. Spoon soup on top of chicken.
     Cover with waxed paper, cook 20 to 28 minutes or until fork tender, turning dish twice during the cooking period. 5 servings.

Poulet Parisien

This chicken is browned on a surface unit before cooking in the microwave oven. In France, they serve it with fine parsleyed noodles and baby green peas.

3-lb.	broiler, cut up	$^1/_2$	cup consommé
2	tablespoons butter	$^1/_4$	cup dry sherry
2	large onions, thinly	$^1/_8$	teaspoon thyme
	sliced	1	bay leaf

Place chicken pieces in frying pan or 10-inch CORNING WARE skillet and brown in the butter, over medium heat on surface range. Season with salt and pepper. When ready, place in an oblong baking dish or keep in skillet. Arrange sliced onions over chicken. Mix remaining ingredients, pour over all. Cook, uncovered, for 10 minutes. Turn dish, cook another 10 minutes, turn dish again, cover with waxed paper and cook 5 minutes or until fork tender. Let stand 10 minutes before serving. 4 to 5 servings.

Citrus Baked Chicken

Fresh lemon and orange juices spiked with rosemary give a Provençale flavor to this chicken.

3-lb.	broiler, cut up	$^1/_2$	cup each fresh orange
1	teaspoon rosemary		and lemon juices
$^1/_2$	teaspoon basil		grated rind of 1 lemon
$^1/_4$	teaspoon pepper	$^1/_2$	teaspoon coriander
5	green onions, chopped		(optional)
	fine	1	teaspoon paprika

Pat chicken dry with paper towels. Combine rosemary, basil and pepper. Rub into chicken pieces. Arrange in a glass baking dish or 10-inch CORNING WARE skillet.

Sprinkle chopped green onions on top. Combine orange and lemon juices with lemon rind, coriander and paprika. Pour over chicken. Cook, covered with waxed paper for 15 minutes. Turn dish, cook, uncovered, another 10 minutes or until fork tender. Let stand 5 minutes before serving. 4 servings.

Chicken for Barbecueing

Here's an ideal recipe for complementary cooking. In summer you can cook it partially in the microwave oven and finish out-of-doors on your barbecue; in winter it can be finished under the broiler. You can even start it in the microwave oven early in the morning, refrigerate and finish cooking when needed.

2½ to 3-lb. broiler, cut up   or
     Basting Sauce   Barbecue Sauce
     (see p. 87)   (see p. 85)

Arrange broiler in a 12 × 8-inch baking dish. Place large pieces toward outside of dish. Cook, uncovered, 15 minutes. Dip each piece in barbecue sauce or brush with basting sauce.

Barbecue over charcoal 15 to 20 minutes, turning often, or broil 6 inches away from direct heat in the oven broiler for 10 to 15 minutes, turning once.

Chicken Teriyaki

Dry Sake wine or dry sherry and fresh ginger roots make this dish quite special. Serve with boiled rice.

2 to 3-lb. broiler
½ cup soy sauce
¼ cup Sake wine or dry sherry
1 clove garlic, chopped fine
2 tablespoons brown sugar
1 teaspoon grated fresh ginger root

Wash chicken and place in plastic bag. Mix the remaining ingredients and pour over the chicken. (Set bag with chicken in a bowl, then it is easy to add liquid.) Secure the bag. Stir around to coat the chicken with the marinade. Refrigerate 2 to 6 hours.

Remove chicken from bag, reserving marinade, and place in an oblong baking dish. Cook, uncovered, for 14 minutes. Turn dish, baste with marinade, cook, uncovered, another 8 to 10 minutes or until fork tender, depending on size of chicken. Let stand 5 minutes before serving. 2 to 3 servings.

Leftover Chicken Casserole

Delicious for lunch or light supper.

2	cups cooked chicken, diced		grated rind and juice of 1 lemon
2	cups celery, diced	1/8	teaspoon nutmeg
1/2	cup salted nuts of your choice, chopped	1/2	cup mayonnaise
1/3	cup diced green pepper or pimiento	1/3	cup grated mild cheddar cheese
3	green onions, diced	2 to 3	cups crushed potato chips
1/2	teaspoon salt	1/2	teaspoon paprika

Place in a fairly large bowl the chicken, celery, nuts, green pepper or pimiento, onions, salt, lemon juice and rind, nutmeg and mayonnaise. Mix together and turn into a buttered 2-quart glass casserole dish. Mix cheese and chips, spoon over casserole. Sprinkle paprika on top.

Bake, uncovered, 10 minutes. 6 servings.

Roast Turkey

Because a turkey is large, the period for defrosting a frozen one in the microwave oven is fairly long. During that period some cooking may begin, which means that some of the flavor is lost and that the turkey must be cooked as soon as defrosted. For these reasons, I think it advisable to defrost a turkey the conventional way, i.e., refrigerate 2 to 3 days, still wrapped, then open package, dry inside and out with paper towel and prepare for microwave oven cooking.

The 8 to 13-lb. turkeys can all be successfully roasted in the microwave oven. The ideal weight for perfect results and ease of work is 10 lbs.

Cooking Time

8 to 10-lb. turkey: 8 minutes per pound, 20 minutes standing time
10 to 13-lb. turkey: 9 minutes per pound, 25 minutes standing time

Meat thermometer at end of cooking should register 170°F. Test outside of oven, put bird back if necessary, *but do not leave* thermometer in bird. When 170°F. is reached remove turkey from oven, cover with foil and insert thermometer, let stand 20 to 25 minutes—the thermometer will climb to 180°-190°F.

How to Prepare the Turkey

Wash turkey and wipe inside and out with paper towels. Sprinkle the inside with 1 teaspoon coarse salt, $1/2$ teaspoon freshly ground pepper, 1 teaspoon savory. Add 1 onion cut in four, 1 large stick of celery with leaves, cut in three. Close the opening with a slice of bread, tie legs to tail end with a wet string. Fold wings under.

Prepare turkey basting sauce as follows:

Melt $1/4$ cup margarine or butter in measuring cup for 1 minute, add 2 tablespoons paprika, 1 tablespoon Kitchen Bouquet and 1 tablespoon dry sherry or brandy. Keep warm. When ready to cook the turkey, brush all over with basting sauce.

A. In a 12 × 8-inch baking dish place prepared turkey breast side down on inverted saucer or casserole cover.
B. Divide total cooking time, not including standing time, in four and turn turkey 3 times during cooking period at regular intervals. Thus it is first cooked breast down, then on each side. Cooking is finished with the bird breast up.
C. Baste with pan drippings or basting sauce each time turkey is turned, using drippings when all sauce has been used. Also rotate pan. Make sure legs and wings are covered with foil for the first half of the cooking period.
D. Keep turkey covered loosely with waxed paper up to the last 15 minutes of cooking.
E. When done, remove from oven. Set turkey on warm service platter. Wrap in foil. Insert thermometer and let stand for the necessary time.

F. Make **Gravy** with drippings as follows:
   To the fat in the baking dish, add 2 tablespoons flour, a small onion, chopped fine or grated, 1/2 teaspoon sage or savory. Stir until well mixed. Cook, uncovered, for 8 minutes, stirring once. Add 1 cup hot water, 1 cup undiluted canned consommé or giblet stock (cooked giblets can be chopped and also added). Mix well. Salt and pepper to taste. Cook, uncovered, 5 minutes or until creamy, stirring once after 3 minutes of cooking. Serve separately.

Cooking Turkey Ahead of Time

A turkey can be cooked a day ahead, then wrapped, cooled and refrigerated until ready to use.

To serve, place turkey on platter or baking dish. Cook, uncovered, 15 to 18 minutes or until heated through.

If you prefer to carve the cold turkey, you can do so before heating. Arrange slices on cold platter. Pour 1 cup gravy on top, cover with waxed paper and reheat 5 to 10 minutes, depending upon the amount of meat.

These 2 methods are convenient for some occasions, but not as perfect as roasting and serving the turkey immediately.

For a Crisper Skin

Although the turkey is in the oven long enough to get a golden brown skin, it does not have the crispness that some people prefer. To achieve this, cook turkey as directed, but reduce cooking time 1 minute per pound. Then as soon as cooking is finished, place in a *preheated* 450°F. oven for 15 to 20 minutes or until skin is browned and crisp.

When Turkey Is to Be Served Cold

Cook turkey and let stand wrapped in foil according to rule. Make gravy. Cool and refrigerate, still wrapped, until ready to serve.

Turkey Stuffing

For perfect texture and flavor, I prefer to cook the stuffing during the standing period of the cooked turkey, rather than the usual way.

1/2	cup butter or margarine	8	cups dry toasted bread cubes
1	large onion, chopped	1	teaspoon salt
1	cup chopped celery	1/8	teaspoon allspice
	the giblets chopped or minced	1	teaspoon savory
		1/2	teaspoon sage
1	cup (8-ounce can) well drained canned mushrooms	1/2	cup consommé or water

Place in a large glass mixing bowl the butter, onion, and celery. Cook, uncovered, 8 minutes, stirring once. Add giblets, cook, covered, 3 minutes. Add remaining ingredients. Blend thoroughly. Place in a large glass dish. Brush top with some of the turkey basting sauce. Cook, covered, 10 to 15 minutes or until hot. Let stand 10 minutes. Makes 10 cups.

Duck à l'orange

The duck skin browns and has some crispness. If you prefer a crisper skin, place it under broiler until crisped after standing time.

a 4 to 4¹/₂-lb. domestic duck		*2*	*medium unpeeled apples*
1	*teaspoon salt*		*grated rind of 1 orange*
1	*tablespoon brown sugar*	*1*	*clove garlic*
		6	*peppercorns*
		1	*slice of bread*

Orange sauce:

2	*tablespoons brown sugar*	*3*	*tablespoons duck drippings*
1	*tablespoon cornstarch*	*3*	*tablespoons brandy (optional)*
	grated rind of 1 orange		
²/₃	*cup fresh orange juice*		

Wash duck inside and out with vinegar. Sprinkle inside of cavity with the salt. Stuff with the brown sugar, the apples cut in eighths, the orange rind, garlic and peppercorns. Close cavity with a slice of bread. Tie legs with a wet string.

Cover the ends of legs, tail and the wings with foil. Place breast side down on inverted saucer or casserole cover in a glass baking dish. Cook, uncovered, 20 minutes. Drain juices. Turn duck onto its back. Cook, covered with waxed paper, another 20 minutes. Remove from oven, wrap in foil, let stand 10 minutes.

In a 2-cup measure combine the brown sugar and cornstarch. Stir in the orange rind, orange juice and duck drippings. Mix well and cook, uncovered, 4 minutes, stirring once. When mixture is creamy and transparent, stir in the brandy. Serve separately. 4 servings.

Cranberry Duck

The exact cooking time for duck depends on age and tenderness of the duck. A 3 to 4-lb. domestic duck usually takes 7 to 8 minutes per pound with 10 minutes standing time. Wild duck takes 6 minutes per pound, also with 10 minutes standing. When cooked, after standing, the thermometer should read between 180° and 185°F.

3 to	4-lb. duck, cut in quarters	2	tablespoons dry vermouth or water
1/2	teaspoon freshly ground pepper	2	tablespoons fresh lemon juice
1/2	teaspoon ground cumin	1/4	teaspoon ground ginger
1/2	cup whole cranberry sauce or black currant jam	1	teaspoon salt
		3	whole cloves
		1	stick cinnamon (1 inch)

Season duck with pepper and cumin. Place in a 12 × 8-inch glass baking dish. Cook, uncovered, 5 minutes.

Remove from oven, place duck on a plate, drain all pan drippings, reserving 2 tablespoons. Pour reserved drippings into jug or bowl and stir in cranberry sauce, vermouth or water, lemon juice, ginger, salt, cloves and cinnamon. Mix well. Place duck back in dish and pour sauce over.

Cook, uncovered, 22 minutes, turning duck pieces every 8 minutes. It can be covered with waxed paper in the last 10 minutes of cooking. Test for doneness with a fork.

Remove from oven, discard cloves and cinnamon. Cover and let stand 10 minutes. 4 servings.

Stuffed Cornish Hens

The small 1 to 1½-lb. type is delicious done in the microwave oven. Use the packaged white and wild rice mix as stuffing, adding to it 1 teaspoon curry powder mixed with 1 tablespoon brandy or whisky. Place the 6-ounce package of rice with the above flavoring in a 3-quart casserole, add 1¾ cups hot water and 2 tablespoons butter. Cook, covered, 15 minutes. Let stand 10 minutes. Cool, and it is ready to use as stuffing.

4	small Cornish hens	1	teaspoon paprika
	wild rice stuffing	1	tablespoon dry
4	slices bread		Madeira
¼	cup butter		

Sprinkle the inside of the cavities with salt. Fill with the rice stuffing. Place a slice of bread in the opening, tie legs with a wet string, fold wings under body. Cover the end of legs with foil. Melt the butter 30 seconds and stir in the paprika and Madeira. Baste birds all over with mixture.

Place birds in a 12 × 8-inch baking dish, breast side down, on inverted saucers. Cook, covered with waxed paper, 15 minutes. Turn, breast side up, and reverse outside edges to inside. You will be able to tell by looking which side is cooked most and you'll be turning the pink side to the outside and browner side to the inside. Brush with remainder of basting sauce or drippings.

Cook, covered with waxed paper, another 15 minutes or until fork tender. Remove from oven, wrap in foil and let stand 15 minutes. Thermometer should register 185°F. For a sauce, add ½ cup consommé (or giblet stock with chopped giblets) to drippings in the pan. Heat 3 minutes. Pour over hens. 4 servings.

12.Fish and Shellfish

If fish has not been a favorite on your family table, try it in your microwave oven and you will realize just how good it really is. When cooked properly the results will be tender, delicate, flaky fish and seafood, but care must be taken not to overcook it as this will toughen the fish.

To defrost frozen fish, I prefer to unwrap a 1-lb. package and place the block on a paper towel set on a plate. It will take 2 minutes, covered, on regular cook cycle or 4 minutes on defrost, turning twice in either case. I then separate the pieces under running cold water and cook as soon as defrosted. If you prefer to defrost the fish still wrapped in its package you will also find this satisfactory.

Another point with fish is that your meal planning will have to take into account how fast fish cooks. It is a last minute food, so set the table and make sure other foods you are serving are completely prepared or ready to go into the oven immediately after removing the fish or seafood.

Always defrost and cook fish and seafood covered, keeping it covered during standing time as well. Also it is best to cook it in a shallow baking dish, such as a glass pie plate or a round 8 or 10-inch dish. Try to arrange the fish so that thinner sections overlap slightly for more even cooking, or roll thin fillets such as sole.

I do not recommend cooking a whole fish, even of 2 to 3 pounds, as the shape makes it difficult to cook evenly. Also the turning, which is essential, is difficult to do without breaking the fish and the amount of moisture developed by a whole fish prevents the browning or even the textured topping of the skin.

Fillets and steaks are the most successful and very quick to do. In addition, you have a definite advantage when cooking frozen fish because it does not go mushy as often happens with conventional cooking. Fish overcooks very easily so test often during the cooking period. I found that a fresh filleted fish takes 1 minute less to cook compared to the same type of defrosted fillets. The thickness also changes timing. Once you master the art of fish cookery in the microwave oven, you will find it very hard to go back to other methods.

When cooking seafood such as lobster, crab, shrimp, scallops, fresh or frozen types are equally successful. You can follow recipes calling for fresh seafood using frozen, which has a wide availability, or vice versa. Apply the same principles to defrosting as given for frozen fish—partly thawed by microwave oven, then broken up under cold water. Seafood cooked in the shell is timed as for seafood cooked without the shell.

Remember that for even cooking the thickest ends of fish fillets or seafood should go toward the edges of the dish or container.

Fish

Cornell Fried Fillets

This is a method developed at Cornell University to oven fry fish fillets. Applied to the microwave oven, the results are equally good, although the fish is not quite as brown.

1	lb. frozen fish fillets, any type	1	teaspoon paprika
1	teaspoon salt	1/4	teaspoon thyme
1/2	cup milk	2	tablespoons bacon fat
1	cup fine dry breadcrumbs	2	tablespoons melted butter

Unwrap frozen fish and place in the milk and salt mixed together. Cover with waxed paper and let thaw on kitchen counter until it can be separated. When possible, turn fish 3 or 4 times during thawing period. Cut into individual portions. Mix breadcrumbs, paprika and thyme. Roll fish in mixture. In an 8 × 8-inch glass dish place bacon fat and melt 30 seconds. Place fish, one piece next to the other, in the bacon fat. Melt the butter in small glass dish or measuring cup, 40 seconds, and spoon over each piece of fish.

Cover with waxed paper, cook 4 to 5 minutes, turning dish once. Let stand 3 minutes and serve as is, or with Tartar Sauce. 3 to 4 servings.

Fillets à l'Anglaise

The simplest way to cook fish but so tasty. Use fresh fish or thaw out frozen fillets.

1	lb. fish fillets	3	tablespoons melted
	juice and rind of		butter or margarine
	1 lemon	$1/4$	teaspoon paprika

Cut fillets in individual pieces. Roll each piece in the lemon juice and rind mixed together.

Place in a single layer in an 8 × 8-inch glass dish or a 9-inch glass pie plate. Brush each fillet with melted butter or margarine. Sprinkle with paprika. Cover dish with waxed paper and cook 6 to 8 minutes, depending on thickness of fish. Do not turn. Let stand 5 minutes. Serve with butter remaining in baking dish. Salt and pepper to taste. 3 to 4 servings.

Fillets of Sole Italienne

Serve as they do in Florence, with buttered hot spinach and tomato salad topped with fresh basil.

1	lb. sole fillets	$1/2$	teaspoon salt
$2/3$	cup commercial sour cream	1	teaspoon fresh dill (optional)
2 to 3	green onions, chopped fine	$1/3$	cup grated Parmesan cheese

Thaw fish just enough to separate, and place in an 8 × 8-inch glass dish. Mix remaining ingredients except the cheese and spread evenly over each portion of fish. Sprinkle with cheese. Cover with waxed paper. Cook, 6 to 8 minutes, depending on thickness of fish. Let stand 5 minutes. Salt and pepper to taste. 3 to 4 servings.

Citrus Cod Fillets

I use frozen or fresh fillets, lime or lemon juice, each giving quite a different flavor.

1	lb. cod fillets	1/2	teaspoon salt
1/4	cup fresh lemon or lime juice	1/2	teaspoon grated fresh ginger
2	green onions, chopped		a pinch of thyme
		1	tablespoon butter

Defrost frozen fillets as previously explained in introduction to chapter. Separate fillets and place in 8 × 8-inch glass dish.

Combine lemon or lime juice with onions, salt, fresh ginger and thyme. Pour over fish. Dot with butter.

Cover with waxed paper, cook, 3 minutes, turning dish once. Cook 2 to 3 minutes longer or until fish flakes easily. Let stand 3 minutes. Sprinkle with paprika and serve. 3 to 4 servings.

Haddock "à la Grecque"

Frozen cod, halibut or perch can also be prepared in this manner. Serve with parsleyed noodles or rice.

1	(16-ounce) can tomatoes, drained		fish of your choice
1/2	cup cracker crumbs	3	green onions, chopped fine
1	teaspoon sugar	1/4	cup chopped parsley
1/4	teaspoon basil	1/4	cup vegetable oil
1/2	teaspoon salt	2	tablespoons flour
1	lb. frozen haddock or	1	teaspoon paprika

Place tomatoes and cracker crumbs in bottom of 8 × 8-inch glass dish. Sprinkle with sugar, basil and salt. Mix together with a fork. Place partially defrosted fish in one block over tomatoes. Mix the remaining ingredients until well blended. Spread over fish.

Cover with waxed paper. Cook, 8 to 10 minutes, or until fish is cooked in the middle, turn dish twice during cooking period. Let stand 5 minutes. 4 to 5 servings.

Fish Polonaise, page 162
Sole Amandine, page 161

Buttered Lobster Tails, page 164
Coquilles St-Jacques, page 169

Poached Cod

Fresh cod, contrary to popular belief, is delicious and doubly so poached in a microwave oven. Frozen cod can also be used where fresh is not available. You can serve it with melted butter and parsley.

2	lbs. fresh codfish steak	4	peppercorns
1¼	cups water or milk	2	tablespoons butter
1	medium onion, sliced	2	tablespoons flour
1	bay leaf	1	tablespoon lemon juice
3	slices unpeeled lemon	¼	cup fresh parsley or
1	teaspoon salt		2 tablespoons fresh dill

Place fish in single layer in a 12 × 8-inch baking dish. Pour the water or milk over top. Add slices of onion, bay leaf, slices of lemon, salt and peppercorns. Heat, uncovered, for 3 minutes. Turn dish, cover with waxed paper, cook 4 to 5 minutes or until fish flakes easily. Let stand, covered, 3 minutes, then lift with a slotted spatula to a hot dish. Drain liquid from dish and reserve.

Place butter in a measuring cup, melt 40 seconds, add flour, stir until well blended. Add reserved fish liquid, stirring constantly. Add lemon juice, parsley or dill. Heat, uncovered, 1 minute 30 seconds, stirring once. Pour over fish. 5 to 6 servings.

Poached Haddock

Fish is first on the list for any figure-conscious cook. Try it this way. The following method is perfect because the oils cook out of the fish and yet it retains its iodine and other minerals. Omit the sauce if you are on a diet.

4	1-inch thick slices of fresh haddock or 4 frozen steaks, defrosted	1	teaspoon salt
		½	teaspoon pepper
		3	tablespoons melted butter
1	cup hot water	¼	teaspoon curry powder
2	tablespoons fresh lemon juice	1	minced green onion

Place the individual portions in an 8 × 8-inch glass dish. Mix the hot water, lemon juice, salt and pepper. Pour over the fish. Cover with waxed paper. Cook, 6 minutes or until water simmers, turning dish twice. Let stand 4 to 6 minutes. You will notice that the water will be coated with oil.

Lift the fish carefully with a slotted spatula to a hot platter. In a measuring cup, melt the butter with curry powder and green onion, uncovered, 40 seconds. Pour over fish and sprinkle with parsley or dill or chives. For diet purposes, simply sprinkle fish with fresh herbs of your choice and garnish with sections of lemon. 4 servings.

Halibut "à la Russe"

One-and-a-half-inch thick haddock steaks can be cooked in the same manner. Serve with buttered Kasha (Buckwheat).

4	small halibut steaks	4 to 6	thin slices unpeeled
$1/2$	teaspoon salt		lemon
$1/2$	teaspoon paprika	1	tablespoon butter
$1/2$	teaspoon sugar	2	tablespoons chili
1	medium onion, thinly sliced		sauce

Place fish steaks in 8 × 8-inch glass dish. Mix the salt, paprika, and sugar, sprinkle over fish. Break onion into rings. Spread over fish, top with slices of lemon. Melt the butter and chili sauce in a small dish, 40 seconds. Spread over fish. Cover with waxed paper. Cook 6 to 7 minutes, turning dish twice. Let stand, covered, 4 minutes. 4 servings.

Dover Sole

Although it's hard to beat the English Dover Sole, the fresh or frozen type prepared like this can be as near as possible to the true English flavor.

2	lbs. fresh or frozen sole fillets, thawed	the juice and grated rind of 1 lemon
1/2	cup butter (unsalted if possible)	salt and pepper to taste finely chopped parsley
2	tablespoons cornstarch	

In a 12 × 8-inch baking dish, melt the butter 1 minute. Add cornstarch, mix thoroughly. Add lemon juice and rind. Dip each fillet in this butter, then turn buttered side up in dish. Salt and pepper to taste. Cover with waxed paper, cook 8 minutes, turning dish once. Let stand, covered, 2 to 3 minutes to finish cooking. Spoon sauce in dish over each serving. Serves 6.

Variation

To make *Sole Amandine*, proceed in the same manner as above. While fish is standing, place in a 1-cup measure 1/3 cup butter and 1/3 cup slivered blanched almonds. Cook, uncovered, 4 minutes, or until nuts are light brown, stirring twice. Sprinkle over cooked fish as soon as ready. Serve. This makes an extremely rich sauce together with the lemon butter sauce and it could be served equally well over plain cooked fish.

Chinese Fish Fillets

Frozen or fresh fillets of any type can be used in this easy fish dish. Serve with buttered or plain rice.

2	tablespoons soy sauce grated rind of 1 lemon	1	clove garlic, minced
1	tablespoon lemon juice	1	tablespoon fresh ginger root, grated
1	tablespoon ketchup	1	lb. fresh or frozen fish fillets, thawed

In an 8 × 8-inch glass dish, combine soy sauce, lemon rind and juice, ketchup, garlic and fresh ginger root. Cut fish into individual portions, place in dish and roll each piece in sauce. Cover with waxed paper. Cook, 5 to 6 minutes or until fish flakes easily, turning dish once. Let stand, covered, 5 minutes. Pour remaining sauce in the dish over the fish to serve. 3 to 4 servings.

Fish Polonaise

In Poland they make a sauce from fresh, wild mushrooms. Here we can simplify by using a can of mushroom soup. I like to break 3 to 4 dried mushrooms into mine to give it the special Polish flavor.

2	lbs. fillets of sole or haddock	1	can (10-ounce) condensed cream of mushroom soup
1	small cucumber, peeled and diced	1/3	cup commercial sour cream
1	tablespoon chopped fresh dill	1	medium tomato, diced
2	tablespoons butter	1/2	teaspoon sugar salt, pepper to taste

Use fresh fish or frozen, thawed as described in the introduction to this chapter. Place cucumber, fresh dill and butter in 1 quart dish. Cook, uncovered, 4 minutes, stirring once. Stir in soup, sour cream, tomato and sugar. Arrange fish in a 12 × 8-inch glass dish, left whole or each piece rolled or cut into individual portions. Cover with waxed paper. Cook 6 minutes. Spoon sauce on top, cook, covered, 3 to 4 minutes. Let stand 5 minutes. Salt and pepper to taste. 6 servings.

Salmon Loaf In-The-Round

A fish loaf that can be cooked and ready to serve in 15 minutes.
Serve with Parsley, Caper or Hollandaise Sauce.

1	can (16-ounce) salmon	2	tablespoons chopped celery leaves
1	egg, lightly beaten	1/2	teaspoon dill or curry powder
1	cup soft breadcrumbs	1	small onion, grated
1/4	cup rich cream	1/4	teaspoon salt
1/4	cup diced celery		juice of 1/2 lemon

Flake and remove bones from salmon, but do not drain. Add egg, breadcrumbs, cream, diced celery and leaves, dill or curry powder, onion, salt and lemon juice. Mix well. In the middle of an 8-inch glass cake dish or 9-inch pie plate, place a small custard cup open side up. Spoon mixture equally around cup. Cover with waxed paper, cook, 9 minutes, turning plate once. Let stand, covered, 5 minutes and serve with the sauce of your choice. 4 to 5 servings.

Tuna Casserole

Vary the soup for different flavors.

2	cups elbow macaroni	2	tablespoons chopped parsley
1	teaspoon salt		
2	cups boiling water	1 1/2	teaspoons curry powder
1	can (6 1/2-ounce) flaked tuna	1	can (10-ounce) cream of chicken soup
1	small onion, chopped fine	1/2	cup buttered breadcrumbs
1	pimiento, drained (optional)		

Place macaroni in a 2-quart casserole. Add salt and pour boiling water on top. Cook 8 minutes. Stir thoroughly. Let stand 5 minutes, drain.

Place all the remaining ingredients except the buttered bread-crumbs in the casserole and stir until well mixed. Add the macaroni. Mix well, top with buttered crumbs, cook, uncovered, for 6 to 8 minutes. Let stand, covered, for 5 minutes. 4 to 5 servings.

Shellfish

Buttered Lobster Tails

Simplicity is often the very best. Make this dish sophisticated by serving with a bowl of imported chutney stirred with a few spoonfuls of brandy.

1   *10-ounce package frozen lobster tails*
3   *tablespoons butter*
2   *teaspoons lime or lemon juice*

Remove wrapping around lobster tails or remove from bag. Place in an 8-inch round cake dish or 9-inch pie plate. Heat, uncovered, 2 minutes 30 seconds. Let stand, covered, 5 to 10 minutes or until well thawed.

With kitchen shears cut lengthwise down the underside of the lobster through the hard shell. Press tails open flat. Set one next to the other in shallow dish, meat side up.

Melt butter for 1 minute in a small dish or measuring cup. Stir in lemon juice. Brush each lobster tail generously with butter mixture. Cook, covered, 2 minutes, turning dish after 1 minute, or until lobster meat loses its transparent color and becomes pink. 2 servings.

Steamed Lobster

Hot butter, crisped crusty bread and a glass of cooled white wine with steamed lobster. What more can one ask for?

2	lobsters about 1 ½ pounds each	2	bay leaves
3	cups boiling water	3	slices unpeeled lemon

To cook lobsters one at a time, place in a 12 × 8-inch glass dish. Pour boiling water on top. Add bay leaves and lemon slices. Cook, covered, 5 minutes, turning lobster twice. Remove from water.

Cook the second one in the same way. To serve, split cooked lobster lengthwise, remove stomach and intestinal veins. Crack claws. Serve on hot plate with a bowl of hot butter. 2 servings.

Lobster Newburg

Serve in hot pastry shells or on a nest of parsleyed rice or simply on buttered toast. If you are using frozen lobster tails, thaw as directed on page 164 and let stand while making sauce.

¼	cup butter	2	tablespoons dry sherry
3	tablespoons flour	2	cans lobster or
2	cups light cream	1	10-ounce package frozen lobster or lobster tails
1	well-beaten egg		
1	teaspoon salt		

In a 1½-quart casserole, melt butter, uncovered, 1 minute. Stir in the flour until thoroughly mixed. Add the cream and cook 4 to 5 minutes or until thickened and creamy, stirring twice. Add the egg gradually, beating with a whisk until well mixed. Add the salt and sherry. Add well drained and flaked lobster, or meat from thawed lobster tails, to sauce.

In either case, heat, uncovered, 2 minutes. Taste for seasoning and serve. 4 servings.

Fresh Shrimp Cocktail

Good shrimps and a true Créole Shrimp Sauce are delectable.

1	lb. medium size unpeeled shrimps	1/4	cup fresh lemon juice
1	thick slice unpeeled lemon	1	teaspoon A-1 Sauce or chutney
1/2	cup water	1	teaspoon drained horseradish
1/4	cup chili sauce	1	teaspoon sugar

Place in a 1-quart casserole the shrimps, lemon slice, and water. Cover with waxed paper. Cook, 8 to 10 minutes or until shrimps are pink, turning dish twice. Cool and shell. In a 1-cup measure place the remaining ingredients. Stir well. Cool and refrigerate. To serve, place a small container of sauce in a dish and surround with shelled shrimps. 2 to 4 servings.

Shrimp Superb

Use only fresh, uncooked shrimps to prepare these.

1 to 1 1/2 lbs. fresh unpeeled uncooked shrimps	1	teaspoon coarse salt
juice and grated rind from 2 limes	3	tablespoons vegetable oil or butter

Split the shrimps in half lengthwise through the shell and tail. To do this, set shrimp on a table on its back and cut through with sharp knife. Rinse out dark vein but leave shrimp in shell. Dry shrimps on a paper towel. On a 10-inch pie plate place shrimps in a circle, cut side up. Sprinkle with the lime juice, rind, and salt mixed together. Cover with waxed paper and let stand for 3 to 6 hours, refrigerated. Rub top of shrimps with vegetable oil or butter. Cover with waxed paper, cook 4 to 6 minutes or until shrimps are pink and fragrant. Heap on warm platter, surround with quartered limes to taste. 3 to 4 servings.

Barbecued Shrimps

These are excellent for a party and can be bought in large quantities — a 7-pound box of frozen, uncooked shrimp, purchased if possible from a fish dealer, will serve 12.

3 to 3 ¼ lbs. uncooked frozen shrimps	½ teaspoon garlic powder
⅓ cup olive or vegetable oil	1 teaspoon salt
⅓ cup lemon juice	1 cup chutney
1½ teaspoons curry powder	2 tablespoons brandy

Place shrimps on a plate and defrost 4 minutes or cook 45 seconds, rest 1 minute and repeat 4 times. Shell shrimp and mix with the oil, lemon juice, curry powder, garlic powder and salt. Stir until well blended, cover and refrigerate 3 to 6 hours, stirring twice if possible. Set half the shrimps in a circle on a 10-inch pie plate (you will have to use 2 plates or cook them one after the other). Spoon some of the liquid mixture on top. Cover with waxed paper. Cook each plate 4 to 6 minutes or until shrimps are pink. Serve with a bowl of the chutney and brandy mixed together, to be used as a dip. 6 servings.

Shrimp Curry

When serving rice with the curry, cook rice first while mixing curry and cook the curry while rice stands.

¼ cup butter	1 chicken bouillon cube
1 large onion, diced	3 tablespoons flour
2 cloves garlic, minced	1 cup water or ½ water, ½ milk
2 teaspoons curry powder	3 cups frozen uncooked cleaned shrimps
1 tablespoon grated fresh ginger root	

In a 1¹/₂-quart casserole, combine butter, onion and garlic. Cook, uncovered for 5 minutes, stirring twice. When onions start to brown, add the curry powder and stir well for 30 seconds. Add the ginger root, chicken bouillon cube and flour. Mix well, add water. Cook, uncovered, 5 minutes. Stir, add shrimps, mix well. Cook, covered, 8 to 10 minutes or until shrimps are pink. Stir once. 4 to 5 servings.

Shrimp Marinière

Parisiens are fond of this dish in the spring time. They follow it with a thick wedge of Brie cheese. Fresh or frozen shrimps can be used.

1	10-oz. package uncooked frozen shrimps (shelled)	¹/₃	cup dry white wine
		¹/₂	teaspoon sugar
		2	tablespoons oil
¹/₄	cup hot water	1	clove garlic, minced
2	teaspoons lemon juice	1	medium tomato, peeled and chopped
¹/₄	teaspoon salt		
¹/₄	teaspoon basil or thyme	2	green onions, chopped fine

Place frozen shrimps in a 2-quart glass casserole. Defrost 2-3 minutes to thaw. Let stand 2 minutes. Separate shrimps. Place shrimps in a 1-quart casserole. Combine hot water, lemon juice, salt, basil or thyme, wine and sugar. Pour over shrimps. Cook, uncovered, 4 minutes. Let stand 1 minute. Drain and set aside. Pour oil in the 1-quart casserole, heat 1 minute. Add garlic, tomato and green onions. Cook, covered with waxed paper, for 3 minutes. Add shrimp, heat 2 minutes. Serve with parsleyed rice. 4 servings.

Coquille St-Jacques

These can be made ahead of time and refrigerated or frozen. Simply reheat when ready to serve. If refrigerated they will reheat in 2 minutes. If frozen, defrost for 2 minutes, then heat 1 minute.

1/4	cup butter	1/2	cup dry white wine or dry vermouth
1/2	cup (4-ounce can) drained sliced mushrooms	1	lb. fresh or frozen thawed scallops
2	green onions, diced	1/4	cup rich cream
2	tablespoons flour	1	egg yolk
1/2	teaspoon salt	2	tablespoons fine dry breadcrumbs
1/4	teaspoon thyme or tarragon	2	tablespoons grated cheese

To thaw out frozen scallops: Place a 16-ounce package in a 2-quart casserole. Heat, uncovered, 2 minutes, 30 seconds. Separate scallops under running cold water. Drain well before using.

In a 2-quart casserole combine butter, mushrooms and green onions. Cook, uncovered, 3 minutes, stirring twice. Stir in flour, salt, thyme or tarragon. Mix well, add wine and scallops. Cook, covered, 5 minutes, stirring twice. Beat together the cream and egg yolk and stir into mixture. Taste for seasoning. Spoon into 4 or 5 shells or individual serving dishes. Mix breadcrumbs and cheese. Sprinkle over each shell. Cook, uncovered, 1 minute, or place under broiler to brown crumbs.

Scallops Amandine

Very simple and very tasty.

1	lb. frozen scallops	1 1/2	teaspoons cornstarch
1	tablespoon butter	1/4	teaspoon salt
1/4	cup diced green onions	1/4	cup butter
		1/4	cup slivered almonds

Thaw out frozen scallops (see previous recipe). Place the tablespoon of butter in a 1 1/2-quart casserole, heat, uncovered, 30 seconds or until melted.

Add green onions and scallops. Cook, uncovered, 4 minutes, stirring twice. Combine the cornstarch and salt and add 2 table- spoons liquid from scallop casserole. Blend to a smooth paste. Add to scallops, stirring to blend. Cook covered, 2 minutes, stirring once.

Place butter and almonds in a 1-cup measure. Cook uncovered, 4 minutes or until nuts are light brown, stirring twice.

Pour over scallops as soon as ready.

4 servings.

Luncheon Crab Casserole

It is easy to double or triple this quick recipe, which can be made in individual casseroles and cooked two at a time. The mixture can also be served on shells as an entrée. This dish can be made ahead and refrigerated to reheat when required.

3/4 to	1 cup drained and flaked crabmeat	2	tablespoons mayonnaise (not salad dressing)
1/2	cup grated Swiss cheese	2	tablespoons cream or milk
2	tablespoons dry breadcrumbs	1	small onion, chopped fine
2	tablespoons diced celery		grated rind of 1 lemon
		1/4	teaspoon nutmeg
		1/8	teaspoon pepper

In a 1-quart casserole combine all the ingredients. Cook, un- covered, 3 minutes or until edges bubble, turning dish once. Serves 2.

For individual servings, divide or multiply above quantity and place in individual casseroles as required.

1 dish takes 2 minutes
2 dishes take 3 minutes
3 dishes take 4 minutes
4 dishes take 5 minutes

or until each is bubbly around the edges, remembering to turn each dish once during cooking period.

13. Vegetables

When you cook vegetables the microwave way, whether they are fresh or frozen, their color and flavor are far better than when cooked by all other conventional methods, and because very little water is used, or sometimes none at all, the loss of nutrients as well as color is minimal. Even when reheated the vegetables will retain their original flavor and color and will not dry out, because the heat is generated internally, as opposed to the conventional way of cooking where external heat tends to dry out items that are reheated. If you want to cook a vegetable with a sauce nothing could be easier, as sauces vie with vegetables as the easiest foods to cook the microwave way.

The best way to cook most vegetables, fresh or frozen, is to put them in a casserole with the required amount of water and cover with the casserole lid. You can also use plastic wrap or waxed paper to cover. Some vegetables such as potatoes or squash, when kept whole, can be cooked without a covering because their skin acts as the cover.

Most vegetables need a very small quantity of water—generally no more than a tablespoon or two — but this is for the most part absorbed by the time the vegetables are cooked and ready to be served, so no draining is necessary. The water is necessary because it creates steam which in turn provides more even cooking. The lid helps to keep the steam in and also hastens the cooking time.

The water can be replaced by a different liquid, such as cider, white or red wine, consommé, tomato juice, etc. You can also add a pinch or two of herbs, but these should be placed at the bottom of the dish before adding the vegetables on top. Add salt only when the vegetables are cooked so that they do not dry out during the cooking period. Add $1/8$ to $1/4$ teaspoon of sugar to all vegetables being cooked to accentuate the fresh flavor.

Vegetables should still be a little firm when removed from the oven, because, as with most items cooked in the microwave oven, they will continue to cook while standing. The standing time for most vegetables is between 3 and 5 minutes.

It is best to eat cooked vegetables when they are still fairly crisp, but if your personal preference is for vegetables with a soft texture, simply increase the cooking time by 1 to 3 minutes. Age and freshness, and the way a vegetable is cut, will also affect the cooking time. One vegetable that is a good test for all these factors is cabbage, for by cutting it fine, medium, or coarse, and whether you prefer it crisp or soft, the cooking period will vary from 6 to 10 minutes.

The variation in size of vegetables can also, of course, affect the cooking time. This is particularly evident in vegetables such as French artichokes, for instance, which can be from 3 to 8 inches in diameter and can vary the cooking period from 4 to 10 minutes. But you will soon begin to judge cooking time to suit your own tastes and preferences in the same way as if you were cooking conventionally.

Vegetables require stirring at least once during the cooking period to distribute the heat evenly and care should be taken at this time to bring the inside portions to the outside.

If a vegetable become dehydrated and tough after being cooked, it indicates it has overcooked.

Frozen vegetables can be cooked right in their carton or plastic pouch, but they must be rearranged or stirred or shaken halfway through the cooking period. A slit should be made in the pouch to let the steam out. Also when cooking frozen packed vegetables in a casserole they should be placed ice-side up, so there is a more even distribution of heat as water penetrates through vegetables. If not placed ice-side up vegetables would dry out on top.

If you buy your frozen vegetables in bulk in the 2 or 5 lb. plastic bags, rather than the packages, then you can easily remove individual servings and cook according to the general directions.

Canned vegetables should be drained completely first, then simply reheated as they are already cooked. I like to add a pinch of sugar and a teaspoon of butter to mine as it gives them a fresher taste.

To reheat cooked vegetables just heat, covered, for 1 or 2 minutes until hot. No additional liquid is required.

Basic Cooking Chart for Fresh Vegetables

Vegetable	Quantity	Cooking Instructions	Stir or Rearrange Once	Time
French artichokes	2 large	Soak 1 hour, covered in cold water. Drain. Wrap in waxed paper or place in covered dish.	Turn dish Twice	10 min.
Asparagus	1 lb.	Add 2 tbsp. water	Yes	8 mins.
Beans, green or waxed	1 lb.	Add ¼ cup water	Yes	6 to 8 mins.
Beets	4 medium	Cover with water	No	17 to 20 mins.
Broccoli	3 to 4 spears	Add ¼ cup water. Split spears in half if very long.	Yes	8 to 9 mins.
Brussels Sprouts	½ lb. (2 cups)	Add 2 tbsp. water	Yes	5 to 6 mins.
Cabbage	4 cups shredded	Add 2 tbsp. water	Yes	6 to 7 mins.
Carrots (slivered or sliced)	2 medium,	Add 2 tbsp. water	Yes	4 to 5 mins.
	4 medium	Add 2 tbsp. water	Yes	7 to 8 mins.
	6 medium	Add 2 tbsp. water	Yes	9 to 12 mins.
Cauliflower	1 medium flowerets	Add 2 tbsp. water	Yes	6 to 7 mins.
	1 medium whole	Add ¼ cup water	No	10 to 11 mins.
Celery	4 cups, sliced	Add 2 tbsp. water	Yes	8 to 9 mins.
Corn on Cob	2 ears	Place in covered dish or wrap in waxed paper	Yes	3 to 4 mins.
	4 ears		Yes	8 to 9 mins.
	6 ears		Yes	9 to 10 mins.
Corn cut from cob	1½ cups	Add 2 tbsp. cream or water	Yes	5 mins.
Onions	1 lb. equal size	No water	No	6 to 7 mins.
	2 to 4 large & quartered	No water	No	9 to 11 mins.
Parsnip	4 medium quartered	Add ¼ cup water	Yes	8 to 9 mins.
Peas, green	2 lbs. (2 cups)	Add 2 tbsp. water	Yes	7 to 8 mins.
Potatoes, baked	1 medium	Place on paper towel. Leave 1 inch space between each.		4 to 5 mins.
	2 medium	Do not rearrange during cooking period.		7 to 8 mins.
	3 medium			9 to 10 mins.
	4 medium	Wrap in foil until		11 to 12 mins.
	5 medium	ready to serve		14 to 15 mins.

Basic Cooking Chart for Fresh Vegetables

Vegetable	Quantity	Cooking Instructions	Stir or Rearrange Once	Time
Potatoes, baked (continued)				
	6 medium			16 to 18 mins.
	7 medium			19 to 20 mins.
	8 medium			22 to 23 mins.
Potatoes, boiled	4 medium	Add 2 cups water		14 to 18 mins.
Potatoes, sweet	1 medium	Prepare as for baked potatoes		6 to 8 mins.
	2-4 medium			15 to 18 mins.
Spinach	1 lb. (4 cups)	Only water that clings to leaves	Yes	4 to 5 mins.
Squash Acorn or Butternut	1 medium, 1-1½ lbs.	Place whole on plate, uncovered, prick with a fork.	No	8 to 12 mins.
Turnip	1 lb. (3 cups cubed)	Add ⅓ cup water	Yes	10 to 12 mins.

Cooking Chart for Frozen Vegetables

Use a 1½ or 2-quart casserole covered. As a general rule, add between 2 and 4 tablespoons of hot water and stir or rearrange the vegetables once or twice. Times given are for standard frozen packages from the supermarket.

Vegetable	Quantity	Time (mins.)	Comments
Artichoke hearts	10 oz.	6	
Asparagus	10 oz.	5-6	
Beans, green cut	10 oz.	7	Stir twice
Beans, wax	10 oz.	6-7	
Beans, baby lima	10 oz.	7	
Broccoli, chopped	10 oz.	5	Stir twice
Broccoli, spears	10 oz.	8	
Brussels sprouts	10 oz.	9-10	
Carrots	10 oz.	6	Add butter
Cauliflower	10 oz.	5-6	
Corn-on-the-cob	2 ears	5-6	Wrap in waxed paper, add a little butter
	4 ears	9-10	
Niblets	10 oz.	4	Add butter
Mixed vegetables	10 oz.	5-6	
Okra	10 oz.	6-7	

Vegetable	Quantity	Time (mins.)	Comments
Onions, small white	10 oz.	5	
Peas	10 oz.	5-6	
Spinach	12 oz.	5	Ice side up, no water
Squash	12 oz.	5-6	Do not add water. Add butter

Allow a 2-3 minute standing time after cooking.

Frozen vegetables packed in pouches do not need to be unpacked. Remember to pierce one corner of the pouch to allow steam to escape during cooking.

Artichokes Barigoule

Serve hot, serve cold, as an entrée, as a light meal, with toasted, unbuttered, crispy bread. Different, elegant and so good!

4	medium size artichokes	2	onions, chopped fine
5	cups cold water	1/2	teaspoon thyme
3	tablespoons white vinegar	1	bay leaf
3	tablespoons butter	3	tablespoons cider vinegar
1	tablespoon vegetable oil	1/4	cup dry French vermouth
			salt, pepper to taste

Slice off 1/3 of upper tip of each artichoke with a sharp knife, trim and cut off thorny tips of leaves with scissors. Cut off stem evenly. Place in a bowl, cover with the cold water, add the first 3 table-spoons vinegar and let stand until ready to cook, at least 30 minutes.

Place butter and oil in a 10 × 6-inch baking dish. Add the onions. Cook, uncovered, 6 to 8 minutes, or until onions are soft and translucent, stirring once during the cooking period.

Remove from oven. Stir in the thyme, bay leaf, vinegar and vermouth. Place the well-drained artichokes around the dish, leave center free. Cover with waxed paper. Cook 20 minutes, turning artichokes in the sauce at 5 minute intervals. Remove from oven, let stand, covered, 15 minutes. Salt and pepper the sauce in the cooking dish to taste and serve with artichokes.

Artichokes Hollandaise

A perfect entrée before a light dinner or a main course at lunch. You can make the sauce while artichokes are standing or make in advance and reheat at the last minute.

4	medium size artichokes	1	teaspoon vegetable oil
5	cups cold water	2	tablespoons fresh lemon juice
1	tablespoon white vinegar		True Hollandaise Sauce (see p. 80)
1	cup water		

Prepare and soak the artichokes in 5 cups water and white vinegar as for Artichokes Barigoule (see preceding recipe). Drain. Place 1 cup water in a 2 or 3-quart glass casserole. Add oil and lemon juice. Cook, covered, 4 minutes or until water boils. Add prepared artichokes. Cook, covered, 20 minutes, turning artichokes 3 times during that period. Let stand, covered, 5 minutes. Drain. Place each artichoke on a warmed serving plate. Set small individual bowl next to it, fill with Hollandaise Sauce and serve. 4 servings.

Asparagus Mousseline

This is where you will see the advantage of making a sauce in the microwave oven. "Mousseline" is a rich, creamy, yet light sauce which can be made easily while asparagus is standing. If you wish, you can sprinkle some cheese or a flurry of finely chopped parsley over all.

1 to	1 1/2 lbs. fresh asparagus	1/4	cup rich cream
2	tablespoons water	1/4	teaspoon salt
	salt and pepper to taste	1	tablespoon fresh lemon juice
1/4	cup butter	1/2	teaspoon dry mustard
2	lightly beaten egg yolks	1/4	cup rich cream

Place cleaned asparagus in a 1 1/2-quart casserole. Add the water, cook, covered with waxed paper, 8 to 12 minutes, rearranging asparagus once during the cooking period.

Remove from oven, let stand 5 minutes. Salt and pepper to taste.

To Make Sauce: Place the butter in a measuring cup. Heat 1 minute to melt. Add the egg yolks, the first 1/4 cup rich cream, salt and lemon juice. Cook, 1 minute, stirring 3 times during that period. Stir in the mustard and remove from oven. Whip the last 1/4 cup of cream, fold into the cooked sauce. Return to oven, uncovered, for 25 seconds. Stir and serve over asparagus. 4 servings.

Asparagus Maline

A specialty of the delightful town of Maline in Belgium, where cooking is four-star. The ingredients for the sauce can be prepared ahead of time so that when asparagus is standing, just melt the butter and add to chopped eggs mixture.

1 to	1½ lbs. fresh asparagus	1	tablespoon finely chopped fresh parsley
2	tablespoons water salt and pepper to taste	½	teaspoon salt a pinch of pepper
2	hard cooked eggs	¼	lb. unsalted butter

Place cleaned asparagus in a 1½-quart glass casserole. Add the water, cook, covered with waxed paper, 8 to 12 minutes, rearranging asparagus once during the cooking period. Remove from oven, let stand 5 minutes. Salt and pepper to taste. Place on a warm serving platter.

To Make Sauce: Coarsely chop the hard cooked eggs, add the parsley, salt and pepper. Melt the butter in a small dish or measuring cup, 1 minute, and pour over the eggs in a thin stream, while stirring constantly. Pour over asparagus. 4 servings.

Asparagus Teriyaki

Frozen asparagus, crunchy celery, almonds, and water chestnuts are combined in this unusual dish.

2	tablespoons butter or margarine	½	cup celery, sliced on the bias
2	tablespoons slivered blanched almonds	½	cup (5 ounce can) water chestnuts (optional)
1	(10 ounce) package frozen cut asparagus	1	tablespoon soy sauce

Place the butter or margarine and almonds in a 1-quart casserole. Cook, uncovered, 3 to 4 minutes or until almonds are golden brown stirring a few times during cooking period. Remove almonds with a perforated spoon, set aside.

To butter remaining in dish, add asparagus, iced side up, celery and well-drained and sliced water chestnuts. Cook, covered, 7 to 8 minutes, stirring twice during last half of cooking. Stir in soy sauce and almonds. Cover, let stand 10 minutes. 4 servings.

Green Beans Lyonnaise

Lyonnaise means a plain vegetable topped with a good cover of fried onions garnished with buttered croutons — all easily accomplished with a microwave oven. The topping is quickly made while the beans are standing.

1	*lb. fresh green beans*	1	*cup thinly sliced*
1/4	*cup water*		*onions*
	salt and pepper to taste	1	*tablespoon butter*
2	*tablespoons butter or*	1	*cup fresh bread,*
	margarine		*cubed*
		1/8	*teaspoon thyme*

Green beans can be cut lengthwise into slivers or left whole. Place in a 1½-quart casserole dish with water. Cook, covered, 6 to 8 minutes when beans are slivered; 10 to 12 minutes when left whole. Salt and pepper to taste. Let stand, covered, while making topping. Drain if necessary. Place butter and onions in small glass dish or 2-cup measure. Cook 6 to 8 minutes, uncovered, or until onions are golden brown. Salt and pepper and place over green beans.

Melt the tablespoon of butter in a 9-inch glass pie plate, 30 seconds. Add bread cubes and thyme. Stir until coated with butter; cook, uncovered, 3 to 4 minutes, or until browned, stirring often. Pour over onions. 4 servings.

Green or Wax Beans in Walnut Sauce

A Russian specialty, equally good served hot or cold. The sauce can be made right in a measuring cup, thus saving an extra dish.

1	lb. wax or green beans	1	teaspoon paprika
1/4	cup water	1	teaspoon salt
1/2	cup chicken stock	2	tablespoons red wine vinegar
1/4	cup minced green onions	1/2	cup finely ground walnuts
1	small clove garlic, chopped fine	2	tablespoons parsley, chopped fine

Place beans in a 1½-quart casserole with the water. Cook, covered, 10 to 12 minutes. Let stand, covered, 8 minutes.

To Make Sauce: Chicken stock can be fresh, canned, or made from cubes. Place stock in a 2-cup measure, add the onions, garlic, paprika, salt and vinegar. Heat for 1 minute or until hot. Add walnuts and parsley. Stir thoroughly and pour over cooked beans. 4 servings.

Pink and Green Beans

Deep green beans topped with a delicious pink cream sauce. Excellent with roast chicken or veal.

1	lb. green beans	1	teaspoon paprika
1/4	cup water	2	tablespoons flour
	salt and pepper to taste	1	cup commercial sour cream
2	tablespoons butter		
1	cup finely chopped onion	1/2	teaspoon salt

Cut beans into 1-inch pieces. Place in a 1½-quart glass casserole. Add water. Cook, covered, for 6 to 8 minutes, stirring twice. Remove from oven, salt and pepper to taste. Let stand, covered, while making sauce.

To Make Sauce: Place the butter in a 1-quart casserole dish or a 4-cup measure and melt 30 seconds. Add the onions. Stir well. Cook, uncovered, 5 minutes. The onions should be soft and translucent, but not brown. Remove from oven. Stir in the paprika and flour until well blended, beat in the sour cream and salt. Return to oven and cook, uncovered, for 3 minutes, stirring 4 times. When creamy, pour over beans. 4 servings.

Frozen Green Beans "Nouveau Genre"

Cream cheese and sour cream combined for a cream sauce made in seconds while beans are standing. Curry powder gives the zip.

1	10-ounce package or 1½-2 cups frozen green beans salt and pepper to taste	2	green onions, chopped fine
3	ounces cream cheese	½	teaspoon curry powder
2	tablespoons commercial sour cream	¼	teaspoon salt

Place green beans in a 1½-quart glass casserole. If beans are a solid pack, place ice side up with ¼ cup water. For loose package, add 2 tablespoons water. In either case, cook, covered, 8 to 10 minutes, stirring once. Salt and pepper to taste. Let stand 5 minutes, covered. Drain if necessary. Heat remaining ingredients in a measuring jug for 20 seconds, mix well. Spread over beans. Heat, uncovered, for 2 minutes. 4 servings.

Harvard Beets

A favorite of all.

3 to	4 cups cooked beets, diced or sliced or a 16-ounce can of beets, well drained	1/2	cup sugar
		1/3	cup cider vinegar
		1/3	cup water
		3	tablespoons butter
4	teaspoons cornstarch		salt and pepper to taste

Cook beets according to directions on Fresh Vegetable Chart (see p. 173), or dice or slice canned beets. Place in a fairly large casserole dish. Place the cornstarch and sugar in a measuring cup, mix well. Add the remaining ingredients except salt and pepper. Mix well. Cook, covered, for 3 minutes. Stir well, cook another 3 minutes or until creamy and transparent. Pour over beets, stir well. Cook 1 minute or until hot. Salt and pepper to taste. 4 to 5 servings.

Pickled Beets

This recipe calls for canned beets, but the same technique can be used with microwave oven cooked beets following directions in Fresh Vegetable Chart (see p. 173).

2	cups canned sliced or whole beets	1/3	cup cider vinegar
		1	teaspoon pickling spices
1/3	cup sugar		
1/3	cup beet liquid or water	1	small clove garlic left whole

Drain beets, reserving 1/3 cup liquid. Place in a 1 1/2-quart casserole dish. Add reserved liquid and remaining ingredients. Cook, covered, 4 minutes or until mixture boils, stirring once. Cool. Place beets in glass jar, strain vinegar mixture on top. Cover, keep refrigerated. Will keep for 5 to 7 weeks.

Beets Poblano

Peeling and grating the raw beets makes the preparation somewhat messy, but the recipe is fast and the result is well worth the trouble.

4	medium size beets	1	tablespoon butter
1/4	cup fresh orange juice	1	cup green seedless
1/2	teaspoon sugar		grapes
			salt and pepper to taste

Peel and grate the raw beets and place in a 1½-quart casserole. Add the orange juice, sugar and butter and mix well. Cook, covered, 5 minutes. Stir. Add the grapes. Cook, uncovered, 2 minutes. Cover and let stand 5 minutes. Salt and pepper to taste. 4 servings.

Note Remove beet stains from your hands with a little vinegar and salt.

Beets Quebec Style

Another way to cook grated beets. The perfect vegetable to serve with roasted pork, game, sausages or liver.

4	medium size beets	3	tablespoons butter
1	large apple, unpeeled		a pinch allspice
2	medium onions		

Peel and grate the raw beets, apple and onions. Add the butter and allspice. Stir until well mixed. Place in a 1½-quart casserole and cook, covered, 7 minutes. Salt and pepper to taste. Let stand, covered, 5 minutes. 4 servings.

Polish Beets

In this recipe the beets are cooked first, then grated. Serve with goose, turkey, pork and game.

12	small beets		salt and pepper to taste
1	tablespoon cider vinegar	1	tablespoon butter
2	tablespoons sugar	1	tablespoon flour
2	tablespoons vegetable oil	1/2	cup commercial sour cream

Place washed beets in a 2-quart casserole. Add enough hot water to cover. Cover dish with waxed paper. Cook 17 to 20 minutes. Remove from oven. Let stand 10 minutes, then cool, peel and grate the beets. Mix together the vinegar, sugar, and vegetable oil, stir into the beets. Salt and pepper to taste.

Place the butter in a 2-cup measure and melt 20 seconds. Stir in the flour and the sour cream. Heat 1 minute. Stir thoroughly. Add to the beet mixture. Stir well. Heat 2 minutes. Stir and serve. 6 servings.

Broccoli Florentine

A recipe that is colorful and tasty. Prepare ingredients for sauce while broccoli is cooking and cook while it is standing. Serve with buttered egg noodles, the Florentine way.

1	lb. fresh broccoli		grated rind of 1 lemon
1/4	cup water	2	tablespoons lemon juice
2	tablespoons butter		
4	green onions, sliced	1/2	teaspoon basil
2	canned pimientos, chopped		salt and pepper to taste

Discard large leaves and tough portions of broccoli stalks. Split each stalk lengthwise into halves for more even cooking. Place in a 1 1/2-quart glass casserole. Add water. Cook, covered, 9 minutes or until crisp, yet tender, and green color becomes vivid.

Remove from oven, keep covered and let stand 3 minutes.

To Make Sauce: Melt butter in measuring cup for 30 seconds. Add green onions, stir until well coated with butter. Cook 2 minutes, stirring once. Add remaining ingredients, stir to mix. Pour over cooked broccoli. Taste for seasoning. Heat 2 minutes. 4 servings.

Broccoli Oriental

A very interesting way to cook vegetables. Broccoli can be replaced by another type of green vegetable. This is a perfect example of how vegetables cooked in this way retain their fresh green color.

1	lb. broccoli	1	teaspoon sugar
3	tablespoons vegetable oil	1/2	cup chicken stock or consommé
1	small onion, diced	2	teaspoons cornstarch
2	tablespoons soy sauce		

Cut the broccoli stems on the bias making long cuts and break the heads into small flowerets. In a 12 × 8-inch glass baking dish, heat the vegetable oil 30 seconds, add the onion and cook, uncovered, 5 to 6 minutes, or until onion is brown. Add the broccoli, stir until well coated with the oil and onion. Cook 5 minutes, stirring 2 to 3 times. Blend together the remaining ingredients. Add to the broccoli. Stir thoroughly. Heat 2 minutes. Taste for seasoning. 4 servings.

Broccoli Amandine

The almonds can easily be toasted in the microwave oven while the broccoli is standing. They add an air of elegance to this dish.

1	*lb. fresh broccoli*	2	*teaspoons fresh lemon*
1/4	*cup water*		*juice*
2	*tablespoons butter*		*salt and pepper to taste*
2	*tablespoons slivered blanched almonds*		

Discard large leaves and tough portions of broccoli stalks. Split each stalk lengthwise into halves for more even cooking. Place in a 1½-quart glass casserole. Add water. Cook, covered, 9 minutes or until crisp, yet tender, and green color becomes vivid. Remove from oven, keep covered and let stand 3 minutes.

To Prepare the Amandine: Melt the butter in a flat dish or pie plate, 30 seconds. Stir in the almonds, cook, uncovered, 2 to 3 minutes, or until golden brown, stirring twice. Add the lemon juice. Salt and pepper the broccoli, pour the Almond butter on top. 4 servings.

Quick Creamed Broccoli

Green, crunchy, and saucy. A quick dish when you have to serve 6 to 8.

2	10-ounce packages frozen broccoli spears	2	green onions, chopped fine
1	cup diced or slivered celery	1	tablespoon chopped parsley
1	can (10-ounce) cream of celery soup undiluted		

Place frozen broccoli ice side up in a 12 × 8-inch glass baking dish. Cook, covered with waxed paper, 8 to 9 minutes or until broccoli is just about tender, turning over once. Sprinkle celery on top, cover with the soup. Cook, uncovered, 5 minutes. Top with the onions and parsley mixed together and serve. 6 to 8 servings.

Note Recipe can be halved, or if you don't want half a can of soup left, make the full quantity and freeze half for later use.

Scandinavian Brussels Sprouts

A lemon butter treatment makes these quite different from the usual and it can be prepared while sprouts are soaking.

1	lb. fresh Brussels sprouts		juice and grated rind of $1/2$ a lemon
2	tablespoons water	$1/4$	teaspoon sugar
1	teaspoon butter		salt, pepper to taste

Trim and soak the Brussels sprouts for 15 minutes in enough cold water to cover, with 1 teaspoon vinegar added. Meanwhile place in a $1^1/_2$-quart glass casserole the water, butter, juice and grated rind of lemon and the sugar. Heat, uncovered, 2 minutes. Drain Brussels sprouts, roll in the lemon mixture. Cook, covered with waxed paper, 5 to 6 minutes, stirring once. Let stand 6 minutes. Salt and pepper to taste. 3 servings.

Creamed Brussels Sprouts

The sauce is made while the sprouts are standing, then mixed together for last 5 minutes of cooking. Serve with pork chops or baked ham slice.

1	lb. Brussels sprouts grated rind of ¹/₂ an orange	2	tablespoons flour
¹/₄	cup water	¹/₂	cup cream or milk
2	tablespoons butter or margarine	¹/₈	teaspoon nutmeg salt and pepper to taste

Trim and soak sprouts 15 minutes in cold water with 1 teaspoon vinegar added. Drain, place in a 1¹/₂-quart glass casserole with grated orange rind and ¹/₄ cup water. Cover with waxed paper, cook, 6 to 8 minutes, stirring once. Let stand until sauce is ready.

To Make Sauce: Place butter in measuring cup or bowl and melt in oven, 30 seconds. Add the flour, stir until well mixed, add the cream or milk and nutmeg. Stir to mix and pour over undrained Brussels sprouts. Mix together. Cook, uncovered, 5 minutes, stirring once. When creamy, salt and pepper to taste. 4 servings.

Frozen Brussels Sprouts

Good topped with True Hollandaise Sauce (see p. 80) before serving.

1	10-ounce package (1¹/₂ cups) or 10-ounce pouch frozen Brussels sprouts	2	tablespoons water
		¹/₄	teaspoon sugar
		¹/₂	teaspoon lemon rind (optional) salt and pepper to taste

Remove sprouts from package, unless using pouch (see Note). Place in a 1-quart dish with the water, sugar and lemon rind. Cook, covered, 9 to 10 minutes, stirring after 5 minutes cooking. Let stand 5 minutes. Salt and pepper to taste. Serve with butter or Hollandaise Sauce. 3 servings.

Note When using the frozen sprouts in pouch, set pouch on a plate, make 3 slits in pouch. Cook, uncovered, 6 to 8 minutes, turning pouch once. Let stand 6 minutes. Drain and serve as above.

Golden Cabbage

Chopped or shredded cabbage is always perfect cooked the microwave way.

4	full cups chopped cabbage	1/2	teaspoon black or white mustard seeds (optional)
3	tablespoons peanut oil	2	tablespoons water
1/2	teaspoon turmeric		salt and pepper to taste

If you wish to chop cabbage ahead of time, store in a plastic bag and refrigerate until ready to use. Place cabbage in a 1½-quart casserole or baking dish and cook covered, 4 minutes. Add the oil, turmeric and mustard seeds. Stir until the cabbage is partly coated with the oil. Add the water. Cook, covered with waxed paper, 6 minutes. Let stand 3 minutes. Salt and pepper to taste and serve. 3 to 4 servings.

Bavarian Cabbage

The apple and juniper berries give something special to this cabbage.

2	tablespoons butter	4	juniper berries (optional)
6	cups shredded cabbage	1/2	cup white wine or consommé
1	large peeled apple, thinly sliced	3	tablespoons flour
1	bay leaf		salt and pepper to taste

Melt butter 30 seconds in a 2 or 3-quart casserole. Stir in the cabbage and apple until coated with the butter. Add the bay leaf and juniper berries, white wine or consommé. Stir well. Cook, covered, 6 minutes. Sprinkle the flour on top and stir until well mixed. It will thicken a little as you stir. Cook, uncovered, 2 minutes, stirring once. Salt and pepper to taste. 4 servings.

Finnish Cabbage

Nobody can cook cabbage like the Finnish women. All their recipes for it are unusual and interesting and luckily can easily be translated to microwave cooking.

1/4	cup butter	1	teaspoon caraway
6	cups shredded		seeds
	cabbage	2	tablespoons sugar
1	onion, chopped	3	fresh tomatoes,
	coarsely		unpeeled and diced
			salt and pepper to taste

Melt the butter 30 seconds in a 2-3-quart casserole. Add the cabbage and onion. Stir until coated with the butter. Mix the caraway seeds and sugar together and sprinkle over the cabbage. Top with the tomatoes. Cook, covered, 6 minutes, stirring well after 3 minutes. Let stand 2 minutes. Salt and pepper to taste. 4 servings.

Creamy Sweet and Sour Cabbage

Cabbage makes a nourishing dish cooked in this way, together with a baked potato.

6	cups shredded	1	tablespoon butter or
	cabbage		margarine
1/4	cup water	1/4	cup cider vinegar
1/4	cup flour	1/4	cup sugar
1	cup sour cream		salt and pepper to taste

Place cabbage and water in a 2 to 3-quart casserole. Cook, covered, 4 minutes. Let stand while making sauce.

To Make Sauce: Place in a 4-cup measure, the flour, then the sour cream. Stir until well blended, add the butter, vinegar and sugar. Mix well and cook, uncovered, 2 minutes. Stir well, cook another 2 minutes. Stir and add to the cabbage. Mix thoroughly. Salt and pepper to taste. Heat 2 minutes. 4 to 6 servings.

Asparagus Mousseline, page 177
Cauliflower Cheese and Mushroom, page 192

Confetti Rice, page 221
Green Sauce Pasta, page 226

Parsleyed Carrots

In season replace the fresh parsley with fresh mint or basil.

5 to	6 medium carrots, peeled and thinly sliced	1	tablespoon sugar
3	tablespoons butter	2	teaspoons chopped parsley
2	tablespoons water		salt and pepper to taste

Place in a 1-quart casserole, the carrots, butter, water and sugar. Cook, covered, 8 minutes or until carrots are tender. Add the parsley, salt and pepper to taste and serve. 6 servings.

Buttered Carrots

When finished, these carrots are in a clear, buttery sauce, and, because it is cooked with the carrots, there are no extra dishes to wash up.

2 1/2 to 3	cups carrots, sliced 1/4 inch thick	1/2	teaspoon sugar
1/4	cup butter or margarine	1/8	teaspoon thyme
1/4	cup hot water	3	teaspoons flour
		1/2	cup hot water
			salt and pepper to taste

Place in a 2-quart casserole the carrots, butter and 1/4 cup hot water. Cook, covered, 8 minutes. Add the sugar, thyme and flour. Mix well with the carrots. Add the 1/2 cup hot water. Stir well. Cook, covered, 3 minutes, stirring twice. Salt and pepper to taste. 4 servings.

Ginger Glazed Carrots

Delicious, especially when fresh ginger roots are used. These can be purchased at Oriental food shops and will keep for months in your freezer.

4 to 5 cups peeled and
    sliced carrots
¼ cup honey
¼ cup butter
2 tablespoons brown
    sugar
4 tablespoons vegetable
    oil

¼ cup boiling water
    the grated rind of ½
    a lemon
1 teaspoon grated fresh
    ginger root or 1
    teaspoon ground ginger
    salt and pepper to taste

Place in a 2-quart casserole the carrots, honey, brown sugar, vegetable oil, and boiling water. Cook, uncovered, 10 minutes, stirring twice. Add the remaining ingredients, cook, uncovered, another 8 minutes, stirring twice. Drain and stand 2-3 minutes. 4 to 6 servings.

Cauliflower Cheese and Mushroom

You can cook a whole head of cauliflower to perfection in a microwave oven. It is very tasty topped with the mushroom sauce made while the cauliflower is standing.

1 to 1 ½ lb. cauliflower
¼ cup hot water
2 tablespoons butter
2 tablespoons flour
½ teaspoon salt
1 cup milk

½ cup grated sharp
    cheddar cheese
1 (4-ounce) can
    chopped mushrooms
    with liquid

Clean head of cauliflower and leave whole. With a sharp, pointed knife remove hard core at stem end. Place head up in 2-quart casserole. Pour hot water on top. Cook, covered, 10 minutes, turning casserole around after 5 minutes. Allow to stand while making sauce.

To Make Sauce: To the water remaining in dish, add the butter, melt 30 seconds. Stir in the flour and salt. Mix well. Add milk. Cook, uncovered, 2 minutes, stirring after 1¹/₂ minutes. Add cheese and mushrooms. Stir until well blended. Cook, uncovered, 2 minutes, stirring twice or until creamy. Salt and pepper to taste. Pour over the hot cauliflower. 4 servings.

Marinated Carrots

Serve as a salad. This will keep 6 to 8 days refrigerated in a glass jar, well covered.

4	cups carrots, peeled and sliced ¹/₄ inch thick	1	teaspoon salt
		¹/₄	teaspoon pepper
		¹/₄	cup vegetable oil
¹/₂	teaspoon sugar	2 to 3	tablespoons cider or wine vinegar
¹/₄	teaspoon thyme		
¹/₂	cup hot water	1	teaspoon oregano
1	clove garlic, cut in half		

Place the carrots in a 1¹/₂-quart casserole. Add the sugar, thyme and hot water. Cook, covered, 10 minutes. Let stand 10 minutes. Place the drained carrots in a bowl, add all the remaining ingredients, toss well. Cover and refrigerate 12 hours before serving. 6 to 8 servings.

Cauliflower Gratiné

This time the cauliflower is cut in flowerets topped with cream sauce and a crusty cheese topping. If you wish to brown the topping under the broiler, preheat it while cauliflower is cooking. Serve with roast beef.

1 cauliflower or 2 10-ounce packages frozen cauliflower	2 tablespoons fine dry breadcrumbs
1 tablespoon butter	1/2 teaspoon salt
1 tablespoon flour	1/4 teaspoon pepper
1 cup milk	1/4 teaspoon paprika
	2 tablespoons grated Parmesan

For Fresh Cauliflower: Break cauliflower into flowerets. Place in a 1 1/2-quart casserole. Add 3 tablespoons water. Cook, covered, 5 minutes. Salt to taste. Let stand 2 minutes.

For Frozen Cauliflower: Place cauliflower in a 2-quart casserole and cook, covered, 10-11 minutes, stirring twice. Let stand 2 minutes.

To Make Sauce: Place butter in a medium size measuring cup and melt 30 seconds. Stir in the flour. When well mixed add the milk, stir and cook, uncovered, 2 minutes. Stir well, cook another minute, or until creamy. Stir well and pour over the cauliflower. Mix the remaining ingredients together, sprinkle on top of the sauce. Cook, uncovered, 2-3 minutes, or for a darker brown color, place under broiler in regular oven, for 3 to 4 minutes or until browned. 4 servings.

Carrots and Peas India

An interesting combination that is served with chicken or barbecued steak.

2	tablespoons butter	1	cup fresh or frozen
1/4	teaspoon cumin seeds		green peas
2	cups carrots, peeled		grated rind and juice
	and sliced		of 1/2 a lemon
1/4	cup hot water		salt and pepper to taste

Place the butter and cumin seeds in a 1½-quart casserole. Heat, uncovered, 5 minutes, stirring once. Add the carrots and hot water. Stir well. Cook, covered, 8 minutes, stirring twice. Add the green peas, grated lemon rind and juice. Cook 4 minutes. Salt and pepper to taste. Let stand 3 to 5 minutes. 4 servings.

Steamed Celery

Only the microwave oven can steam celery to retain its texture, color and flavor. This is delicious with all types of meat and egg dishes.

4-5	sticks celery (3-4 cups	3	tablespoons butter
	when cut)		salt, pepper to taste
2	tablespoons water or		
	consommé		

Pull head of celery apart, cut off the green leaves. Scrape and wash the stalks. Cut them into thick matchsticks, 4 to 5 inches long. If cut all the same size they look very attractive. Arrange in a 1½-quart casserole, add the water or consommé. Cook, covered, 8 to 10 minutes, stirring once after 4 minutes cooking. Drain water if any remains. Salt and pepper to taste. Add butter. Cook, uncovered, 2 minutes to melt the butter. Stir well. 4 servings.

Steamed Corn

Corn is especially good cooked in the microwave oven and can also easily be reheated without losing its flavor.

1 to 6 fresh corn ears   sugar
       rich cream or melted
       butter

Remove husks, brush corn with cream or melted butter and sprinkle each ear with ¼ teaspoon sugar. Season to taste with salt. Wrap in waxed paper. Lay corn on a plate.

For 2 ears: Cook 2 minutes, turn corn over, cook another 2 minutes.
For 4 ears: Cook 8 to 9 minutes, turning once.
For 6 ears: Cook 9 to 10 minutes, turning once.

To Cook Frozen Corn: Place 2 to 4 ears of corn on a plate. Rub each one with cream or butter and sprinkle with sugar, as for fresh corn. Wrap each one in waxed paper.

For 2 ears: Cook 8 to 9 minutes.
For 4 ears: Cook 10 to 12 minutes.

To Cook Fresh Corn In Its Husks: Pull outer husks off ears of corn leaving only 3 to 5 leaves covering corn. Carefully pull back remaining husks, remove silk. Butter and season as above. Replace husks, so corn is completely covered. Set on plate and cook as for fresh corn. Let husks remain around ears of corn until ready to eat.

Corn O'Brien

A well-known favorite. You can use frozen instead of canned corn. Cook first according to the directions on the Frozen Vegetable Chart (see p. 174) and add as for canned.

1	green or red sweet pepper, diced	1	to 2 cans (14-ounces each) corn niblets, undrained
2	green onions, diced		
2	tablespoons butter		salt, pepper to taste

Place green pepper, onions and butter in a 1-quart casserole. Cook, covered, 5 minutes, stirring twice. Add corn, mix well. Salt and pepper to taste. Cook, uncovered, 3 minutes or until heated through. 4 to 5 servings.

Creamed Cucumbers

The French chef's way to do it and it takes only 5 minutes cooking time.

3 to	4 cups of cucumber balls	1/4	cup fresh chopped parsley
1/4	cup rich cream		salt, pepper to taste
1	teaspoon butter		

Peel cucumbers and cut into small balls resembling olives, with a special cutter, or in 1-inch squares. Place in a 1 1/2-quart casserole the cucumbers, cream, butter and parsley. Mix well. Cook, uncovered, 5 minutes, stirring twice. Salt, pepper to taste. Let stand 2 minutes. 4 to 5 servings.

Arabic Eggplant

Simple, quick, attractive, tasty — what more can we ask? The dry soup is the modern touch.

1	large eggplant	2	tablespoons dry onion
3	tablespoons butter		or mushroom soup
1	cup commercial sour		mix
	cream		salt, pepper to taste

Peel the eggplant. Cut out small balls with a melon cutter or cut into cubes. Melt the butter in a 1½-quart casserole, 40 seconds. Roll the eggplant balls in the butter. Cook, covered, 5 minutes. Top with the sour cream and powdered soup mix mixed together. Cook, uncovered, 3 minutes. Salt, pepper to taste. 4 servings.

Eggplant Capri

Preparation is fast and simple and in only six minutes this casserole dish is ready to be served. A perfect example of the tremendous time saved by cooking the microwave way. Serve with rice or noodles or as a vegetable with chicken and pork.

1	medium size or 2	1	teaspoon salt
	small eggplants	¼	teaspoon pepper
2	tablespoons flour	3	tablespoons butter or
½	cup fine breadcrumbs		vegetable oil
1	teaspoon sugar	1	cup canned tomato
¼	teaspoon thyme		sauce with
¼	teaspoon basil		mushrooms

Peel eggplant and cut into thin slices. Blend together the flour, breadcrumbs, sugar, thyme, basil, salt and pepper. Dip each slice of eggplant in a little milk and roll in flour mixture. Place a row of eggplant in bottom of an oblong baking dish or 10-inch CORNING WARE skillet, sprinkle with some of the vegetable oil, repeat until all eggplant and oil have been used. Pour the tomato sauce around the edges, leaving the middle free. Cook, covered with waxed paper, 6 minutes. Let stand 2 minutes. 4 servings.

Leeks in Lemon Sauce

An elegant and tasty vegetable to serve in the autumn when leeks are at their best. Make in advance and serve cold.

4 to	6 medium size leeks		juice and rind
1/2	cup hot water		of 1 lemon
1	tablespoon cornstarch	1	teaspoon salt
2	tablespoons vegetable oil		

Clean the leeks, remove outer leaves and cut off half the green top (keep for soup). Split the remaining green part in two from the white part up. Wash under running water, letting the water run through the leaves, where sand is usually lodged. Drain well. Place in an 8-inch square or oblong baking dish, pour hot water on top. Cook, covered with waxed paper, 8 minutes. Let stand 2 minutes. Remove leeks to platter. Mix together cornstarch, vegetable oil, lemon juice and rind and salt and add to water left from cooking the leeks. Stir well. Cook, uncovered, 2 minutes, stirring once or twice. Pour over leeks. Cool, cover and refrigerate. Serve cold. 3 to 4 servings.

Baked Pearl Onions

Another once-a-year treat. At their best in September and October. Superb cooked in the microwave oven at your leisure and served cold.

1	lb. pearl onions	1/2	clove garlic, chopped fine
1/4	cup vegetable oil		
1/2	teaspoon each salt, pepper	1/4	cup finely chopped parsley
1	tablespoon wine or cider vinegar		

Place unpeeled onions in a single layer in a glass pie plate. Cook, 5 minutes. Cool and peel (very easy). Blend remaining ingredients in a large jam jar or other container, pour in onions as they are peeled. Cover, refrigerate, serve cold. Will keep 4 to 6 weeks. 4 servings.

Italian Steamed Onions

Unusual and very good.

4	large onions or 8 medium	1/2	teaspoon each salt and pepper
1	tablespoon water	1/4 to 1/2	teaspoon oregano
2	tablespoons vegetable oil	2	tablespoons chopped fresh parsley
2	tablespoons soft butter		

Peel and cut large onions into quarters, leave medium sized onions whole. Place onions in a 1½-quart casserole with water. Cook, covered, 9 to 10 minutes. As soon as they are removed from oven, mix remaining ingredients together and pour over onions. Stir until butter is melted and coats the onions. 4 to 6 servings.

Green Peas

Everyone's favorite and easily available, frozen or canned or to be enjoyed fresh at the beginning of the summer when at their best. Cooked in the microwave oven they retain their color, shape and flavor. Keep the frozen ones available at all times.

A 10-ounce package or 1½ cups of frozen green peas will cook, covered, without water, in 5 to 6 minutes, stirring or turning them once.

In the summer add butter and fresh chives, chopped fresh mint or basil or diced fresh tomatoes to peas when ready to serve. In the winter, add 1 or a few teaspoons cream, green onions chopped, a few mushrooms chopped fine, a tablespoon or so of chopped water chestnuts, or warm up ½ cup grated carrots with 1 teaspoon cream 3 minutes in the microwave oven, then toss with peas.

If you prefer frozen peas and carrots, cook according to the directions on the Frozen Vegetable Chart, page 174. These are interesting served with 3 slices of crisped, crumbled bacon, cooked in the microwave oven, of course.

Green Peas Parisiens

Two 10-ounce packages frozen green peas or 2-3 cups bulk can replace the fresh peas.

2 to 3 cups shelled green
  peas (2 to 3 lbs.
  unshelled)
3 tablespoons butter
2 cups coarsely
  shredded lettuce

1 tablespoon fresh
  parsley, chopped fine
1 tablespoon sugar
12 very small onions,
  peeled
  salt and pepper to taste

Shell the peas only when you are ready to cook them. Melt the butter 30 seconds in a 2-quart casserole. Add the lettuce, parsley and sugar. Mix the onions and green peas together and place on top of lettuce. Cook, covered, 8 minutes, stirring twice. Salt and pepper to taste. 4 to 5 servings.

Springtime Potatoes and Green Peas

A traditional dish in New England. Serve as they do, for family dinner, with a large basket of hot biscuits followed by fresh strawberries sweetened with maple syrup for dessert.

1 lb. small new potatoes
1 1/2 cups (1 1/2 lbs.) shelled
  fresh peas
2 tablespoons butter
2 green onions, chopped
2 tablespoons flour

2 teaspoons salt
1/4 cup fresh chopped
  parsley
1/4 teaspoon pepper
1 1/2 cups milk

Place washed, unpeeled potatoes on paper towel in oven. Prick each potato once with the point of a knife. Cover with another paper towel. Cook 8 to 9 minutes. Remove from oven and set aside. Place peas in 1 1/2-quart casserole, add 2 tablespoons water, cook, covered, 5 minutes. Set aside.

Place in a 2-cup measure the butter and green onions and cook, uncovered, 1 minute. Blend in flour, salt, parsley, pepper and milk. Mix well, cook, uncovered, 4 minutes, stirring twice.

Meanwhile peel potatoes, add to peas and pour hot creamy sauce on top. It can be reheated, uncovered, for 2 minutes. 4 to 5 servings.

Frozen Peas and Mushrooms

In this combination frozen peas taste as if they were fresh.

2	tablespoons butter or margarine	1	10-ounce package frozen green peas
3	green onions, chopped	1	teaspoon sugar
1	4-ounce can drained mushroom pieces	1/4	teaspoon basil salt, pepper to taste

Place in a 1-quart casserole the butter and green onions. Cook, covered, 2 minutes. Add mushrooms, frozen green peas, sugar, and basil. Cook, covered, 6 to 8 minutes, stirring once. Salt and pepper to taste. 4 servings.

Boiled Potatoes

There is little saving of time when cooking boiled potatoes in the microwave oven, particularly if cooking more than four. However, you may want to use your oven for the variations below.

Cooking time often varies with potatoes, depending on type. It is wise to check if they are done 2 minutes before end of cooking, then add or subtract minutes for total time in the future.

    4   medium size potatoes
    2   cups water
    1/2 teaspoon salt

Peel and quarter the potatoes. Place in a 1½-quart casserole with the water and salt. Cover. Cook 14 to 18 minutes. Drain. Put back in oven, uncovered, for 2 minutes to dry.

Variations

Austrian Potatoes Replace water with consommé. Drain, reserving consommé for soup. Toss with butter and parsley. Heat, uncovered, 2 minutes.

Cheese Topped Boil according to directions. Drain, place in 1-quart glass casserole, top with 1 cup grated cheddar cheese mixed with ¹/₂ cup dry breadcrumbs. Cook, uncovered, 3 minutes.

Hungarian Melt 3 tablespoons margarine in a 1-quart glass casserole, 30 seconds. Add 1 teaspoon paprika, 2 to 4 green onions, chopped fine. Mix with butter. Add drained cooked potatoes. Toss in pink butter until coated. Heat, uncovered, 2 minutes.

Onion Potatoes Add 1 envelope of dry onion soup mix to the water before cooking potatoes. Omit salt. When cooked, drain in sieve. Place potatoes in a 1-quart glass casserole. Sprinkle onions remaining in sieve on top. Dot with butter to taste. Heat, uncovered, 2 minutes.

Baked Potatoes

The easiest of all in a microwave oven, although time can vary slightly, depending on the variety of potatoes used, whether they are new or old and even the part of the country they come from. The Idaho baking type potatoes are the very best.

Select uniform, medium-sized baking potatoes. The best size is approximately 7-ounce. Larger ones will require 1 to 3 minutes more cooking time.

Scrub potatoes thoroughly with a brush. Prick each potato all the way through with a 2-prong fork.

Arrange potatoes on a paper towel in oven. Make sure there is a 1-inch space between potatoes. Never place one potato in the center surrounded with other potatoes. Leave center free and place others in a circle. I always like to turn the potatoes over or around about midway through cooking time, but this is not essential.

When cooked, let stand, uncovered, 5 minutes. They will remain piping hot. To keep them hot 10 to 20 minutes, wrap each one in foil.

1 potato will take 4 to 8 minutes depending on size.
8 medium potatoes 22 to 23 minutes depending on size.
For other quantities, see Fresh Vegetable Chart, p.173.

Note Potatoes can also be pricked with a fork, wrapped in plastic wrap and cooked as above.

Do-Ahead Baked Potatoes

Prepare, keep refrigerated or freeze. Perfect to have on hand when time is short and for last minute occasions.

4	(7-8 ounces each) baking potatoes	1/4	teaspoon summer savory
2	tablespoons butter	2	green onions, chopped fine
1/4-1/2	cup milk or cream or sour cream	1/4-1/2	cup grated cheddar cheese
1/2	teaspoon salt	1	teaspoon paprika

Bake potatoes according to directions in preceding recipe. Let stand 10 minutes. Then cut a thin oval slice through skin from the top of each potato. Scoop out potato with a spoon, leaving the skin intact to form a boat shape. For quick work, cut each potato in half and empty shell. Mash the potatoes with the butter, milk or cream or sour cream, salt, pepper, savory and green onions. When mixture is light and fluffy, lightly spoon back into potato shells. Top each with 1 tablespoon cheese and a generous sprinkling of paprika. Place potatoes in a circle on paper towels in the oven and heat, uncovered, 4 to 5 minutes. 4 to 6 servings.

Deep-Browned Potatoes

These are very tasty and reheat beautifully. A favorite way to serve potatoes around a roast or with steaks and chops.

2	tablespoons butter or fat of your choice, or 4 tablespoons gravy from roast	1/4	teaspoon paprika
		1/4	teaspoon herb of your choice (optional)
1/2	teaspoon Kitchen Bouquet	4 to 6	medium-size potatoes, peeled

In a 1½-quart casserole, place the butter or other fat, or gravy from roast, Kitchen Bouquet, paprika and herbs. Cook 1 minute. Stir well. Roll potatoes in mixture until well coated. Cook, covered, 4 minutes. Stir potatoes to coat with mixture again. Cook, uncovered, another 4 to 5 minutes or until potatoes are tender.

When prepared ahead of time, leave cooked potatoes, uncovered, on kitchen counter. When ready to serve, reheat 1 minute. Stir well. Heat 30 to 40 seconds. Serve.

Mashed Potatoes

Cooked in a microwave oven and whipped with an electric mixer, everything is done and ready to serve six in 20 minutes.

4	large or 6 medium potatoes (2 lbs.)	1	tablespoon butter
1½	cups hot water	¼	teaspoon savory
½	teaspoon salt	⅛	teaspoon garlic salt or powder (optional)
¼	cup milk or cream		

Peel potatoes, cut into eights and place in 2-quart casserole with water. Cook, covered, 15 minutes or until tender, turning dish halfway through cooking period. Drain. Whip potatoes with remaining ingredients. If you have an electric mixer, place hot potatoes in bowl, add all other ingredients and whip 2 to 3 minutes at medium speed. If necessary, warm up 1 minute in oven. 6 servings.

Scalloped Potatoes

The Idaho baking potatoes give the best results, although any variety can be used. When milk is scalded first in the microwave oven or on top of stove, the potatoes are creamier and lighter. Leftovers reheat beautifully in the microwave oven. Just heat them, covered, 1 to 3 minutes, depending on quantity.

4 to 5 cups, peeled and
    thinly sliced potatoes
2   tablespoons flour
1   teaspoon salt
$1/2$ teaspoon savory
$1/4$ cup chopped onion

$1^{1}/_{2}$ cups hot milk*
2   tablespoons butter or
    margarine
    paprika
    chopped or flaked
    parsley

Toss together in an 8 × 8-inch glass baking dish the potatoes, flour, salt, savory and onion. Stir in the hot milk, spread evenly and dot all over with the butter. Cook, covered, 15 minutes or until potatoes are done, stirring 3 times during the cooking period. Sprinkle top, to taste, with paprika and chopped or flaked parsley. Let stand, covered, 10 minutes to finish the cooking. 5 servings.

*Milk can be heated 3 to 4 minutes in a measuring cup in the oven.

Potatoes au Gratin

These cheesy scalloped potatoes are delicious with steak or roast beef.

4   cups thinly sliced
    potatoes
$3/4$ cup milk
$1/4$ cup cream
3   tablespoons flour
1   teaspoon salt

$1/8$ teaspoon celery seeds
1   cup grated cheddar
    cheese
2   tablespoons butter
$1/2$ teaspoon paprika

Arrange half of the sliced potatoes in an 8 × 8-inch baking dish. Heat the milk and cream together in a 2-cup measure, uncovered, 2 minutes. Meanwhile combine the flour, salt, celery seeds and cheese and sprinkle half the mixture over potatoes. Arrange remaining potatoes on top. Sprinkle with remaining flour mixture. Pour hot milk and cream over potatoes. Do not stir. Dot with butter. Sprinkle with paprika. Cook, uncovered, 13 to 15 minutes or until potatoes are done. Let stand, covered, 10 minutes. 4 to 5 servings.

Potatoes Chantilly

A very elegant and tasty way to serve instant mashed potatoes for company dinner. The potatoes can be prepared and placed in a pie plate early in the morning, but do not refrigerate. Add topping when ready to serve.

4	servings of instant mashed potatoes	$^1/_2$	cup whipping cream
		$^1/_2$	cup grated sharp cheddar
1	tablespoon chopped parsley		
2	green onions, chopped fine	$^1/_2$	teaspoon salt
		$^1/_4$	teaspoon pepper

Prepare instant potatoes according to package directions. Add parsley and green onions. Mix well. Place in buttered 9-inch glass pie plate. Whip cream until stiff, fold in cheese, salt and pepper. Spread attractively over potatoes, as you would a meringue on lemon pie. Heat, uncovered, 4 minutes, and serve immediately. 4 servings.

Lemon Potatoes

A recipe from California, which is delightful when cooked in the microwave oven.

2	teaspoons butter or margarine	2	teaspoons lemon juice
3-4	potatoes, quartered	3	tablespoons grated Parmesan cheese
2	teaspoons grated lemon peel	1/2	teaspoon paprika

Melt butter in an 8 × 8-inch baking dish for 1 minute. Peel potatoes and cut into quarters, roll in the melted butter, add remaining ingredients. Cook, uncovered, 12 to 14 minutes. Let stand 2 minutes and serve.

Baked Sweet Potatoes or Yams

These bake well in a microwave oven proceeding in the same manner as for white potatoes, scrubbing, pricking with fork, placing on paper towel.

What is important, when more than one is baked, is to make sure they are all the same weight—again 7 or 8 ounces each is the best weight.

It is not advisable to cook more than 4 at a time.

1 sweet potato will cook in 6 to 8 minutes.
2 to 4 will take 15 to 18 minutes.

Glazed Sweet Potatoes or Yams

This is an ideal recipe to prepare early in the day. Keep on kitchen counter and reheat, covered, 3 minutes before serving.

4	medium sweet potatoes	1/8	teaspoon each cinnamon and allspice
1/2	cup firmly packed brown sugar	1/4	cup butter or margarine

Bake potatoes according to directions in preceding recipe. Let cool. Peel. Slice and arrange in a 1¹/₂-quart casserole. Mix brown sugar with spices and sprinkle evenly over the potatoes. Dot all over with butter. Cook, covered, 8 minutes, spooning glaze twice over potatoes during that period. 6 to 8 servings.

Sunshine Sweet Potatoes

Prepare ahead of time and keep refrigerated until ready to cook, or package and freeze for later use.

3	large oranges	¹/₂	teaspoon salt
4	sweet potatoes (7-8 ounces each)	1	tablespoon brandy or dry Madeira
4	teaspoons butter	¹/₈	teaspoon nutmeg or allspice
4	tablespoons brown or maple sugar		

Wash oranges and cut in half. Squeeze out juice and reserve. Remove membrane from shells, leaving them whole. Set aside.

Scrub sweet potatoes, prick with a fork and place on a paper towel in oven. Cook 18 minutes or until done. Peel while hot. Add butter, 2 tablespoons of the brown sugar and salt, whip until fluffy. Gradually add ¹/₂ to ³/₄ cup of the orange juice, while whipping. Fill orange shells with mixture.

Place in shallow glass dish or pie plate. Combine remaining sugar, brandy and nutmeg or allspice. Spoon an equal amount over top of each shell. If using immediately, cook, uncovered, 2 to 4 minutes or until hot. 6 servings.

Note If prepared and refrigerated, cook, covered, 10 minutes. If frozen, cook, covered, 20 minutes.

Gratiné Spinach

This can be prepared ahead of time. Do not refrigerate, keep on your kitchen counter. When ready to serve, reheat, covered, for 5 minutes.

2	lbs. spinach	1/2	teaspoon dry mustard
1	cup diced bread	1/4	cup grated cheese
3	tablespoons butter	3	tablespoons spinach
2	tablespoons flour		water
1	cup milk		salt, pepper to taste

This is done in 3 operations. First clean and then cook the spinach, covered, without water, for 5 minutes. Drain well, reserving 3 tablespoons of the water.

Next place bread in a glass pie plate with 1 tablespoon of the butter and cook, uncovered, for 5 to 8 minutes, stirring 3 to 4 times, or until browned. Set aside.

Then make sauce in a 2-cup measure. Melt remaining butter, 1 minute. Add remaining ingredients. Cook, uncovered, 3 to 4 minutes, stirring once. When sauce is creamy, pour over spinach placed in serving dish. Top with the buttered bread cubes. Heat, uncovered, 3 minutes. 6 servings.

Creamed Spinach

There is little time advantage when cooking spinach in the microwave oven, but the color and flavor are better than with any other method.

1	lb. (4 cups well packed) fresh spinach	2	tablespoons cream
			salt, pepper to taste
1	tablespoon flour		a pinch of nutmeg or
1	tablespoon butter		garlic powder

Clean spinach, cut coarsely or break up and pack into a 2-quart casserole. No water is needed, enough clings to leaves. Cook, covered with waxed paper, 5 minutes. Turn spinach over once.

Add remaining ingredients to cooked *undrained* spinach. Stir well. Cook 3 minutes, stirring once.

For plain buttered spinach, simply drain well, add butter, salt and pepper to taste, stir and heat 1 minute, stir again. 4 servings.

Note One half teaspoon grated lemon rind added to the butter gives a very tasty flavor.

Creamy Onion Spinach

This is inspired by the famous sour cream – onion soup dip. Quick and easy.

1 *package (10 ounces) frozen chopped spinach*
1/2 *cup commercial sour cream*
3 *tablespoons dry onion soup mix*

Place spinach in a 1-quart casserole, ice side up. Cook, covered, 6 minutes, turning once. When almost defrosted, stir in sour cream and onion soup mix. Cook, covered, 1 minute. Let stand, covered, 2 minutes. Stir and serve. 3 to 4 servings.

The Family of Squash

There are many varieties of squash which can be quickly cooked in the microwave oven with the advantage, over other methods, that each type keeps its delicate, elusive flavor and its attractive color.

I have given the basic cooking directions as well as my favorite serving suggestions.

Stuffed Acorn Squash

Choose a squash weighing between 1 and 2 lbs. Scrub. Leave whole. Using metal skewers, pierce holes right through squash in several places. Place on glass plate. Cook, uncovered, 8 to 12 minutes, depending on size. Let stand 3 minutes. Cut in half lengthwise, remove seeds and stringy fibers.

For Filling: While the squash is cooking combine 4 teaspoons soft butter, $1/2$ teaspoon salt, 1 tablespoon fresh ginger root grated, $1/8$ teaspoon each cinnamon and allspice, 1 tablespoon honey, 2 tablespoons brown sugar. Fill each cavity with mixture. Return to oven 2 minutes. Turn plate and cook 2 minutes more. Add 1 tablespoon brandy to each half. Serve.

Butternut Squash

Choose one that weighs 1 to $1 1/2$ lbs. Large ones are too watery to cook successfully. Scrub. Make 2 slits on sides of the neck with knife, then make 2 more slits in body of squash. Place on plate. Cook, uncovered, 8 to 12 minutes, depending on size. Let stand 5 minutes. Cut in half lengthwise. Discard seeds. Scoop squash out of shell.

Serving Variations: Mash squash with grated rind of 1 orange, juice of $1/2$ orange, 1 teaspoon salt, $1/2$ teaspoon pepper, 3 tablespoons chopped parsley, 2 tablespoons molasses or maple syrup or brown sugar. Beat thoroughly. Taste for seasoning. Place on serving dish and reheat, uncovered, 1 minute. For a different flavor: Replace orange juice and rind by an equal quantity of lemon. When prepared with lemon, you can also add 2 medium-sized unpeeled tomatoes, diced.

Summer Squash

Summer squash should be at most 1 pound to be cooked successfully.

Take 2 to 3 yellow summer squash about 1 pound each. Scrub them, cut stem ends, then cut crosswise into 1/2-inch slices. Place slices in a 1 1/2-2 quart casserole. Add 2 tablespoons consommé or use 1 beef or chicken cube broken up into 2 tablespoons water. When using cubes, heat first in oven, 2 minutes. Stir the mixture, pour over squash. Cook, covered, 6 to 8 minutes or until tender. Drain well. Add butter, chopped chives or green onions, salt and pepper to taste. You could also sprinkle with lots of parsley or a generous portion of grated cheddar or Parmesan. Reheat, uncovered, 1 minute.

Stuffed Tomatoes

A dish for the fall when vegetables are plentiful. Vary the stuffing to suit your fancy.

6 to 8	medium tomatoes	2 to 3	tablespoons chopped green pepper
1	teaspoon salt		
1/2	teaspoon thyme	1	can (14 ounces) drained corn niblets
2	teaspoons sugar		
2	tablespoons butter or margarine	1/4	cup crushed potato chips or crackers
3	green onions, chopped fine		grated cheese (optional)

Cut off top of tomatoes and hollow out inside with a spoon. (Save inside to use in salad or soup.) Place hollowed out tomatoes on serving dish. Sprinkle with salt, thyme and sugar. Place butter, onions and green pepper in a glass dish. Cook, uncovered, 2 minutes, stirring once. Stir in corn and crushed chips or crackers. Mix well and spoon into tomatoes. Sprinkle top with grated cheese. Cook, uncovered, 5 minutes or until hot. 6 servings.

Bacon Crumb Tomatoes

Tomato and bacon are excellent companions at any time.

4 *medium or large firm*	½ *cup dried*
tomatoes	*breadcrumbs*
3 to 4 *slices bacon*	¼ *teaspoon thyme*
2 *tablespoons bacon*	
drippings	

Cut the unpeeled tomatoes in half crosswise and arrange on glass pie plate, cut side up. Sprinkle with salt and pepper to taste. Place bacon on a pie plate, cover with paper towel and cook 2 to 4 minutes or until bacon is crisped. Remove bacon from fat, set aside to cool. Measure 2 tablespoons of the bacon drippings and place in a bowl. Add the breadcrumbs and thyme, stir well, sprinkle some over each tomato half, then top with crumbled bacon. Cook, uncovered, 4 minutes or until hot. 4 servings.

Buttered Tomatoes

Tomatoes can be heated right on a serving dish and they heat so quickly that a cover is not necessary. A true last minute vegetable.

4 to 6 *very firm tomatoes*	½ *teaspoon pepper*
3 *tablespoons butter*	¼ *teaspoon basil or*
1 *tablespoon sugar*	*marjoram*

To peel the tomatoes, place in microwave oven and heat for 15 to 20 seconds. Let stand 10 minutes and the skin will come off easily. Press gently to extract the seeds. Cut each tomato in four.

Melt butter in a 1-quart casserole, 30 seconds. Place the tomatoes in the butter. Stir the remaining ingredients together. Sprinkle over the tomatoes. Cook, uncovered, 2 to 3 minutes. Serve as soon as ready. 4 servings.

Cucumber and Tomato Casserole

Unusual, light and pleasant, served at a summer barbecue. This is like a fresh vegetable sauce.

2 medium size cucumbers	1/2 teaspoon sugar
4 medium size tomatoes	4 soda crackers, crumbled
3 tablespoons butter	juice of 1/2 a lemon
1 to 2 teaspoons chopped fresh dill	salt and pepper to taste

Pare cucumbers and remove seeds, peel tomatoes (see previous recipe), dice both. Place butter, dill, sugar and crackers in 1 1/2-quart casserole. Add cucumbers and tomatoes. Cook, uncovered, 5 minutes, stirring twice. Add lemon juice, salt and pepper. 6 servings.

Curried Tomatoes

Surround with a crown of parsleyed rice; a pleasant light lunch.

4 unpeeled tomatoes, cut in half	1 small onion, chopped fine
2 teaspoons sugar	1-2 teaspoons curry powder
2 tablespoons butter	

Place the tomatoes on a glass pie plate, cut side up. Sprinkle each with some of the sugar. Melt the butter in a measuring cup, 30 seconds, add the onion and curry powder. Stir together. Cook, covered, 4 minutes. Pour this butter on the tomatoes. Cook, uncovered, 3 minutes. 4 servings.

Turnips

Turnips can be cooked shredded or thinly sliced, diced or cut in small wedges. The small white or purple turnips can be peeled and cooked whole. There is no smell of any kind and cooked turnips have a very nice color and flavor cooked in the microwave oven.

Peel turnips immediately before cooking, removing a thicker peel than for other root vegetables. Cut to taste as indicated above. You will need a 1½-quart casserole for about 3 cups turnip. A smaller quantity can cook in a smaller dish. Add ¼ cup water and 1 teaspoon sugar. Cook, covered, 15 to 22 minutes, depending on the size of the pieces. Stir turnip and turn dish twice during cooking period. Let stand 3 minutes.

Sauce for Turnips

Place in a small dish 2 tablespoons butter, 1 small onion, chopped fine and ¼ teaspoon freshly ground pepper. Cook, uncovered, 3 to 4 minutes or until brown. Stir well, add the grated rind of ½ a lemon. Cook another minute. Pour over cooked turnip before the standing time. Reheat 30 seconds if necessary.

Variation 1   Add 1 cup peeled and diced apples to 2 cups grated turnip. Cook as given for turnip. After standing period, add butter, salt, pepper to taste, mash or pass through a sieve or blend 1 minute. Place purée in serving dish. Sprinkle top with 1 tablespoon brown sugar. Cook, uncovered, 1 minute. Serve.

Variation 2   Cook 3 slices of bacon according to direction (see p.138). Remove from oven to cool. Place in small glass dish, 4 tablespoons cream cheese, 3 tablespoons sour cream or rich cream or fresh lemon juice, chives or parsley to taste. Heat in oven, covered, 2 minutes. Stir until creamy, add crumbled bacon, mix well. Cook, covered, another 2 minutes. Pour over cooked turnip.

Zucchini Italian

In Bologna they have a delectable way to prepare zucchini. Served usually with steamed shrimps.

1 lb. small zucchini	1/2 teaspoon salt
4 stalks celery	1/4 teaspoon oregano or basil
1 can (8-ounces) tomato sauce	2 tablespoons vegetable oil
1/2 teaspoon sugar	2 to 4 tablespoons grated Parmesan cheese
1/8 teaspoon garlic powder	

Scrub zucchini, slice 1/4-inch thick. Slice celery in long slivers. Mix both vegetables in a 1 1/2-quart casserole. Combine tomato sauce with sugar, garlic powder, salt, oregano or basil and vegetable oil. Pour over zucchini. Sprinkle with cheese. Cook, covered, 7 minutes. Stir for a minute. Cook 6 to 7 minutes longer. Let stand 5 minutes before serving. If you prefer a thicker sauce, stir in 1/2 cup fine breadcrumbs when cooking is finished. It will thicken during the standing period. 4 servings.

14. Cereals, Rice and Pasta

Breakfast Cereals

Cooking cereals, whether instant or regular, in the microwave oven is both simple and convenient.

Quick-cooking or instant cereals are most convenient and the job is so easy that anyone in the family can prepare his own hot cereal on chilly winter mornings. The ingredients are simply measured right into the serving bowl or dish, mixed with water and heated to bring to a boil and then left to stand for 3 to 5 minutes.

If the cereal is not quick cooking, it should be covered, brought to a boil and then cooked for the time given on the package. This way it is not a time saver, but definitely a flavor saver.

As cereals tend to boil over quickly, use a larger bowl than usual and if you are preparing a large quantity of cereal, use a casserole dish.

A real time-saver is to make a large quantity of creamy old-fashioned oatmeal the night before, refrigerate and reheat in individual servings for breakfast the following day.

Hot Quick-Cooking Cereal

³/₄ cup water	pinch salt
¹/₃ cup quick-cooking rolled oats or cream of wheat	

In a cereal bowl, combine all the ingredients. Cook, uncovered, 2 minutes or until mixture boils, stirring once. Let stand 2 minutes. Serves 1.

When preparing more than one serving, the cereal can be prepared in a casserole dish and then served in individual dishes.

For 3 servings: Cook 5 minutes. Let stand 2 minutes.
For 4 servings: Cook 6 to 7 minutes. Let stand 3 minutes.

Note Cooked as above, texture will be creamy. For a thicker texture, heat water first to boiling then stir in cereal. Cook, covered, 1 to 3 minutes per serving. Stir and let stand 2 minutes.

Creamy Old-Fashioned Oatmeal

This is so easily and quickly prepared that there is little excuse not to serve the best porridge. The following quantity will serve 4 to 6.

3   *cups water or half water, half milk*
1¹/₂   *cups old-fashioned or regular oatmeal*
¹/₂   *teaspoon salt*

Place the water or milk and water in a 2-quart casserole. Heat, uncovered, 8 minutes or until boiling. Stir in oatmeal and salt. Cook, uncovered, 4 to 6 minutes, stirring twice. Let stand 5 minutes and serve.

To reheat, place desired portion in bowl, add milk or cream to taste. Heat, uncovered, 1 to 2 minutes or until hot.

Red River Cereal

3   *cups water or half*   ¹/₂ *teaspoon salt*
      water, half milk   1   *teaspoon brown sugar*
1¹/₄ *cups Red River Cereal*

Place the water or milk and water in a 2-quart casserole. Heat, uncovered, 8 minutes or until boiling. Stir in Red River Cereal, sugar and salt. Cook, uncovered, 4 to 6 minutes, stirring twice. Let stand 9 minutes and serve.

To reheat, place desired portion in bowl, add milk or cream to taste. Heat, uncovered, 1 to 2 minutes or until hot.

Rice or Pasta

Rice is very easy to cook in the microwave oven although it is fair to point out that little time is saved as you are actually just rehydrating it. There is, though, the definite convenience factor of being able to use the same dish to cook and serve in and often to cook a complete rice or pasta dish such as rice and beef casserole or even spaghetti and meat sauce.

It is important to start cooking any rice or pasta in boiling water —it is quicker to boil the water conventionally but it can be done in the oven. This makes the cooking period fairly short and allows a longer standing time, very useful when you are making a sauce or other foods to serve with the rice or pasta.

One of the real advantages afforded by the microwave oven is the ease with which you can reheat rice or pasta. I find it simple to keep a quantity of cooked rice in my refrigerator so that I have it on hand when needed either for part of a rice dish or as an accompaniment to the meat or fish course.

Cooking Regular Short and Long Grain Rice

1 cup rice	$^1/_2$ teaspoon salt
2 cups water for short grain	1 teaspoon vegetable oil or butter
$2^1/_4$ cups water for long grain	

Pour required water into a 2-quart casserole. Cook, uncovered, 8 to 10 minutes or until boiling. Stir in the rice, salt and vegetable oil or butter, stir well. Cook, covered, 9 minutes for short grain, 10 minutes for long grain. Let stand, covered, for 10 minutes. Fluff with a fork before serving. Yield: 3 cups.

To Reheat Rice

For 2-3 cups cold cooked rice, cook in a dish, covered, for $2^1/_2$ minutes. Stir well and cook again for 50 seconds.

Note Pasta can be reheated in the same way.

Quick-Cooking Rice

Pour 1¹/₂ cups water into a 1-quart casserole. Cook about 5 to 6 minutes or until boiling. Add 1¹/₂ cups rice, ¹/₂ teaspoon salt. Stir well. Let stand, covered, for the time indicated on package. Fluff with a fork. Season and serve. Makes 3³/₄ cups.

Vegetable Rice Pilaff

Serve as a luncheon casserole or as a vegetable in place of potatoes.

¹/₃	cup butter or margarine	¹/₄	cup chopped parsley
1¹/₂	cups uncooked long grain rice	3	cups water
		2	chicken bouillon cubes
1	large onion, chopped finely	¹/₄	teaspoon thyme or tarragon
¹/₂	cup diced celery		

Place in a 2-quart casserole the butter or margarine, rice, onion and celery. Cook, uncovered, 5 minutes, stir well, add remaining ingredients. Cook, covered, 10 minutes, stirring twice. Let stand, covered, 10 minutes, to finish cooking. 6 servings.

Confetti Rice

This recipe is full of color and flavor. Peas or other vegetables can be used, or leftovers. Perfect with pork, veal or lamb chops.

2	cups boiling water	1	cup or ¹/₂ box frozen green peas
1	teaspoon salt		
1	cup long grain rice	1	tablespoon butter or margarine
2	carrots, peeled and shredded		fresh parsley, chives or dill to taste
¹/₂	cup finely diced celery		
4	green onions, chopped fine		

Place all the ingredients in a 2-quart casserole. Stir well. Cook, covered, 10 minutes, stirring once. Let stand 10 minutes. Stir, taste for seasoning. 4 servings.

Vegetarian Casserole

If you really want some meat at each meal a cup or two of leftover cooked chicken or turkey can be added to the rice when cooked. This casserole can be prepared, cooked, then refrigerated, but shorten baking time to 10 minutes if this is done. Finish cooking when ready to serve.

1	*cup uncooked long grain rice*	6	*chopped green onions, with tops*
1/4	*cup margarine grated rind and juice of half a lemon*	1	*teaspoon salt*
		1	*10-ounce package frozen, chopped spinach, thawed*
1/8	*teaspoon garlic powder*		
1/8	*teaspoon nutmeg*	1/2	*cup chopped parsley*
		1	*egg*
		1	*cup milk*

Cook rice according to directions on page 220.

Add to cooked rice the margarine, lemon juice and rind, garlic powder, nutmeg, green onions, salt, spinach and parsley. Mix thoroughly with a fork. Turn mixture into a 2-quart glass casserole. Beat egg and milk together, pour over mixture.

Bake, uncovered, for 15 minutes, or until custard just begins to firm, turning casserole every 4 minutes. Let stand 10 minutes. Stir lightly and serve. 6 servings.

Rice and Beef Casserole

It is advisable to keep a pound of ground beef in your freezer at all times for something like this casserole in which a pound of ground beef goes a long way. Rice can also be precooked and at the ready in your refrigerator.

1	cup cooked long or short grain rice	$^1/_2$	teaspoon cumin powder or allspice
1	tablespoon butter or margarine	$^1/_2$	teaspoon thyme
1	pound ground beef	1	cup commercial sour cream
2	cups diced celery	1	teaspoon paprika
2	large onions, chopped fine	2	tomatoes, cut in wedges
2	cloves garlic, chopped fine	$^1/_2$	cup grated cheddar cheese
1	teaspoon salt		

Place butter or margarine in a 2-quart casserole for 30 seconds. Add beef, cook 5 minutes, stirring 2 to 3 times to break up meat. Add celery, onions and garlic. Cook, covered, 8 minutes, stirring three times.

Combine salt, cumin or allspice, thyme and sour cream. Add to meat mixture along with the cooked rice. Mix thoroughly. Sprinkle with paprika. Place tomato wedges on top of casserole mixture. Cook, covered, 5 minutes. Stir well, sprinkle cheese on top. Cook, uncovered, another 4 minutes. Let stand 10 minutes before serving. 6 to 8 servings.

Pasta

Macaroni, Spaghetti, Noodles

Place 8 ounces of uncooked pasta in a 3-quart casserole. If you use wide pasta such as lasagna, use a 9 × 5-inch loaf dish. Add 2 teaspoons salt and 6 cups boiling water. (It is quicker to boil this quantity of water on stove than in the microwave oven.) Stir well and cook, uncovered, 5 to 6 minutes, stirring once. Let stand, covered, 10 to 12 minutes. Drain thoroughly before serving.

To serve plain, add butter and salt and pepper to taste to drained pasta. Return dish to oven, covered, and reheat 2 minutes. Serve.

Macaroni and Cheese

Everyone's favorite and just as easy and quick to cook as the pre-packaged type. You can vary the topping to your own taste.

2	cups elbow or fancy macaroni	1	teaspoon salt
2	tablespoons butter	2	green onions, chopped
2	tablespoons flour	2	cups grated cheddar cheese
2	cups milk		

Cook and drain macaroni according to directions at beginning of chapter and place in a 2-quart casserole. While it is standing, melt the butter in a 4-cup measure, 30 seconds. Add the flour, stir until well blended. Add the milk. Stir and cook, uncovered, 3 minutes. Stir well, cook another minute or until sauce is bubbling. Add salt and green onions. Stir in cheese until melted. Pour over cooked macaroni. Mix well.

You might like to vary the proportions of macaroni and sauce. 4-6 servings.

Topping Suggestions: Sprinkle with paprika or cover top completely with sliced fresh tomatoes. Mix together $1/2$ teaspoon sugar, 1 tablespoon vegetable oil, pour over tomatoes. In either case, cook, uncovered, another 3 minutes.

Two-Cheese Macaroni

Diced and grated cheddar cheese combine to make a truly unusual macaroni.

8	ounces elbow macaroni	1	small onion, diced
1/2	cup grated strong cheddar cheese	2	tablespoons flour
1/2 to	1 cup diced medium cheddar cheese	2	cups milk
		1/2	cup cream
2	tablespoons butter		salt, pepper to taste
1/4	cup celery, diced	1	tablespoon butter
		1/2	cup bread, cubed.

Cook and drain macaroni, according to directions on page 224. Place half the macaroni in a 1½-quart casserole, sprinkle with half of the grated cheese and half of the diced cheese. Add the rest of the macaroni and cheese in the same manner.

Melt 2 tablespoons butter 30 seconds in a 4-cup measure, stir in the celery and onion. Cook, uncovered, 5 minutes. Stir well, add the flour, mix thoroughly and stir in the milk and cream. Cook, uncovered, 5 minutes, or until creamy. Salt and pepper to taste. Pour over macaroni, but do not mix.

Melt the remaining tablespoon of butter in a glass pie plate, add the bread cubes, stir until coated with butter. Pour over macaroni. Cook, uncovered, 5 minutes, turning dish 3 times. 4-6 servings.

Macaroni Hélène

Interesting and different and very easy to make.

8	ounces elbow macaroni	3	teaspoons butter
¹/₂	lb. strong or mild cheddar cheese, grated	1	cup commercial sour cream
			paprika to taste

Cook and drain macaroni according to directions on page 224. Place half the cooked macaroni in a 1¹/₂-quart casserole, sprinkle with half the cheese, top with half the sour cream and dot with half the butter. Repeat procedure with the remaining ingredients. Sprinkle with paprika. Cook, uncovered, 10 minutes, turning dish 3 times. 4 servings.

Green Sauce Pasta

In Italy, Cilantro or Italian parsley is used. Its flavor is unusual and interesting. It can be grown in your garden or balcony or sometimes found in special markets. The more generally available green curly parsley, when fresh, is equally good in this sauce.

8	ounces pasta of your choice	1	cup fresh parsley, chopped
¹/₂	cup butter	¹/₂	cup grated Parmesan or medium cheddar cheese
1	clove garlic, minced		

Cook pasta and drain according to directions on page 224. While pasta is standing, melt butter in serving dish for 30 seconds. Add garlic and cook, uncovered, 5 minutes. Add well drained pasta, parsley, cheese, salt and pepper to taste. Toss together and serve. 4-6 servings.

Florentine Pasta

Cottage cheese and grated Parmesan combine to give a special texture and flavor to the pasta and can be prepared while the noodles are cooking. In Italy this is served in the spring with a big dish of tiny fresh green peas for an interesting lunch.

8	ounces egg noodles	1/2	cup grated Parmesan cheese
1	cup creamy cottage cheese		salt, pepper to taste
		1/4	cup butter

Cook and drain noodles according to directions on page 224. Cream together the cottage cheese and Parmesan cheese until smooth. Add salt and pepper to taste. Melt the butter in the serving dish for 30 seconds. Toss in the noodles and the cheese. Toss well and serve. 4-6 servings.

Spaghetti and Meat Sauce

A strong or medium cheddar or a processed cheese will give a different taste to this sauce, so one can easily vary according to taste or mood. Make the sauce while the spaghetti is standing.

2 to 3	cups (4 to 8 ounces) spaghetti	1	bay leaf
1/2 to 1	lb. ground beef or pork	1	can (10 ounces) tomato soup
1	large onion, chopped	3/4	soup can water
1	green pepper, diced	1	teaspoon salt
1/2	teaspoon oregano or basil	1/4	teaspoon pepper
		1/2	lb. cheese of your choice, cubed

Cook and drain spaghetti according to directions at beginning of chapter. In a 2-quart casserole, combine beef or pork, onion, green pepper, oregano or basil and bay leaf. Cook, covered, 10 minutes, stirring 3 times. Add tomato soup, water, salt and pepper, cook, uncovered, 5 minutes. Stir in cheese cubes, let stand, covered, 5 minutes. Pour over spaghetti. 4 servings.

"Alfredo" Noodles

Made famous by the well-known Roman chef of the same name.

8	ounces of fine noodles	1	cup (1/2 lb.) unsalted
4	cups boiling water		butter*
1	teaspoon salt	1	cup grated Parmesan
			cheese

Cook and drain noodles according to directions in preceding recipe. Place in large bowl, add butter, cut in slices, and the cheese. Mix quickly and lightly with 2 forks so that butter and cheese melt to a creamy sauce. Return to oven and cook for 30 seconds. Stir again quickly and serve. 4-6 servings.

*The original recipe calls for this quantity but 1/2 cup (1/4 lb.) could be sufficient if preferred.

Leghorn Spaghetti

This sauce is at its best made with olive oil. When leeks are not available, substitute 2 more medium onions.

8	ounces spaghetti	2	leeks, thinly sliced
1/4 to 1/2	cup olive or vegetable oil	1	can (26 ounces) tomatoes
2	carrots, peeled and grated	1	tablespoon sugar
2	onions, thinly sliced	2	teaspoons salt
		1	teaspoon basil

Cook and drain spaghetti according to directions on page 224. Heat the oil for 30 seconds in a 2-quart casserole. Add the carrots, onions and leeks. Stir well. Cook, covered, 5 minutes. Stir, add remaining ingredients. Cook, covered, 20 minutes. Taste for seasoning and serve over spaghetti.

15. Desserts and Dessert Sauces

What do we have for dessert? This is no longer a problem when the microwave oven is there to help.

Custards, many types of puddings, creams or combined fruit desserts, sweet sauces, etc., can all be very successfully cooked in your oven. Fruits and fruit desserts cooked in the microwave oven retain their delicious fresh fruit flavor. Learn to understand their cooking time and the amount of sugar used, as both vary depending on ripeness of fruit and variety. I always check them at half time, then I add sugar or syrup or add to or subtract from the cooking period. Remember, too, that during the 5 or 10-minute standing period the fruits keep on cooking.

When cooking cut fruit, be sure that pieces are uniformly sized and well spaced in the baking dish.

You can use fresh, frozen and canned fruits in a variety of ways; they cook quickly and there are never any problems of burning or sticking to the pan. Fruit desserts also are easy to rewarm if they have cooled between cooking and serving, so dessert can be made earlier in the day if you find it more convenient.

Caramel Pudding

The well-known French Flan Caramel. Light and creamy when done in the microwave oven.

1¹/₂ cups milk	a pinch of salt
¹/₂ cup rich cream	1 teaspoon vanilla
1 cup sugar*	¹/₂ teaspoon almond
4 tablespoons cornstarch	extract

Pour 1¹/₄ cups of the milk and all the cream into a 2-quart casserole. Cook, uncovered, 6 to 7 minutes or until scalding but not boiling, stirring twice. Remove from oven. Keep covered.

Place sugar in a 2-quart glass casserole, cook, uncovered, 5 to 6 minutes. Stir well, cook 4 to 6 minutes longer, stirring often, until sugar is golden brown.

Pour the hot milk mixture into the sugar, heat 2 minutes, uncovered, stirring once. Heat until all the sugar is melted. Blend the cornstarch with the remaining ¹/₄ cup of milk. Stir into hot milk. Stir in salt. Heat 2 to 3 minutes, stirring three times. Stir in vanilla and almond extract. Let stand 10 minutes. Stir well. Pour into dish or individual custard cups, cover and refrigerate. Serve cold.

*Do not use demerara sugar.

Fruits Belle-Aurore

A warm, creamy sweet sauce poured over mixed fresh fruits, served very cold. A creation of the well-known French chef Abelard.

2 tablespoons butter	2 to 3 cups fresh peeled and sliced fruits of your choice
2 tablespoons flour	
1 cup cream, light or heavy, to taste	
	3 tablespoons brandy
¹/₂ cup sugar	1 tablespoon sugar
1 teaspoon orange flower water	

Place butter in a 1-quart casserole or a 2-cup measure and heat 1 minute to melt.

Stir in the flour, mix well, add the cream and sugar. Stir to mix. Cook, uncovered, 1 minute. Stir thoroughly, cook 1 to 2 minutes longer, stirring twice or until sauce is creamy.

Add orange flower water (purchase at drugstore or food specialty shops).

Use one fruit or a mixture. Canned fruits, well drained, can be used but the result is not as delicate in flavor and texture. Sprinkle fruits with the brandy and the tablespoon of sugar.

Pour the hot sauce over all. Do not mix. When available, sprinkle top with fresh mint leaves, left whole (off the stem) as a flavoring. Serve the fruit well chilled.

Peach Custard

I bake this in my serving dish, a blue ceramic bowl.*

2	cups sliced fresh or canned peaches	1/4	cup flour
3	eggs	1	teaspoon vanilla
1/2	cup sugar	1	cup heavy cream
1/2	teaspoon ground nutmeg	1/2	cup dry vermouth or dry white wine

Peel the fresh peaches or drain the canned type. Slice into a 1½-quart dish.

Place the remaining ingredients in a bowl. Mix thoroughly with a whisk or rotary beater. Pour over the peaches. Bake uncovered, 8 to 9 minutes, turning dish around four times. Let stand 15 minutes. Serve at room temperature or refrigerate until well chilled.

For a variation, coat top with black currant jelly, melted 40 seconds in the microwave oven.

*See note on earthenware dishes on page 16.

Chocolate Bread Pudding

For a special occasion, serve with brandy poured over each portion, and topped with mounds of sweetened whipped cream.

3	tablespoons butter	1	cup light cream
1	square (1 ounce) unsweetened chocolate	1¹/₂	cups soft bread crumbs
¹/₂	cup sugar	¹/₄	cup slivered toasted almonds
3	eggs		

Combine butter and chocolate in a 1-quart casserole dish, cook 2 minutes, stirring once. When chocolate is all melted, mix well, stir in the sugar.

Beat the eggs with a rotary beater until fluffy. Add to chocolate mixture. Stir, add cream. Stir and cook, uncovered, 2 minutes 30 seconds, stirring twice. Let stand 5 minutes. Stir in the breadcrumbs and toasted almonds (toast almonds in the microwave oven—see p. 284). Cook, uncovered, 2 minutes, turning dish halfway once. Let stand 10 minutes. Serve warm.

Creamy Rice Pudding

A pudding mix and quick-cooking rice team up to make a creamy rice pudding in a few minutes. It is superb served with maple syrup and brandy sauce.

1	cup quick-cooking rice		pie filling
1	package (3¹/₄ ounces) vanilla pudding and	3	cups milk or 2 cups milk, 1 cup water

Stir all ingredients together thoroughly in a 1¹/₂-quart casserole. Cover with waxed paper. Cook 10 minutes, stirring 3 times during the cooking period. Taste rice and if a little hard, cook another 3 minutes. Stir 3 to 4 times while pudding is cooling.

To make sauce: Add 3 tablespoons brandy to 1 cup maple syrup. Heat 2 minutes.

Tapioca Pudding

Although you do not save too much time here, the deliciously light and fluffy texture cannot be obtained in conventional cooking.

3 tablespoons quick-cooking tapioca	1/2 cup light cream
5 tablespoons sugar	1 egg, separated
a pinch of salt	1/2 teaspoon almond flavoring
1 1/2 cups milk	

In a 1 1/2-quart casserole, combine tapioca, 3 tablespoons of the sugar, salt, milk, cream and the egg yolk. Mix well. Let stand 5 minutes. Then cook, uncovered, 2 minutes. Stir well, cook 2 minutes longer or until mixture bubbles vigorously.

Remove from oven, add almond flavoring. Let stand 3 minutes. Stir well.

Meanwhile, beat the egg white until frothy, add the remaining 2 tablespoons sugar, one at a time. Beat until stiff. Fold into the hot tapioca mixture. Let stand 10 minutes. Serve warm or cold.

Easy Caramel Bread Pudding

Ready in 6 minutes. Vary by using vanilla or chocolate pudding. Leftover cakes or sweet rolls can replace the bread.

1 package (3 1/4 ounces) caramel pudding and pie filling mix	1/2 cup raisins
2 cups milk	1 cup cubed white bread without crust

In a 1-quart casserole combine all ingredients, stirring all to mix well. Cook, uncovered, 6 to 7 minutes, or until mixture boils, stirring 3 times during the last 3-4 minutes of cooking. Serve warm or cooled.

Snow Eggs

Keep this recipe in mind for an elegant and interesting topping.

1½	cups milk	¼	cup sugar
½	cup light cream		a pinch of salt
¼	cup sugar	½	teaspoon vanilla
1	teaspoon vanilla	3	egg yolks
2	egg whites		

Place in a 1½-quart casserole the milk, cream and the first ¼ cup of sugar. Mix well. Heat, uncovered, 3 minutes or until mixture boils. Add the 1 teaspoon of vanilla.

Meanwhile, beat egg whites with remaining ¼ cup of sugar and pinch of salt, until stiff. Add the remaining ½ teaspoon vanilla to beaten whites. Drop 6 tablespoons of the mixture into the boiling milk to form six mounds. Heat, uncovered, 1 minute 30 seconds. Remove meringue with slotted spoon into a serving dish. Repeat this until all the egg whites are cooked. To the remaining milk, add the well-beaten egg yolks. Cook 2 to 3 minutes, stirring very thoroughly, continuing as it starts bubbling around the edges of the dish. Beware of overcooking as it will curdle. Let stand 5 minutes. Stir well, pour over beaten egg whites. Cool, then refrigerate or serve warm.

Chocolate Rum Mousse

Use as individual puddings or as a pie filling in a chocolate cookie crumb crust.

2	squares (1 ounce each) semi-sweet chocolate	3	eggs, separated a pinch of salt
⅓	cup sugar	1	cup milk
1	envelope unflavored gelatine	3	tablespoons rum
		⅓	cup sugar
		1	cup whipping cream

Melt chocolate, uncovered, in a 4-cup measure for 2 minutes. Blend in the sugar and gelatine, mixed together. Then beat in egg yolks and salt. Stir in milk and rum. Cook, uncovered, 4 minutes or until slightly thickened, stirring 3 times. Cool. Beat egg whites until foamy. Gradually add the $1/3$ cup sugar and beat until stiff. Fold beaten egg whites into cooled chocolate mixture.

Whip cream in a large bowl until stiff and fold the chocolate mixture into it. Spoon mixture into 6 to 8 individual dessert cups or into an 8 or 9-inch crumb crust. Refrigerate 3 to 6 hours.

Fudgy Pudding Cake

This is good served hot with cream or ice cream.

2	cups water	$1/2$	teaspoon salt
1	cup flour	1	teaspoon vanilla
$3/4$	cup sugar	$1/2$	teaspoon nutmeg
$1/2$	cup chopped nuts or seedless raisins	2	tablespoons vegetable oil
2	tablespoons unsweetened cocoa	$1/2$	cup milk
1	teaspoon baking powder	$3/4$	cup sugar
		$1/4$	cup unsweetened cocoa

Measure water in a 4-cup measure and heat, uncovered, 4 to 5 minutes or until water boils.

Meanwhile, in a 3-quart casserole, combine the flour, the first $3/4$ cup sugar, the nuts or raisins, the cocoa, baking powder and salt. Add vanilla, nutmeg, vegetable oil and milk. Stir until thoroughly mixed. Spread evenly in the dish.

Combine remaining sugar and cocoa, sprinkle on top of cake. Pour boiling water over all. Cook, uncovered, 9 to 10 minutes, turning dish 4 to 5 times.

Boiled Apples

Do not be deceived by the name or the simplicity of the recipe. It is delicious and one of the famous Shaker desserts.

6	red cooking apples, unpeeled, uncored apple juice or water	1/2	cup sugar

Place apples in a 10-inch CORNING WARE skillet or an oblong baking dish. Add enough apple juice or water to measure 1/2-inch deep. Sprinkle sugar over apples. Do not cover. Cook, 5 minutes, turn apples over carefully with a perforated spoon, cook 2 or 3 minutes. Apples must not break, but should be just puffed and tender. Remove to serving dish with perforated spoon.

Continue to cook syrup 8 minutes, uncovered. Pour over apples. Serve hot or cold.

Applesauce

This is the very first thing I made in my microwave oven. I was so pleased with the result and ease of work, that I never ceased from that moment to try and create and adapt all kinds of foods to microwave oven cooking.

4	cups (4 to 5) apples peeled and sliced	1	tablespoon fresh lemon juice
1/2	cup apple juice or water	1/3	cup sugar

Place apples and apple and lemon juice in 1¹/₂-quart casserole. Cover with waxed paper. Cook, 6 to 8 minutes or until apples are tender.

Add sugar, beat with whisk until creamy or whirl in blender — each method gives a different texture.

More or less sugar can be used to suit personal taste. Yields 3 cups.

Variations: Replace apple juice or water with cranberry juice, *or* the apple and lemon juice with an equal quantity of orange juice or white wine. You could also replace the sugar with an equal quantity of honey, brown sugar or maple sugar.

Baked Apples

Cooking time will vary slightly with size, shape and starting temperature of apples. A stuffed apple will take a few minutes more since there is more food volume to heat and cook. My favorite variety for flavor and texture is the McIntosh apple.

4	medium baking apples	¹/₈ teaspoon of either
4	tablespoons brown or white sugar	mace, nutmeg, ground cardamom, crushed
2	tablespoons butter or margarine	coriander seeds or cinnamon

Wash and core apples. Place in a circle in an 8 × 8-inch baking dish or, if you prefer, in 4 individual custard cups. Place a tablespoon of sugar and 1 teaspoon butter in each cavity. Sprinkle each apple with your choice of flavoring. Cover dish with waxed paper. Cook 6 to 8 minutes or until apples are just tender. Let stand 10 to 15 minutes before serving.

1 apple in custard cup will cook in 3 minutes
2 apples in custard cups will cook in 4 minutes

If more than four apples are required, cook in batches of four. Larger quantities at a time do not cook as successfully.

Normandy Apples

Serve well chilled. A perfect dessert after a rich or heavy meal.

5 apples, peeled juice and grated rind of 1 lemon	2 tablespoons apricot or plum jam
3/4 cup sugar	2 tablespoons dry sherry
1/4 cup water	

Choose apples of equal size. Peel and cut into quarters. Stir with the lemon juice.

Place the sugar and water in a 12 × 8-inch glass baking dish. Cook, uncovered, 6 minutes, stirring twice.

Stir in the apples and lemon rind. Cook, uncovered, 8 to 9 minutes, stirring once. Stop cooking as soon as the apples are tender — they must retain their shape. Using a perforated spoon, remove apples to a serving dish.

Add the jam and sherry to the syrup remaining in dish. Cook 10 minutes, uncovered, stirring twice. Pour over the apples. Cool, then refrigerate until serving time.

Caramel Baked Apples

The touch of rum or brandy makes these quite special.

4 baking apples	2 tablespoons butter
1/2 cup any cream	2 tablespoons rum or
2/3 cup corn syrup or maple syrup	brandy or 1 teaspoon vanilla

Wash and core apples. Place in a circle in a 10-inch CORNING WARE skillet or oblong baking dish.

Stir together the cream, corn syrup or maple syrup and butter. Pour over the apples. Cook, uncovered, 8 to 9 minutes, or until apples are tender. Let stand 3 to 4 minutes, remove apples to a serving dish. Add rum, brandy or vanilla to cream mixture in dish. Mix well. Cook, uncovered, 4 to 5 minutes. Pour over apples.

Caramel Pudding, page 230
Chocolate Rum Mousse, page 234
Mint Tea, page 53

Rum Grapefruit, page 242
Strawberries with Melba Sauce, page 254
Ice Cream with Butterscotch and Chocolate Sauces, pages 253 and 258

Apple Delight

A light, creamy pancake filled with buttered apples. The glazing must be done in the broiler of a conventional oven. Remember to preheat oven while the apples are cooking.

4	tablespoons butter	3	tablespoons sugar
6	medium size apples		grated rind of 1 lemon
3	eggs		a pinch of salt
3	tablespoons flour	2	cups milk
		1/2	cup icing sugar

Melt the butter in an 8 × 8-inch glass dish, uncovered, 1 minute. Peel and slice the apples. Stir into the melted butter until coated.

Beat the eggs, add the flour and beat with rotary beater or whisk until well blended. Add the remaining ingredients except the icing sugar. Beat thoroughly together. Pour over the buttered apples. Cook, uncovered, 9 minutes, turning dish every 3 minutes. Let stand 5 minutes. Sprinkle icing sugar on top. Place under direct heat of conventional oven, 3 to 4 minutes, until blistered brown here and there. Serve warm. This dessert reheats very well, covered, for 3 minutes.

Crouton Applesauce

The crisp, buttered croutons and the coriander give this applesauce a special appeal.

1	cup apple juice	3/4	cup bread cubes
6	cups peeled and sliced apples	1/2	teaspoon cinnamon
1/4 to 1/2 cup sugar		1/2	teaspoon coriander seeds, crushed
2	tablespoons butter	1	teaspoon butter

Place the apple juice and apples in a 2-quart dish. Cook, uncovered, 6 to 8 minutes. Beat with a whisk or pass through a sieve to purée the apples. Add sugar to taste. Cool. Place butter in a glass pie plate and melt 1 minute. Roll and toss in it the bread cubes, cinnamon and coriander seeds. Cook 8 minutes, uncovered, stirring 4 times. The bread should be buttery crisp and browned. Pour into applesauce while hot. Stir in a teaspoon of butter until melted. Serve hot or warm.

Apple Crisp

For a superlative dessert, serve topped with ice cream and creamy butterscotch sauce.

4	cups apples, pared and sliced	1	tablespoon margarine or butter
1/3	cup sugar	2	tablespoons lemon juice
2	tablespoons flour		
1/2	teaspoon cinnamon		

The topping:

3/4	cup brown sugar	1/2	cup finely chopped walnuts
3/4	cup flour		a pinch of salt
1/3	cup butter		

Arrange apple slices in an 8 × 8-inch baking dish.

Mix together the sugar, flour, cinnamon, margarine or butter. Sprinkle over the apples. Pour lemon juice over all.

To prepare topping: Mix all the ingredients together until crumbly. Sprinkle over the apples, then pat all over until firm on top.

Cook, uncovered, 15 minutes, turning dish every 5 minutes. Let stand 15 minutes and serve.

Rum Bananas

For a variation, brandy can replace rum.

3	tablespoons butter or margarine	1/4	teaspoon each cinnamon and nutmeg
6	tablespoons brown sugar	2	tablespoons cream
		4 to	5 bananas, peeled
		2	tablespoons rum

In a 2-quart casserole melt the butter, uncovered, 1 minute. Add brown sugar, spices and cream. Mix well. Slice peeled bananas once lengthwise and then once crosswise. Add to sugar mixture, turning to coat. Cook, uncovered, for 3 minutes or until syrup bubbles on bananas, rearranging them after 2 minutes. Stir in the rum. Let stand 1 minute and serve.

Bing Cherry Compote

The big, black Bing cherries are a must for this delicious treat.

1	lb. fresh Bing cherries
1/2	cup red or black currant jelly
1/4	cup brandy or orange liqueur

Pit the cherries, place in a crystal bowl or glass serving dish. Place the currant jelly and brandy or liqueur in a measuring cup. Cook, covered, 1 minute 30 seconds. Let stand 2 minutes. Stir well. Pour over the cherries. Mix gently. Cover. Refrigerate 4 to 6 hours before serving.

Rum Grapefruit

Hot grapefruit, excellent as a dessert or as an entrée before a roast beef dinner.

1	large grapefruit	1	teaspoon ground
2	teaspoons brown		ginger
	sugar	1	teaspoon butter
		2	teaspoons rum

Cut grapefruit in half. Take out seeds if necessary. Cut around sections. Place each half on serving dish. Sprinkle the brown sugar and ginger mixed together on top of each half. Dot with butter and pour a teaspoon of rum over each half.

Prepare as many as you require, following the same pattern. To serve, bake one at a time, uncovered, 4 minutes, or bake 1 half at a time for 2 minutes. They will stay hot 8 to 10 minutes, so it is easy to prepare 2 while 2 others are baking.

Orange Fondue

A white wine fondue, unusual and different. Orange segments and slivered peaches are usually served with this fondue, but other fruits, such as apples, grapes, bananas, etc., may be added or substituted. The syrup can be made ahead of time and reheated for 2 minutes in the microwave oven.

1	cup sugar	2	tablespoons brandy
1	cup dry white wine		juice and grated rind
			of 2 oranges
		6	oranges, 6 peaches

In an 8-inch CORNING WARE skillet or buffet dish, place the sugar, white wine, brandy and rind and juice of oranges. Stir well. Cook 18 to 20 minutes, uncovered, stirring twice. The syrup should reach 240°F. Remove dish from oven, test syrup, put back if necessary. When ready, place over a spirit burner. Eat the fondue by spearing the fruit pieces on a fondue fork and dipping them into the pot for a second or two.

Brandied Fresh Peaches

Heat the fresh peaches for 15 to 20 seconds in the microwave oven, then let them stand 10 minutes and peel. This is much easier than the boiling water treatment usually used for peeling peaches.

4 to	5 (about 2 lbs.) peaches	¹/₄	cup chopped blanched almonds
	lemon juice	¹/₄	teaspoon nutmeg
2	tablespoons sugar	2	tablespoons brandy

Peel peaches, cut in half and remove pits. Coat lightly with lemon juice.

Arrange peach halves in an 8 × 8-inch baking dish, open side up. Sprinkle top of each with sugar. Place almonds and nutmeg on a pie plate. Heat in the oven, uncovered, 3 to 4 minutes, or until browned here and there. Use to fill centers of each peach. Bake, uncovered, 5 to 7 minutes, turning dish twice during cooking period.

Pour brandy on top. Let stand 5 minutes. Serve warm or cold.

Superb Peach Berry Compote

A true summer compote. Fresh raspberries can be replaced by frozen—but when possible use all fresh fruits. Delicious served with hot biscuits.

1	cup peeled and sliced peaches	2	cups fresh raspberries
1	cup sliced strawberries or 1 cup blueberries	¹/₂	cup icing sugar

Place peaches, strawberries or blueberries in a glass serving dish.

Mash the raspberries, pass through a sieve if you do not want the seeds. Add the icing sugar. Stir well. Pour over the fruits, but do not mix.

Heat dish in oven, uncovered, for 3 minutes. Cool and refrigerate until ready to serve. Stir only when ready to serve.

Lemon Mousse

A very attractive light, cool dessert.

1/2	cup sugar	1/2	cup lemon juice
1	envelope unflavored		grated peel of 1 lemon
	gelatine	3	eggs, separated
1/4	teaspoon salt	1/3	cup sugar
1/2	cup water	1	cup whipping cream

In a 4-cup measure, combine the 1/2 cup of sugar, gelatine, salt, water, lemon juice and peel.

Beat the egg yolks and add to mixture. Cook, uncovered, 3 to 4 minutes or until mixture bubbles, stirring 3 times. Cool until mixture is thickened, but not set.

Prepare a 3 to 4-cup soufflé dish by forming a collar of waxed paper around top of dish so that it extends about 3 inches above top edge. (You can grease inside upper edge of dish to hold paper in place or tie with paper clip.)

Beat egg whites until frothy, beat in the 1/3 cup sugar and fold into cooled lemon mixture. Whip cream and also fold into mixture. Pour into prepared dish.

Refrigerate 6 to 12 hours or until ready to serve. Remove waxed paper from soufflé dish before serving.

Molded Pears

This will keep 2 days if covered and refrigerated.

1 tablespoon unflavored gelatine	6 to 8 canned pear halves
2 tablespoons cold, strong coffee	1 teaspoon grated orange rind
6 tablespoons sugar	1 cup whipping cream
1/2 cup pear syrup	1/2 teaspoon almond extract
1 cup coffee	

Sprinkle gelatine over the 2 tablespoons coffee in a 4 cup-measure. Let stand 3 minutes. Add the sugar, pear syrup and the cup of coffee. Cook, uncovered, 4 minutes, stirring twice.

Arrange the pear halves in bottom of an oiled 10-inch ring mold. Sprinkle pears with orange rind and add part of the gelatine syrup to a depth of about 1/2-inch. Refrigerate 1 to 2 hours or until set.

Refrigerate remaining gelatine mixture until half set. Whip the cream and almond extract together and fold into the half set gelatine. Mix well. Spoon into the ring mold over the pears when they are set. Refrigerate until set. Then keep covered until ready to serve. Unmold and garnish to taste with whipped cream.

Poached Canned Peaches

The combination of wine and orange peel gives a liqueur flavor to the peaches.

1/2 cup sugar	1/2 cup sherry or sweet white wine
2 tablespoons cornstarch	1 large can (29 ounces) undrained peaches, sliced or halved
grated rind of 1 orange	

Combine all the ingredients in a 2-quart casserole. Cook, uncovered, 9 to 10 minutes, stirring twice. Let stand 5 minutes. Serve warm or cold.

Peach Crumble

At its best served warm with whipped cream or ice cream. Prepare crumble mixture while peaches are standing.

6 to 8	*peaches*	1	*cup brown sugar*
2	*tablespoons lemon juice*	3	*tablespoons butter*
1/4	*cup water*	1/4	*teaspoon salt*
3/4	*cup flour*		*grated rind of 1 orange*
		1/4	*teaspoon nutmeg*

Heat peaches 15-20 seconds in oven, then let stand 10 minutes.

Peel and slice peaches. Place in an 8 × 8-inch baking dish. Combine lemon juice and water and pour over peaches.

Mix together flour, sugar, butter, salt, orange rind and nutmeg and sprinkle over the fruits. Cook, uncovered, 5 to 8 minutes, depending on ripeness of peaches. Let stand 3 to 4 minutes and serve.

Pears de Luxe

Although simplicity itself, a delectable dessert. You will think you are eating fresh pears.

1	*large can pear halves*	1	*cup whipping cream*
3/4	*cup crème de cacao liqueur*	1	*teaspoon instant coffee*

Drain pears, reserving 1/2 cup liquid. Pour this liquid into a 2-cup measure and add the crème de cacao, first reserving 2 tablespoons to add to cream later. Heat, uncovered, for 3 minutes.

Arrange pears, cored side down, in a nice shallow dish. Pour the hot liquid on top. Cover with waxed paper. Refrigerate 2 to 3 hours.

To serve, whip the cream, add 2 tablespoons of crème de cacao when it begins to thicken. Top pears with it and sprinkle a teaspoon of instant coffee over the cream. Serve.

Pears Brillat-Savarin

This great French chef gave many an outstanding recipe to the food world and luckily this one can easily be adapted for microwave cooking.

4	fresh pears	1/8	teaspoon salt
1/2	cup water	1	teaspoon vanilla
1	cup sugar	1/2	cup rum
1 1/2	cups milk		toasted slivered
3	eggs		almonds
1/4	cup sugar		

Peel and halve the pears. Place in an 8-inch round cake dish or 8-inch CORNING WARE skillet. Add the water and 1 cup sugar. Cook, uncovered, 8 minutes, turning dish and stirring gently 3 times. Let stand 3 minutes. Remove pears from syrup with a perforated spoon. Place each half in an individual dessert dish.

Pour milk in a 1-quart casserole or 4 cup measure, heat 4 minutes, uncovered, or until milk is scalded.

Beat eggs until frothy, slowly add 1/4-cup sugar and salt and beat until fluffy. Gradually add scalded milk, vanilla and rum, stirring constantly. Pour an equal amount of custard over each pear.

Pour 1 cup boiling water into an 8 × 8-inch baking dish and set 4 dessert dishes in it. Bake 4 to 5 minutes, uncovered, turning dishes every minute until custard is barely set. It thickens quite a bit when cold. Repeat process with remaining desserts. Refrigerate until ready to serve. Garnish top with toasted slivered almonds.

Pears Caramel

Serve hot over ice cream or a square of plain cake. Delicious!

2 tablespoons butter	1/4 teaspoon ginger
1/3 cup brown sugar	1 large (29-ounce) can
1/4 teaspoon each,	pear halves
cinnamon and nutmeg	

In a 2-quart casserole or 10-inch CORNING WARE skillet, combine butter, brown sugar and spices. Cook, uncovered, 2 minutes, stirring once. Drain pears, stir into the syrup and cook, covered, 4 minutes. Serve by placing pears cut side down over ice cream and spooning syrup over top.

Poires Bordelaises

These pears are poached in red wine. Different wines will give different flavors to the pears. The rather long cooking time for this recipe is to ensure that the sugar and wine form a delicious syrup.

6 pears	1 2-inch cinnamon stick
2 cups red wine of your	1/4 cup sugar
choice	

Peel the pears, cut in two, core and sprinkle generously with sugar (not the 1/4 cup above). Let stand 1 hour.

Place the sugared pears in an 8 × 8-inch dish. Pour on top the red wine, cinnamon stick and sugar. Cook 8 minutes, uncovered, turning dish twice.

Remove pears with a perforated spoon, to a serving dish. Cook syrup 18 minutes. Cool and pour over pears. Refrigerate until ready to serve.

Summer Pudding

An English classic, to be made when fresh raspberries are in season. Frozen berries can be used, but will not have the flavor of the pure English summer pudding.

3	cups fresh raspberries	10	paper-thin slices white bread, buttered
1/2	cup sugar		whipped cream
1	teaspoon lemon juice		

Place the cleaned berries in a 2-quart casserole, add the sugar. Cook 10 minutes, uncovered, stirring twice. Add lemon juice, stir well. (Mixture should not be strained.)

Place a few slices of buttered bread in the bottom of a glass dish. Pour over as much of the raspberry syrup as the bread will absorb. Repeat procedure until all is used.

Cover and refrigerate 6 to 8 hours. Unmold or serve from dish with a bowl of whipped cream.

Baked Rhubarb

The perfect way to cook garden fresh rhubarb. Do try it once with the rose water.

2	cups rhubarb	1/2	cup sugar
2	tablespoons water	1/8	teaspoon rose water (optional)
	a pinch of salt		

Clean and cut the rhubarb in 1/2-inch pieces. Place in a 2-quart casserole, add water and salt. Cook, 4 to 5 minutes, covered, stirring once.

Add sugar and rose water. Let stand 3 minutes. Stir thoroughly. More sugar can be added to taste. Remember it will be much sweeter when cold. Serve cold plain or with cream.

Variation: Proceed as above, but replace sugar by an equal quantity of honey. Sprinkle top with grated rind of 1 orange and a dash of nutmeg.

Rhubarb Crisp

Winter or summer, a pleasant dessert.

2	cups rhubarb	1	cup brown sugar
2	tablespoons lemon juice	3/4	cup flour
		1/4	cup rolled oats
1/2	cup sugar grated rind of 1/2 a lemon	1/2	cup soft butter

Cut cleaned rhubarb in 1/2-inch pieces. Add lemon juice and sugar. Mix well. Spread in bottom of an 8 × 8-inch baking dish and sprinkle lemon rind on top. Combine brown sugar, flour, rolled oats and butter. Mix together until crumbly. Sprinkle on top of rhubarb. Cook, uncovered, 15 minutes, turning dish 3 times. Let stand 5 minutes. Serve hot or at room temperature.

Note For frozen rhubarb, use a little more than 2 cups; cook 1 minute, drain, then follow recipe above.

Jellied Rhubarb

A pleasant dessert to have on hand in the refrigerator, for emergencies. Will keep 3 to 5 days.

3	tablespoons cold water	1	cup boiling water
1	envelope unflavored gelatine	1/2	cup sugar
		2	cups baked rhubarb (see p. 249)
1/4	cup lemon juice		

Measure cold water into a 1½-quart dish, sprinkle the gelatine on top. Let stand 3 minutes. Add the lemon juice, boiling water and sugar. Stir well. Cook 3 minutes, uncovered, stirring once. Add the hot or cold baked rhubarb. Stir thoroughly. Pour into an oiled mold. Refrigerate until set. Unmold and serve to taste with whipped cream.

Minted Rhubarb Compote

Fresh mint and the orange give a special character to this compote.

4	cups rhubarb	1	orange, peeled and
	1-inch cinnamon stick		thinly sliced
2	tablespoons water	3	tablespoons chopped,
1	cup sugar		fresh mint
	grated rind of 1 orange		

Clean and cut the rhubarb into ½-inch pieces. Place in a 2-quart casserole. Add the cinnamon, water, sugar and orange rind. Cook, covered, 4 to 5 minutes. Let stand 3 minutes. Pour into a glass serving dish. Refrigerate until cold. To serve, garnish with a ring of orange slices. Sprinkle the mint in the center.

Rhubarb Strawberry Compote

Fresh, colorful and so good.

4	cups rhubarb	2	cups fresh
½	cup orange juice		strawberries, washed
¾	cup sugar		and halved

Clean and cut the rhubarb into ½-inch pieces. Place the orange juice and sugar in a 2-quart casserole. Cook, uncovered, 5 to 6 minutes or until it is boiling and sugar is dissolved. Add the rhubarb, stir well and cook, uncovered, 4 to 5 minutes, stirring once. Cool 10 minutes. Add the strawberries. Serve very cold with a bowl of sour cream.

To Thaw Frozen Fruits

Remove fruits from package and place in a 1-quart casserole. If they stick in package, place the box under running hot water for 30 to 40 seconds, tap fruit out. Cover frozen fruit with waxed paper while cooking.

Fruit	Size	Time
Strawberries	10-oz. package	1½ to 2 minutes
Sliced peaches	10-oz. package	2 to 3 minutes
Raspberries	10-oz. package	1½ to 2 minutes
Blueberries	10-oz. package	2 minutes

If fruits are in a plastic bag, place bag in dish, punch a few holes so steam can escape. There's no need to cover the bag. Thaw as for packaged fruits above.

For fruit that is packaged in bulk, use 1-1½ cups, place in bowl, cover with waxed paper and cook following the time table above.

Home frozen fruit may take 1 to 1½ minutes longer than the commercial type. Often the block of fruit can be broken easily in a few pieces after 1 minute, which will hasten the thawing. Check often and avoid overheating.

Dessert Sauces

As with meat or vegetable sauces, making dessert sauces in the microwave oven is a joy. Nothing could be easier and failures are a thing of the past. Many of the sauces will keep for several weeks in your refrigerator for use whenever needed.

Creamy Butterscotch Sauce

A great all-purpose sauce. Try it sometimes over a microwave oven baked apple.

1¼	cups brown sugar or half maple sugar, half brown sugar	¼	cup butter
		⅛	teaspoon salt
1	cup light or heavy cream	1	teaspoon vanilla
			a pinch of mace or nutmeg
2	tablespoons corn syrup		

Combine sugar, cream, syrup, butter and salt in a 1-quart casserole. Cook 4 minutes. Stir, cook 4 minutes. Add vanilla and mace or nutmeg. Stir until smooth. If not to be used at once, refrigerate and reheat sauce in microwave oven for 2 minutes, uncovered. Yields 1½ cups.

Variations:

For a caramel walnut sauce: Use dark brown sugar and add ½ cup chopped walnuts when adding vanilla.

For a caramel brandy sauce: Follow as given for Creamy Butterscotch Sauce, adding 4 tablespoons brandy after the corn syrup. Wonderful over sliced fresh peaches or custard.

Rum Chocolate Sauce

Keep in covered glass dish or jam jar. To serve hot, cook for 2 minutes, uncovered, in your microwave oven.

2	squares (1 ounce each) unsweetened chocolate	4	tablespoons butter
		1/4	teaspoon salt
1/2	cup water	2	tablespoons rum or 1 teaspoon vanilla
3/4	cup sugar		

Place chocolate and water in a one-quart casserole and heat, uncovered, 3 minutes. Stir until creamy. If chocolate is not all melted, heat another minute.

Add sugar, stir until well mixed with the chocolate. Heat 2 minutes. Remove from oven. Add butter, salt, rum or vanilla. Stir and use. Yields about 1 1/3 cups.

Sauce Melba

This can be served over fruits, over ice cream, custard or pound cake. One of the tastiest dessert sauces. Will keep for 2 weeks covered and refrigerated.

1	10-ounce package frozen raspberries	1/2	cup currant jelly
		1	teaspoon lemon juice
1/2	cup sugar	1	tablespoon brandy (optional)
1	tablespoon cornstarch		

Place frozen raspberries, unwrapped, in a one-quart casserole. Cook, uncovered, 4 minutes, turn over or stir and cook another 2 to 3 minutes.

Blend the sugar and cornstarch. Stir into the raspberries, with the currant jelly, lemon juice and brandy. Cook, uncovered, 5 minutes, stirring thoroughly after 3 minutes.

To have a perfectly smooth sauce, strain while hot. This removes the raspberry seeds. Yields 1 1/2 cups.

Sauce Jubilée

The Victorian glory. It can dress ordinary ice cream in party glamor in only 4 minutes. Use canned Bing cherries when available.

1	(20 ounce) can pitted cherries		cherry liquid
2	tablespoons sugar	1	tablespoon butter
1	tablespoon cornstarch	1	teaspoon lemon juice
	pinch salt		or 1 tablespoon brandy

Drain cherries, pour liquid into 1-cup measuring cup. Combine sugar, cornstarch and salt in a 1-quart dish. Add enough water to the cherry liquid to make 1 cup. Stir into sugar mixture. Cook, uncovered, 3 minutes. Stir well. Cook another 3 minutes or until sauce is thick and clear. Stir in the butter, lemon juice or brandy and cherries. Heat 2 minutes. Pour warm over ice cream or use hot or cold as you please. Will keep 3 weeks refrigerated. Yields 1½ cups.

Hot Vanilla Sauce

There are many uses for this sauce. For a quick, creamy rice pudding, warm up 1 to 2 cups leftover rice, covered, for 3 minutes. Pour hot sauce on top. Serve.

3	tablespoons soft butter	½	cup boiling water or hot cream
1	teaspoon cornstarch		pinch of salt
¼ to	½ cup sugar	1	teaspoon vanilla
⅛	teaspoon nutmeg		
2	egg yolks, slightly beaten		

Cream the butter, cornstarch and sugar in a 1-quart casserole. Beat in the nutmeg and egg yolks, add the boiling water or cream and the salt. Heat, uncovered, for 4 minutes, stirring after 2 minutes. When creamy, add vanilla.

Apple-Raisin Sauce

Nice on hot gingerbread but just as good with ham steak or steamed pudding.

1 tablespoon cornstarch	1 cup apple or
4 tablespoons brown	cranberry juice
sugar	1/4 cup seedless raisins
a pinch of salt	1/2 cup diced unpeeled
1/4 teaspoon allspice	apples
grated rind of 1 lemon	

Combine cornstarch, sugar, salt, allspice and lemon rind in a 1-quart casserole. Blend in apple or cranberry juice. Cook, uncovered, 2 minutes; stir, cook another 2 minutes. Add remaining ingredients and cook another 2 minutes; stir well. Sauce should be creamy and transparent. Depending on the variety of apples you use, it may be necessary to cook a minute more. Yields 1 1/2 cups.

Raspberry Sauce

1 (10 ounce) package	1/2 cup red wine or apple
frozen raspberries	juice
1/4 cup sugar	grated rind of half
2 tablespoons	an orange
cornstarch	

Put raspberries in a 1-quart casserole. Cook, uncovered, 2 minutes. Turn fruit over, cook another minute.

Combine sugar and cornstarch and add to fruit, stir well. Cook 2 minutes, stirring once. Add wine or apple juice and grated orange rind. Cook, uncovered, 1 minute, or until creamy and bubbly. Cover, cool, stir well, refrigerate until ready to serve. Yield: about 2 cups.

Lemon Sauce

Lemon Sauce is always attractive served over cake, pudding and fruits.

1/2	cup sugar	grated rind and juice
1	tablespoon cornstarch	of 1 lemon
1	cup water	a pinch of salt and
2	tablespoons butter	mace

Combine sugar and cornstarch in a 1-quart casserole. Stir in water. Heat, uncovered, 2 minutes, stirring 3 times. To this creamy mixture add butter, lemon rind and juice, salt and mace. Stir, cook 20 to 25 seconds. Stir well. Serve warm. To reheat, place in oven 20 to 30 seconds. Yields 1 1/4 cups.

Old-fashioned Canadian Lemon Sauce

Tasty and quite different from the usual type.

1	cup brown sugar	2	teaspoons cornstarch
1	cup water	2	tablespoons cold
1	lemon, unpeeled, thinly sliced		water

In a deep 1-quart bowl place the brown sugar, water and lemon. Cook, uncovered, 10 minutes, stirring once. Let stand 10 minutes. Mix cornstarch and cold water. Add to sauce. Stir well. Cook, uncovered, 3 to 4 minutes, stirring twice or until bubbly and slightly creamy. Yields 1 3/4 cups.

Golden Sauce

A hot sauce to be served over hot pudding or cake.

1/4	cup butter	2	tablespoons cream or
1	cup icing sugar		milk
1	whole egg	1	teaspoon vanilla

Cream the butter in a 2-cup measure and gradually add the remaining ingredients. When well mixed cook, uncovered, 30 seconds. Stir well, let stand 10 minutes, stirring twice. Yields 1 cup.

Super Rich Chocolate Sauce

Try it on coffee ice cream or on any of your favorite flavors.

1/2	cup butter	2	tablespoons rum
1	cup sugar	1/3	cup cocoa
1/8	teaspoon salt	1	cup cream, rich or
1	teaspoon instant coffee powder		light
		2	teaspoons vanilla

In a 1-quart casserole, melt the butter, uncovered, for 1 minute. Blend in remaining ingredients. Stir with a whisk or rotary beater. Cook, uncovered, 5 minutes. Serve warm or cold. Sauce thickens quite a bit on cooling. Yields about 2 cups.

16. Cakes and Pies

Both cakes and pies can be cooked successfully in the microwave oven although it is only fair to say that there are certain limitations. On the other hand, pie crusts become exceptionally flaky and a cake can be whipped up in next to no time if you are suddenly confronted with unexpected guests.

Making cakes may take a time to master and the amount of browning may not be what you are normally accustomed to, but this can be overcome with a topping or icing and I've included several of these in my recipes. Cakes should also be eaten fairly soon after they are cooked, as they tend to dry out slightly faster than cakes cooked the conventional way.*

Pie crusts do not brown either, but you can use either pie crust sticks, a mix or home recipe—all of which are equally good in terms of texture and taste—and if you prefer a better color, you could add a few drops of yellow coloring to the water used in the recipe. A sprinkle of sugar before the last minute of cooking helps.

A double crust pie can be baked only if both the microwave oven and a conventional oven are used. The pie is first cooked rapidly in the microwave oven, then finished in a preheated conventional oven.

Cookie crumb crusts are very successful and fast.

Only a microwave oven can rewarm an individual slice of pie and recapture that straight-from-the-oven taste in 15 seconds. Try it sometime.

Baking a Cake from a Mix

Line the bottoms of two 8-inch round glass cake dishes with lightly buttered waxed paper or spray with PAM.

Important: When baking a cake, ALWAYS place a glass cup, open side up, in the middle of the dish. Pour batter around. This gives a perfect cake everytime.

Prepare 1 package of cake mix according to package directions. Pour half of batter into each prepared cake dish.

Cook a layer at a time, 5 minutes, turning the dish halfway every minute, testing with knife or toothpick until it comes out clean. Let stand in dish 5 minutes. Unmold onto a wire cake rack. Cool.

To bake the whole amount at once, place a custard cup in center of a 13 × 9*-inch glass baking dish and pour batter into dish. Bake 9 minutes, turning dish halfway every 2 minutes. Finish as for layer cake above.

*If this size of dish does not fit your oven it will be necessary to cook 2 layers separately.

Cupcakes

Two cupcakes are ready to serve in 1 minute. As they do not brown on top, they can be covered with icing, melted chocolate chips or sprinkled with cocoa before cooking. Of course, this does not apply to chocolate or spice cupcakes which are naturally colored. I have found that it is best to place filled baking cups in small glass cups for a higher cupcake.

Lemon Cupcakes

When baking more than two at a time, place in a circle in the middle of the oven.

$1/2$	cup margarine (at room temperature)	$1^1/2$	cups all-purpose flour
$3/4$	cup sugar	$2^1/2$	teaspoons baking powder
	grated rind of 1 lemon	$1/2$	teaspoon salt
2	eggs	$1/2$	cup milk

In a mixing bowl, place the margarine, sugar and grated lemon rind. Beat with electric mixer at high speed until fluffy, about 10 minutes. Add the eggs, one at a time, beating well after each one is added.

Sift together the flour, baking powder and salt. Add to the mixture in two batches, alternating with the milk and beating at low speed.

To bake: Place 2 or 4 1-inch high paper baking cups in individual glass custard cups, or set on a glass pie plate. Fill each one with 2 teaspoons batter. Sprinkle top with cocoa. Cook as follows:

2 cupcakes: 1 to $1^1/4$ minutes
4 cupcakes: 2 to $2^1/2$ minutes
6 cupcakes: 3 to 4 minutes

Give dish half a turn halfway through baking time. Yield: 2 dozen cupcakes.

Note   It is not advisable to cook more than 6 cupcakes at a time.

Variations:

Orange Cupcakes: Replace the lemon rind with an equal quantity of orange rind. Reserve juice of orange and when the cupcakes are baked and cooled, make icing by adding some of the juice to a small amount of icing sugar. When it has reached desired consistency, spread over cakes.

Vanilla-Chocolate Cupcakes: Replace lemon rind with 1 teaspoon vanilla, $1/4$ teaspoon mace or nutmeg. Place 4 to 6 chocolate chips on top of batter. Cook for times as above. Let cool 1 minute and spread softened chocolate over top of cakes.

Double-Take Orange Cake

You can make this unusual cake, plus some cupcakes from just one package of cake mix.

$3/4$	cup water	1	package (18.5 ounces)
1	package (3 ounces)		yellow cake mix
	orange flavor gelatine		ingredients called for
$1/4$	cup fresh orange juice		on cake package
	grated rind of 1 orange	$1/2$ to 1	cup whipping cream
		2	tablespoons sugar

Place water in small bowl and heat 2 minutes or until boiling in microwave oven, or boil in the conventional way. Add gelatine, stir until dissolved, then add the orange juice. Reserve the grated rind.

Prepare cake mix according to package directions. Pour two-thirds of the batter into a buttered 8-inch round cake dish. Bake, uncovered, 2 minutes, give a quarter turn, cook 2 minutes, turn dish again. Cook 2 more minutes. Test with a wooden pick to see if cooked enough. Place on cake rack. Make holes in cake with a pick, 1 inch apart. Reserve $1/2$ cup orange jelly, then carefully pour remainder into the holes and on top of cake. Cool 15 minutes. Refrigerate both cake and reserved jelly.

To serve: Dice set jelly, fold into cream, whipped and sweetened to taste, and use as a topping for the cake.

With batter remaining make:

Orange Cupcakes: Spoon two tablespoons batter into paper baking cups and set them in small glass custard cups. Mix the reserved orange rind with 2 tablespoons of sugar. Sprinkle each cupcake with mixture. Cook as for Cupcakes. Cool on cake rack.

Note   The reserved cream jelly can be used on the cupcakes instead of above topping in the same manner as on the cake, if preferred.

Egg White Frosting

This is the well-known "7-minute frosting" which can now be done in 3 minutes in the microwave oven. The result is always perfect.

1	*egg white*	6	*tablespoons corn*
	a pinch of salt		*syrup*
2	*tablespoons sugar*	1	*teaspoon vanilla or*
			almond extract

In a small mixing bowl, beat egg white until foamy. Add salt and sugar, beating until soft peaks form.

Measure corn syrup in 1-cup measure. Cook, uncovered, 1 minute 30 seconds or until mixture boils. Slowly pour over egg white, beating constantly until frosting is stiff. Beat in extract of your choice.

For a colored icing, add a few drops of vegetable coloring of your choice while adding extract.

Spread on cooled cake. Will frost an 8 or 9" square or layer cake.

Ever-ready Chocolate Syrup and Icing

This syrup can be used as is over ice cream, pudding or cake, or used to make a quick icing.

1/2	cup corn syrup	2 to 3	squares (1 ounce each) semi-sweet chocolate
1/4	cup water	1	teaspoon vanilla

Measure corn syrup and water into a 4-cup measure or large bowl. Add chocolate squares. Cook, uncovered, 3 minutes, or until chocolate melts, stirring once. Blend until smooth. Stir in vanilla and cool.

To Make Icing: To the cold syrup, add enough icing sugar to make it creamy. For a richer icing, add 1 or 2 tablespoons soft butter. Any excess icing can be refrigerated and used later (see p.284).

German Frosting

A very nice, creamy frosting. Prepare it before making your cake, then cool until the cake is ready to be frosted.

3/4	cup sugar	1/2	cup butter or margarine
1/4	cup flour	1	teaspoon vanilla
3/4	cup milk or cream		

In a small mixing bowl, combine sugar and flour. Stir in milk and cook, uncovered, 3 minutes or until mixture thickens and boils, stirring twice. When ready, stir thoroughly. Place butter on top, then pour vanilla over butter. Do not mix, cover and refrigerate until cold, about 1 hour. Then beat with mixer at high speed or with a hand mixer until light and fluffy. Will frost an 8-inch layer cake.

For a Mocha Frosting: Add 1 teaspoon dry instant coffee and 1 tablespoon unsweetened cocoa to flour. Then proceed as above.

For a Lemon or Orange Frosting: Omit vanilla. Replace 1/4 cup of the milk with orange or lemon juice. Proceed as above, then sprinkle the grated rind of 1 orange or 1 lemon over butter.

Noël Fruit Cake

To obtain the best flavor, store for 7 to 8 weeks before eating. This cake will even keep for 7 months well wrapped in an airtight box.

1/2	lb. cut up candied cherries	1	cup flour
4	ounces coarsely chopped dates	1/2	cup sugar
4	ounces chopped citron peel	1	teaspoon baking powder
8	ounces cut up candied pineapple	1/4	teaspoon salt
4	ounces orange peel	1	teaspoon ground cardamom
4	ounces seedless raisins	4	well-beaten eggs
2	cups walnuts	1	teaspoon vanilla
1	cup coarsely chopped Brazil nuts	1	teaspoon almond extract

Combine the first 8 ingredients in a bowl. Then combine in another bowl the flour, sugar, baking powder, salt and cardamom. Mix well, pour over the fruits and nut mixture. Stir and lift with your hands, until fruits are well coated with the flour. Add eggs, vanilla and almond extract. Stir everything together until well blended. Divide mixture in two well-greased 9 × 5-inch loaf dishes. (No custard cups need to be placed in the dishes.)

Cook each cake separately 8 to 9 minutes, turning dish every 2 minutes. Set dishes on a wire cake rack for at least 1 hour to cool, then remove from dish and wrap each cake in cheesecloth dipped in rum. Then wrap in foil. Store in a cool place.

Carrot Cake

Nice served hot with brandy hard sauce. There is no liquid in this recipe as it is replaced by the grated carrots.

1/2	cup butter or margarine	1/2	cup currants grated rind of
1/2	cup brown sugar		2 oranges
1	egg	1 1/4	cups flour
1	cup grated raw carrots	1	teaspoon baking powder
3/4	cup seedless raisins	1/2	teaspoon soda
		1/2	teaspoon cinnamon
		1/4	teaspoon nutmeg

Cream butter or margarine and brown sugar until fluffy. Add the egg. Beat together 2 minutes.

Add carrots, raisins, currants and orange rind. Mix thoroughly.

Stir the remaining ingredients together. Add to carrot mixture, blend well. Turn batter into a buttered 8 × 8-inch glass dish with glass custard cup in center. Cook 10 to 12 minutes or until surface is slightly firm when touched lightly, turning dish every 2 minutes.

Remove from oven. Let stand on cake rack 15 minutes. Cut into squares to serve.

Variations: To form a crusty top, mix together in a bowl 4 tablespoons butter, 1/3 cup brown sugar, 1/4 cup cream, 1 cup coconut, 1/2 teaspoon vanilla. Cook, 3 minutes, stirring once halfway through. Spread over hot cake before unmolding. Place under broiler of conventional oven for 2 to 3 minutes or until caramelized, watching closely, as it burns easily. Cool on cake rack and cut when cold.

Swedish Walnut Cake

A tasty pound cake that doesn't require any liquid. It will keep 3 to 4 weeks, well wrapped, in a cool place. The lemon glazing is optional. Before mixing cake, make sure that all ingredients are at room temperature.

2/3	cup butter or margarine	1/2	teaspoon baking powder
2/3	cup fine granulated sugar	1/4	cup coarsely chopped walnuts
3	eggs	1	cup icing sugar
1/2	teaspoon vanilla	2	tablespoons water
1	cup flour	1	teaspoon lemon juice

When possible, beat this cake in a cake mixer or use a hand beater.

Cream butter or margarine until fluffy. Add the sugar, 1 tablespoon at a time, beating well each time. Add the eggs, one at a time, beating 1 minute after each one is added. Add vanilla.

Stir together the flour, baking powder and walnuts. Add to batter. Mix until well blended. Turn mixture into a well-buttered 8 × 8-inch cake dish, with glass custard cup in center.

Cook 8 to 11 minutes, turning dish every 2 minutes, until surface is slightly firm when touched lightly. Cool on cake rack.

For the Glaze: Mix together the icing sugar, water and lemon juice, pour over cake after it has been removed from oven. Let stand 2 hours before unmolding.

Old-Fashioned Gingerbread

The crumbly mixture on top gives it a pleasant texture and appetizing appearance.

1	cup flour	1/4	cup chopped nuts
1/2	cup sugar	1/4	cup coconut
1/2	teaspoon baking soda	1	well-beaten egg
1/4	teaspoon salt	1	tablespoon molasses
1/4	teaspoon cinnamon	1/2	cup buttermilk or
1	teaspoon ginger		sour milk
1/4	cup shortening or		
	margarine		

Combine the flour, sugar, soda, salt, cinnamon and ginger. Cut in shortening with a pastry blender or 2 knives, until mixture is crumbly. Remove 1/4 cup of mixture and add to it the nuts and coconut. Set aside to be used as the topping.

Add egg, molasses, buttermilk or sour milk to remaining flour mixture. Mix just enough to blend.

Spread in a greased 8 × 8-inch glass cake dish with glass custard cup in center. Cook 3 minutes, turning dish half-way once. Sprinkle the reserved crumb mixture over entire surface. Cook 3 minutes longer, turning dish twice.

Let stand 5 minutes. Cut in wedges. Serve hot or cooled.

Cookie Crumb Crusts

Type	Amount	Sugar	Butter or Margarine	Cooking Time
Graham Cracker	1 1/2 cups (18 to 20 squares)	1/4 cup	1/3 cup	1 minute, 45 seconds
Vanilla Wafer	1 1/2 cups (36 wafers)	none	1/4 cup	2 minutes
Gingersnap	1 1/2 cups	none	1/3 cup	2 minutes
Flaked or Shredded Coconut	2 cups	none	1/4 cup	2 minutes

Quantities are given for a standard 9" pie plate. Place butter in pie plate and melt for 30 seconds. Add cookie crumbs and sugar if needed and press well into bottom and up sides of dish. Cook, following times above, turning plate twice. Brown spots should begin to appear when crust is cooked.

How to Bake Pastry Shells

Pastry shells can be made from any of the commercially prepared pastry sticks or mixes (with the exception of the frozen prepared pie shells which do not appear to cook satisfactorily in the microwave oven); use my recipe, or your own favorite pastry recipe or any of the cookie crumb crusts.

By using the microwave oven, your pastry will be baked to perfection and the shell will never shrink in the middle or break. If you prefer a browner shell, you can cook the pastry shell in the microwave oven first, then in the conventional oven for a few more minutes until it is brown, but you will not save time this way and the end product is not as good. Fillings, too, are best cooked separately and then combined with the baked pie shell as I've suggested in the following recipes.

To Bake: Roll out the pastry of your choice. Shape into a 9" glass or CORNING WARE pie plate. Flute edges with a fork or your fingers. Do not prick shell.

Cover shell with 1 layer of waxed or absorbent paper, making sure to cover the edges. Place another pie plate over the paper. Cook 3 minutes. Remove covering pie plate and paper. Cook 1 minute, 30 seconds longer. Let cool completely before filling.

If you wish to have a brown crust, place pie in a preheated 400°F oven as soon as pie is taken out of the microwave oven — 2-4 minutes or until browned.

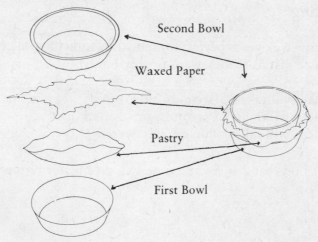

Second Bowl

Waxed Paper

Pastry

First Bowl

My Favorite Pastry

This pastry will keep for 3 weeks in the refrigerator wrapped in foil or plastic wrap. Cook it in the microwave oven or partly in the microwave oven and finish off in a conventional oven.

5	cups all-purpose flour	1	egg
1	teaspoon salt	3	tablespoons white
1	tablespoon sugar		vinegar or fresh lemon
1/4	teaspoon soda		juice
1	lb. pure lard or		cold water
	shortening		

Stir together in a large bowl the flour, salt, sugar and soda. Cut in the fat in fairly large pieces.

Beat together the egg, vinegar or lemon juice. Add enough cold water to fill a 1-cup measure. Add all at once to flour mixture. Work together until dough is partly formed. Turn onto a floured table and knead and roll together until it forms a soft ball of dough. Wrap tightly in foil or plastic wrap. Tap all over to form a square. Refrigerate until ready to use.

When ready to roll, flour table generously. You will need a lot of flour but this does not harm the texture, giving a perfect, flaky crisp dough. Yields 4 two-crust or 8 single 8 or 9-inch pies. Use for any of the following recipes.

Reheating

The microwave oven is perfect for reheating individual slices of pie, which taste just as if they were freshly baked.

    1 slice will take 15 seconds, uncovered
    2 slices will take 25 seconds, uncovered
    4 slices will take 1 minute, uncovered

Note   I find that 2 slices at a time will give better results than 4.

Old-Fashioned Gingerbread, page 268
Pecan Pie, page 272
Lemonade, page 50

Turtles, page 278
Rocky Fudge, page 278
Raspberry Jam Cookies, page 276
Dried Flowers, page 288

Lemon Meringue Pie

So easy and so good! The filling is cooked in the microwave oven and the meringue browned in the conventional way.

1	cup sugar	2	tablespoons butter
4	tablespoons flour		juice and grated rind
	pinch of salt		of 1 lemon
1/2	cup water	3	egg whites
3	eggs yolks, well beaten	6	tablespoons sugar nutmeg to taste
1	cup water		

Place the sugar, flour, salt and the 1/2 cup water in a 1 1/2-quart casserole. Stir until well mixed. Add egg yolks and the 1 cup of water. Mix well. Cook, uncovered, for 6 minutes, stirring twice or until light and creamy. Remove from oven, stir well, add butter and lemon juice and rind. Cool.

When cold, pour into baked pie shell of your choice.

Prepare meringue by beating the 3 egg whites until firm, add 1 tablespoon sugar at a time, beating thoroughly as each spoonful is added. Pour and spread meringue over lemon filling in pie shell and sprinkle with 1 teaspoon sugar and nutmeg to taste. Bake in a preheated 375°F oven until golden brown. Cool and serve.

California Raisin Pie

The combination of sour cream and raisins gives a creamy raisin pie.

1	egg	1/4	teaspoon cinnamon
1/2	cup sugar		a pinch of salt
3/4	cup seedless raisins	1	tablespoon lemon
1/2	cup commercial sour cream		juice
		1	9" baked pastry shell

Beat all the ingredients together in the order given. Pour into baked pie shell. Cook, 8 to 9 minutes or until set in a cream. Let stand 15 minutes. Cool and serve with whipped cream or ice cream.

Pumpkin Pie

One of the best pumpkin pies I have ever made.

2	tablespoons butter	1/4	cup cream
2	cups fresh cooked or canned pumpkin	3	tablespoons molasses
		1/2	teaspoon ginger
1/2	cup white sugar	1/2	teaspoon nutmeg
2	eggs, lightly beaten	1 1/2	teaspoons cinnamon
1/4	teaspoon salt	1	9" baked pie shell
1	cup milk		

In a 2-quart casserole melt butter one minute, add remaining ingredients. Mix well. Pour into baked pie shell. Cook, uncovered, 4 to 6 minutes or until edges just begin to set. Carefully stir the middle part to move cooked portion from edges to center. Cook another 3 minutes or until knife inserted in the center comes out clean.

Pecan Pie

When pecans are expensive, use walnuts and pecans, half and half.

1 1/2	cups pecans	1/2	teaspoon vanilla
1/4	cup butter	1/8	teaspoon nutmeg
1/2	cup brown sugar	3	eggs
1	cup corn syrup	1	9" baked pastry shell

Spread pecans or pecans and walnuts in glass baking dish. Heat, uncovered, 3 minutes, stirring twice. Set aside.

Cream the butter and sugar together until fluffy. Add corn syrup, vanilla and nutmeg. Beat well. Add eggs, one at a time, beating well after each one is added. Spread pecans evenly in pastry shell. Pour mixture carefully over the top. Cook, uncovered, 8 to 9 minutes, turning once. Let stand 10 minutes. Serve cold, but not refrigerated.

English Pie

A combination of mincemeat and custard which results in a very interesting pie.

1	9" baked pastry shell	1	cup milk
1	cup mincemeat	1/2	cup cream
1/3	cup sugar	1	teaspoon vanilla or 1
3	eggs, well beaten		tablespoon brandy

Pour mincemeat into baked pie shell. Spread evenly. Beat the remaining ingredients together with a hand beater until foamy. Pour over mincemeat.

Cook, uncovered, 4 to 5 minutes, turning plate twice and stirring very lightly from edges to middle if necessary. Let stand 15 minutes. Serve cold.

Maple Syrup Pie

A favorite of so many!

1	cup maple syrup	1/4	cup chopped walnuts
1/2	cup water	1	or 2 tablespoons
3	tablespoons cornstarch		butter
2	tablespoons cold water	1	9" baked pastry shell

Place in a 4-cup measure the maple syrup and 1/2 cup water. Bring to boil, uncovered, 3 to 4 minutes. Stir cornstarch with the 2 tablespoons of water and stir thoroughly into the boiling syrup until creamy.

Cook 40 seconds, or until creamy and transparent. Stir in walnuts and butter until butter is melted. Cool and pour into baked pie shell. Serve cold alone or topped with whipped cream.

17. Cookies, Candies and Jams

Cookies

Ginger Cookies

A rolled cookie with an old-fashioned flavor. Dough will keep 1 week refrigerated. Handy to have when you need cookies in a matter of minutes.

4	cups all-purpose flour	1/4	teaspoon ground
1	teaspoon salt		cardamom seeds or
1 1/2	teaspoons ginger		fennel seeds
1 1/2	teaspoons baking soda	1	cup margarine
1	teaspoon cinnamon	1/2	cup brown sugar
1/2	teaspoon allspice or	1	cup molasses
	nutmeg	1/2	cup cold water

Sift together the flour, salt, ginger, baking soda, cinnamon, allspice or nutmeg, cardamom or fennel seeds.

Beat the margarine and sugar with a rotary beater until creamy, add the molasses and water. Mix well and add the flour mixture. Stir until well mixed. If dough seems a bit too soft, add a few more spoonfuls of flour. Cover and refrigerate 3 to 4 hours. The colder the dough, the better the cookie.

To cook: Divide dough into 4 portions. Roll each one on a generously floured board, 1/8-inch thick. Cut with a 1 1/2-inch cookie cutter.

In place of a metal cookie sheet, cover a piece of stiff cardboard to fit oven with waxed paper. Carefully place the cookies on it in a circle if cooking more than three on a sheet. Cook as follows:-

2 cookies - 1 minutes
3 cookies - 1¹/₄ to 1¹/₂ minutes
6 to 8 cookies - 2¹/₂ to 3 minutes

Cool on cake rack. Yield: About 2¹/₂ dozen cookies.

Double Chocolate Chip Cookies

A combination of cocoa, chocolate chips and nuts makes these quite special.

³/₄	cup all-purpose flour	¹/₂	cup butter or margarine
¹/₄	cup unsweetened cocoa	1	egg
¹/₂	teaspoon baking soda	1	teaspoon vanilla
¹/₂	teaspoon salt	¹/₂	cup chocolate chips
¹/₂	cup white sugar	¹/₂	cup walnuts, chopped
¹/₄	cup brown sugar, well-packed		

Sift together the flour, cocoa, baking soda and salt.

Cream together the white sugar, brown sugar, butter or margarine, egg and vanilla. Add the sifted dry ingredients, mix well. Add the chocolate chips and walnuts. Mix thoroughly. Drop by teaspoon onto prepared cardboard and bake as for Ginger Cookies (see p.274). Yield: About 3 dozen cookies.

Raspberry Jam Cookies

These are my favorites, but they can also be made with apricot jam, marmalade or any jam of your choice.

1	cup shortening or margarine	1	teaspoon almond or vanilla extract
1	cup brown sugar, well packed	3¼	cups all-purpose flour
		1	teaspoon baking soda
¼	cup white sugar	1	teaspoon salt
2	eggs	1½ - 2	cups coconut
½	cup water		raspberry jam

Cream the shortening or margarine with the brown and white sugars. When creamy, add the eggs, the water and extract. Beat until well mixed.

Stir together the flour, baking soda and salt. Add to cream mixture, mix, add the coconut, mix thoroughly.

Prepare a baking cardboard, topped with waxed paper as explained in previous recipe. Drop batter by teaspoons onto sheet. Make a small depression in the middle of each cookie with the tip of a wet spoon and fill with ½ teaspoon raspberry jam. Place ½ teaspoon batter over jam. Bake as for Ginger Cookies. Yield: 30-40 cookies.

Candies

New England Fudge

The true fudge is made with unsweetened chocolate, but, if preferred, it can be replaced by ½ cup unsweetened cocoa, mixed with the sugar before adding the other ingredients.

3	cups sugar	2	tablespoons corn syrup
¼	teaspoon salt	3	tablespoons butter
3	squares (1 ounce each) unsweetened chocolate	1	teaspoon vanilla
1	cup rich or light cream	1	cup coarsely chopped walnuts

In a large mixing bowl, place the sugar, salt, chocolate, cream and corn syrup. Cook, uncovered, 10 minutes, stirring 3 times during this period. Remove bowl from oven and test to see if ready with a candy thermometer (it should read 234°F), or until a little of the mixture forms a soft ball in ice cold water. If necessary, cook another few minutes and retest.

When ready, add the butter and vanilla, but do not stir. Let the fudge stand 15 minutes, then stir thoroughly until creamy and dull, about 5 minutes. Pour into buttered 8 × 8-inch dish or pan. Sprinkle chopped nuts on top. Refrigerate, covered, until cold. Cut and serve.

Rocky Fudge

These take 3 minutes to cook, 5 minutes to cool, and the result is 16 squares of crunchy fudge.

4	(4 to 5-ounce) chocolate bars of your choice	$^1/_2$ to $^3/_4$	cup coarsely chopped walnuts or unsalted peanuts
3	cups miniature marshmallows		

Break chocolate bars into pieces. Set in a glass dish. Melt 2 minutes in oven. Well-butter an 8 × 8-inch baking dish. Mix the marshmallows and nuts together and place in dish. Pour well-stirred, melted chocolate on top. Stir gently with a fork, until chocolate blends into mixture. Cool. Cut and serve.

Homemade Turtles

Everyone loves Turtles!

$^1/_2$	lb. (8 ounces) semi-sweet chocolate
4	ounces pecans or walnuts
16	ounces vanilla or assorted caramels

Place the chocolate in a small bowl. Melt, covered with waxed paper, 3 to 4 minutes. Stir thoroughly. Set aside.

Place the pecans or walnuts in small mounds on a buttered cookie sheet.

Unwrap caramels, place in a 1$^1/_2$ quart casserole and melt, uncovered, 3 minutes, stirring once while cooking. If not all melted, cook another minute.

Pour a teaspoon of caramel over each mound of nuts. If mixture spreads too much, it is because it is not sufficiently cooled. Refrigerate 20 to 30 minutes.

To finish, dip each turtle in the melted chocolate. Place, rounded side up, on waxed paper. Let stand in cool place until set.

Candied Apples

Big red candied apples are always a delight to young ones.

2	cups sugar	¹/₄	cup cinnamon candies
2	teaspoons cider		or 4 drops of red
	vinegar		vegetable coloring
1	cup water	8 to	10 medium sized
			apples

Place sugar, cider vinegar, water and cinnamon candies in a 1¹/₂-quart casserole. Stir to mix. Cook 18 to 20 minutes. Stir well. Add coloring if you are not using candy. Let stand 5 minutes, then test with candy thermometer (it should register 295°F) or until syrup forms threads or hard ball when tested in ice cold water. If it has not reached this point, cook another 2 to 5 minutes.

While candy is cooking, insert wooden stick into stem end of washed apples. Be sure apples are well dried. Dip and roll each apple in heavy syrup mixture. Let stand on buttered baking sheet or on greased waxed paper. If syrup gets too hard, return to oven for 30 seconds. Refrigerate until coating is set.

Jams and Jellies

Jams cooked in the microwave oven have the freshest taste of all because they are barely cooked. They will keep for 5 to 6 months refrigerated, or 12 to 16 months frozen, and will keep their summer texture, color and taste.

Blueberries, raspberries, gooseberries, Saskatoon berries, red and black currants and rhubarb all freeze well.

Raspberry Jam

I use my blender to crush the raspberries in seconds, but a fruit press or masher can also be used. To make 3 cups of crushed berries you will need 2 full quarts of raspberries.

3	cups crushed fresh raspberries	1	package powdered pectin
4	cups sugar	3/4	cup water
2	tablespoons fresh lemon juice		

Measure the crushed raspberries into a 2-quart casserole, stir in the sugar and lemon juice. Cook, uncovered, 2 minutes. Stir well. Let stand 10 minutes. Meanwhile, place the powdered pectin and the water in a bowl. Heat 30 to 40 seconds, or until mixture becomes clear. Stir well and add to berries. Stir together 2 minutes. Pour into 6 to 8 jelly jars or freezer container (not metal). Cover with waxed paper and let stand at room temperature 24 hours. Cover and store.

Red Cherry Jam

Use the small autumn red cherries or the early spring black cherries. Measure after being pitted and crushed.

2 1/2	cups crushed, pitted cherries	1/2	teaspoon almond extract
4	cups sugar	1	package powdered pectin
2	tablespoons fresh lemon juice	3/4	cup water

The pitted cherries can be crushed in a blender or meat grinder, then measured. Proceed as for Raspberry jam.

Blueberry Jam

Black currants and Saskatoon berries can be prepared in the same manner. These fruits require a little more water and lemon juice.

3	cups crushed blueberries	1	package powdered pectin
1/4	cup fresh lemon juice	1	cup water
5	cups sugar		

Proceed as for other jams.

Red or Black Currant Jelly

This is made from the currant juice. Other fresh fruit juices can be prepared in the same manner.

2	quarts red or black currants, crushed	1	package powdered pectin
4	cups sugar	3/4	cup water
2	tablespoons lemon juice		

Strain the crushed fruit, pass through a fine sieve and measure the 3 cups of juice. Reserve pulp.* Then proceed to cook and finish as for fresh fruit jams.

Bonus Beverage: Add 2 cups water or apple juice to the reserved currant pulp. Place in a 1½ quart casserole. Cook, uncovered, until bubbly, about 4 to 5 minutes. Strain through a fine sieve. To the juice, add sugar to taste and 2 tablespoons cider vinegar. Put back in casserole. Bring to the boil again. Pour into a sterilized screw-top jar. Keep refrigerated. Very refreshing served with iced soda or lemon-lime soda.

18. Tips Well Worth Knowing

Once you've cooked with your microwave oven for a while you will become more and more aware of the great flexibility it gives your cooking and meal planning — and how you'll love it for that!

So, when you enter your kitchen, and before you begin to cook, reflect a moment and think of what you can do in the microwave oven to shorten and ease the work. Something to defrost, fat to melt, syrup to make, topping to prepare, hard butter to soften, a sauce to make without constant stirring and so on.

The following ideas from my kitchen will help you streamline your cooking and preparation time to an absolute minimum.

1. *Softening Butter*: Place stick of cold butter on serving plate. Heat 5 seconds. Let stand 15 seconds. If necessary, repeat this timing until butter has reached the softness required.

2. *Pancakes and Waffles:* Although they are best cooked conventionally, they are ideal to keep in the refrigerator or freezer, since they can be reheated in the microwave oven. Place on a serving plate one at a time, or stack several, then heat, uncovered, until center of bottom pancake is hot. Waffles reheat more quickly than pancakes.
   If taken from refrigerator:
      2 pancakes will take 35 seconds
      2 waffles will take 25 seconds
   If taken from freezer:
      2 pancakes will take 45 seconds
      2 waffles will take 35 seconds

3. *Heating Corn Syrup or Maple Syrup or Liquid Honey*: Remove metal cap from bottle, heat, uncovered, 30 to 45 seconds for a 13-oz. bottle or until bubbles appear. A pitcher can also be used.

4. *To Soften or Pit Prunes*: Place prunes in glass bowl or jar,

barely cover with leftover tea or coffee or part water, part orange juice. If you so wish, add 1 star anise or 1 stick cinnamon or 2 cloves or the grated rind of an orange or lemon. Heat, uncovered, 8 minutes. Let stand 10 minutes. Warm pitted prunes to serve over your hot cereal. Yummy! They will keep 4 to 5 weeks refrigerated, covered, in their liquid.

5. *To Rehydrate Apricots*: To make jam or cake filling, we often have to soak these for a few hours. With the microwave oven, simply put the needed quantity of apricots in a bowl with just enough water or other liquid of your choice to barely cover them. Heat 6 minutes, let stand 3 to 5 minutes.
Try these for speed:

A Golden Mousse: Soften the apricots with orange juice. Pour into a blender. Blend to a puree. Beat 2 egg whites, fold into puree *or*

Make a Tasty Cake Filling: Soften the apricots with cream. Blend with a small spoonful of butter. Cool and use.

Make a Creamy Cake Topping: Proceed as for Cake Filling. Refrigerate overnight, or place 1 hour in freezer. Fold in whipped cream to taste.

6. *To Soften Raisins*: When your recipe calls for this, pour a little water over raisins. Heat, uncovered, 3 minutes. Let stand 2 minutes, drain and use.

To Make Madeira Raisins to Serve with Curry: Proceed as above, pouring 1/4 cup of dry or sweet Madeira instead of water over 1 cup Muscatel raisins. Heat 3 minutes, let stand 2 minutes. Serve hot or cold, but do not drain.

7. *Convenience Caramel Topping*: Unwrap 20 to 25 caramels, place in bowl with 3 tablespoons cream or 3 tablespoons water or 3 tablespoons rum. Heat, uncovered, 3 minutes or until they are melted, stirring twice. Serve hot or cold.

For a Chocolate Caramel Topping: Use chocolate caramel, proceed as above.

8. *Quick Pudding:* Select your favorite 4-serving size pudding and pie filling mix. In a 4-cup glass measure, pour in milk as directed on the package. Stir in pudding mix until dissolved. Cook, uncovered, 5 minutes or until mixture starts to boil, stirring twice during last 2 minutes. Pour into a dish and cool.

9. *Melting Chocolate:* Melt the 1-ounce squares of unsweetened or semi-sweet chocolate in their waxed paper wrappers, seam side up, on a plate $1^1/_2$ to 2 minutes. Scrape chocolate from paper with a rubber spatula. The measurements are then very accurate as no chocolate is lost on the sides of the pan—and there's no pan to wash.

10. *Frosting on the Cake:* You may wish to double a frosting or you may have some left over. Simply refrigerate the excess, covered, until needed. Then soften, uncovered, to spreading consistency, for 15 to 20 seconds per cup.

11. *Toasted Almonds:* To toast 1 cup of blanched whole, slivered or halved almonds or other types of nuts, simply spread them on a paper plate or a glass pie plate. Heat 2 to 3 minutes, stirring every minute so they will brown evenly. Let stand 2 minutes as they continue browning. Stir again. I like to keep a cup or two in a covered glass jar, handy to sprinkle on fish, vegetables or desserts.

12. *Crunchy Topping:* Delicious topping that will keep for 7 to 8 weeks in a covered plastic box. Use on puddings, ice cream, cakes, pies or cereal, or just munch away.

    Melt 1 cup margarine in an 8 × 8-inch baking dish. Stir in thoroughly $1^1/_2$ cups brown sugar, 2 cups quick oat flakes or rolled oats, 1 cup coconut, 1 cup whole grape nuts, $^1/_2$ to 1 cup chopped walnuts, $^1/_2$ teaspoon cinnamon and $^1/_2$ teaspoon ground cardamom (optional). When well mixed, cook, covered, 5 minutes, stirring every minute. Cool and store.

13. *To Clarify Honey Turned to Sugar:* Remove metal cap from jar, heat 1 minute. Check after 30 seconds as time will vary depending on quantity of honey. Remove from oven as soon as liquified.

14. *Refresh:* Soggy potato chips or crackers can be refreshed by heating a plateful, about 45 seconds to 1 minute. Let stand 1 minute to crisp. It's nice to serve warm, crispy crackers with your soup.

15. *Leftover Tea or Coffee:* Do not throw away any of your leftover tea or coffee. As soon as meal is finished, pour leftovers in a glass jar. (I use a 1-quart glass jam jar). Refrigerate, covered. You can pour hot tea or coffee into one-day-old tea or coffee. To reheat, place needed quantity in a mug, reheat as for fresh tea or coffee (see p.49) or to 175°F on thermometer.

16. *Barbecuing Chicken:* If you have several chickens to do, it is a good idea to partially precook them in the microwave oven in the morning, then finish the cooking on the charcoal — the advantage is not only the time saved, but also they do not get too brown on the outside before the inside is done.
A cut up fryer or broiler cut in halves can be microwave oven cooked, uncovered, 10 to 12 minutes. I like to dip mine in a mixture of melted butter, lemon rind and juice as I take them out of the oven. Leave them in refrigerator until ready to use. They will take from 10 to 20 minutes to broil on charcoal, to a golden color.

17. *Speedy Seasoning for Chicken:* Roll cut-up chicken in seasonings from your favorite rice mix (use only the contents of envelope of mix). Pour melted butter on pieces and cook (see Chicken chapter for cooking time).

18. *Leftover Ketchup:* Turn into a sauce. Remove metal cap from bottle, add a spoonful or two of leftover red wine or cream or orange juice or Madeira, and a square of butter. Heat 3 to 4 minutes in oven. Cover bottle. Shake well until ketchup no longer sticks to bottom of bottle. Pour into hot sauceboat or add to a brown sauce or spaghetti sauce or serve over rice.

19. *Leftover Cooked Meat:* Meats such as beef, ham, corned beef or veal can easily be heated in sandwiches. Just pile several *thin* slices of meat in a buttered bun and cook on paper napkin until filling is hot: 1 sandwich takes approximately 30 seconds, 2

take 45 seconds. Be very careful not to overcook. If preferred, toast bun before filling with meat to give a slightly better flavor and texture.

20. *Garlic Butter:* Melt 1 cup butter or margarine with 3 cloves garlic, peeled and split in two. Let stand 18 minutes, remove garlic. Pour butter in glass jar. Cover, refrigerate. It will keep for months. When needed for buttering bread, seasoning steak or flavoring chicken, just take out what you need.

21. *White Sauce:* White sauce is so easy to reheat in the microwave oven that a supply in reserve in the refrigerator is most handy. It will keep 4 to 5 weeks. (For recipe see p.76). Reheating will take from 30 seconds to 2 minutes, depending on quantity. Stir often. It is ready to use when it begins to bubble.

22. *Warming Baby Bottles:* Fill a 4-oz. or 8-oz. bottle or plastic nurser with milk. Invert nipple and screw cap on loosely. Heat, 45 seconds for a 4-oz. bottle, 1 minute 20 seconds for an 8-oz. bottle. Turn nipple to outside, tighten cap and shake vigorously. Test temperature on wrist.

23. *Warming Baby Foods:* Strained or junior foods can be heated in their jars, but first always remember to remove cap. (Never heat a sealed or capped jar.) For $3^1/_2$ to $7^3/_4$-oz. jars, heat individually from 30 to 45 seconds. Three jars heated together, placed in a circle, will take 1 minute to 1 minute 30 seconds. These times are for foods started at room temperature. If foods are from refrigerator or jars are only partially full, time will vary slightly.

24. *To Melt Butter or Other Fat:* Place required butter or other fat in a glass dish or measuring cup. Heat, uncovered, from 30 seconds to 2 minutes, depending on quantity and temperature of fat.

25. *To Make Gelatine Desserts:* Pour 1 cup water into a 1-quart dish, heat 2 to 3 minutes. Remove from oven, add flavored gelatine and stir until dissolved. Then proceed with recipe of your choice, or heat water required by recipe, add *unflavored* gelatine, heat 30 seconds and proceed with recipe.

26. *To Get More Juice from Oranges, Lemons or Limes:* Place fruits, one at a time, for 30 seconds in microwave oven before squeezing.

27. *To Peel Peaches:* Heat peaches 15 to 20 seconds, depending on their size, let stand 10 minutes and peel.

28. *Re-heating Leftovers:* All leftovers, whether meats, fish, vegetables, desserts, taste unbelievably fresh when reheated in the microwave oven because there is no drying out or reheated flavor. Keep leftovers in dishes that can be placed in the microwave oven from refrigerator or freezer. Simply place in oven, top with a sheet of waxed paper and reheat in minutes. Of course, time varies depending on quantity or if food is refrigerated or frozen. The easy way to test temperature is to take dish out of oven and use a thermometer. The food should be between 150° and 160°F. If not, return to oven, remembering to remove thermometer first.

29. *To Plump Dried Fruits for Cakes:* When a recipe (even one baked the conventional way) calls for fruits and nuts to be soaked 12 to 24 hours with a quantity of rum or brandy, use same quantity of fruits, nuts and rum or brandy. Mix in a large bowl. Heat 5 minutes, covered with waxed paper. No amount of ordinary cooking can make them as moist or as tasty. I use this with all my favorite festive fruitcakes.

How to Dry Herbs and Flowers in the Microwave Oven

For many years I have dried herbs and flowers in spite of the care, time and work it took to make them perfect. When I became involved in microwave cooking, I felt that maybe all the work could be done in minutes rather than hours or days. My first trial was a disaster! I set a bunch of deep green parsley on a paper towel, then set the cooking time to 1 minute (so little compared to 2 to 3 weeks). Well, I got dried parsley, but it turned almost to powder the moment I touched it! But I did not give up, and soon found out how to do it both superbly and fast.

For All Fresh Herbs

Tarragon, basil, marjoram, savory, sage, thyme, mint, etc., all come out with flying colors.

Separate the leaves from the stem. Spread the leaves on a sheet of transparent kitchen paper set on a sheet of cardboard. Cover the leaves with another sheet of paper and place in oven. Heat 20 seconds. Test by just touching the leaves to see if they are dried. They may take another 10 seconds, but beware of overdoing the heating. Let stand 10 minutes. By this time they should be ready to place in a jar. If they are not yet dried to your taste, give them only another few seconds in the oven.

To dry the stems, spread out in an ordinary paper bag, but do not close the bag. Proceed to dry as for the leaves. I find that a good handful of stems usually takes 25 to 30 seconds to dry. Cool, then if you have a blender, blend them for $1/2$ to 1 minute. They will turn into a coarse powder. I label this and keep to flavor soups, stews or any sauce that is strained before serving.

Herbs all have different textures, thicknesses and humidity, which explains why no absolutely exact time fits them all. After drying a few, you will understand the easy process.

Dried Flowers

Flowers dried in the microwave oven retain their natural colors and shapes. Like herbs they are done very quickly and it takes a little practice. I have found that some flowers dried in silica gel in the usual manner tend to discolor during the time-consuming process. Because the microwave oven does the work of dehydrating and drying in 30 seconds to 1 minute (in silica gel) they are still fresh looking and retain their freshness for a long time.

When you have learnt to do it well, you will find that they look almost like fresh-cut flowers.

The easiest flowers to dry are: roses, daffodils, carnations, wild flowers, pansies, lilies, geraniums, etc.

Half-opened flowers dry very nicely because the petals are so firmly rooted they do not fall or become deformed. Avoid flowers that have thick centers or those with petals growing toward the center such as dahlias or chrysanthemums. Leaves of all types are beautiful.

When I want to make a small arrangement of mixed flowers, I first arrange them in my vase, cutting and placing as I wish to have them. Then I dry them together in the oven so that they are then dried to the same degree and color retention. When ready, I arrange them as before.

To Dry Flowers:

I use a 12 × 8-inch glass baking dish and half fill it with silica gel. I then set some flowers on it, making sure that all petals and leaves are well placed. Then I proceed to sprinkle silica gel on top, slowly and gently, making sure that every area is covered, as the slightest exposure of the petals to the air will spoil the effect of the flower. It is easy to fill the spaces between the petals that are curled inward or are close together if you use a skewer. When they are all covered, place dish in the oven, together with a 1 cup measure of water, placed at back of oven. Heat 30 seconds, remove dish from oven, check a little corner to test texture of flower. Depending on size and type of flower used, the time will vary from 30 seconds to 1 minute. However, it is well to remember that flowers will continue to dry for 10 to 15 minutes after completion of heating time.

It is easy to remove a little of the silica gel and check the dryness and simply recover the flower and put back in the oven for a few more seconds.

Experiment once with 4 or 5 different flowers and you will understand the whole process.

After the flowers are dried and cool, I tilt the dish over a sheet of paper to remove the silica gel that tops the flowers, then remove them with care.

Any silica gel sticking to the flowers can be removed gently with a small paint brush or small metal pick.

Metric Conversion Chart

Conversion to a convenient metric quantity usually means a 5% increase in the quantities of most foods and can be done by using metric measuring equipment. A dual measuring cup is now available. If you prefer to use your existing cups and spoons just follow this guide:

250 ml is approximately equal to an 8 oz. cup + 1 tablespoon

15 ml is approximately equal to 1 tablespoon

5 ml is approximately equal to 1 teaspoon

1 litre is approximately equal to 34 fluid ounces

Roasting Temperatures

Internal Temperature of Meat		Temperatures for syrup and candies	
°F	°C	°F	°C
		230 to 234	110-112
130	55	234 to 240	112-115
140	60	244 to 248	118-120
150	65	250 to 266	121-130
160	70	270 to 290	132-143
170	75	300 to 310	149-154
180	80	320	160
185	85	338	170

Index